Reading Ronell

Edited by Diane Davis

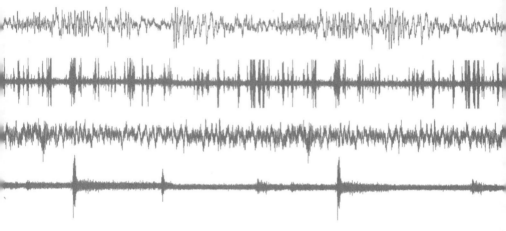

University of Illinois Press
Urbana and Chicago

Reading Ronell

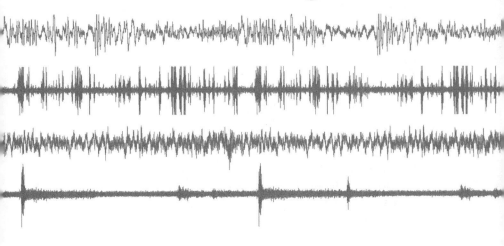

© 2009 by the Board of Trustees
of the University of Illinois
Manufactured in the United States of America
1 2 3 4 5 C P 5 4 3 2 1
∞ This book is printed on acid-free paper.

Publication of this book was supported by a
University Cooperative Society Subvention Grant
awarded by the University of Texas at Austin.

Library of Congress Cataloging-in-Publication Data
Reading Ronell / edited by Diane Davis.
p.   cm.
Includes bibliographical references and index.
ISBN 978-0-252-03450-3 (cloth : alk. paper)
ISBN 978-0-252-07647-3 (pbk. : alk. paper)
1. Ronell, Avital—Criticism and interpretation.
2. Ronell Avital—Philosophy.
3. Critics—United States.
4. Feminists—United States.
5. Philosophers—United States.
I. Davis, D. Diane (Debra Diane)
PN75.R65R43   2009
809—dc22   2008047215

Contents

Reading Ronell

Diane Davis
Introduction

Madame Bovary travels the razor's edge of understanding/
reading protocols. In this context understanding is given as
something that happens when you are no longer reading. It is
not the open-ended Nietzschean echo, "Have I been understood?" but rather the "I understand" that means you have
ceased suspending judgment over the chasm of the real. Out
of this collapse of judgment no genuine decision can be allowed
to emerge.

—AVITAL RONELL, CRACK WARS

Reading Ronell. The simple title names an arduous task—a "mission," we
could say—that is already underway, in medias res, skipping the preliminar-
ies. But what would it take to begin? How might one approach an oeuvre
explicitly designed to "resist you," to get "you" to question what it means
to read anything at all? To open a work by Avital Ronell is, in a sense,
to eavesdrop on a fundamentally dissymmetrical Conversation[1] in which
"your" addresser is first of all an addressee occupying a space of troubled
reception: "Writing," she writes, always takes place "at the behest of another, and is, at best, a shorthand transcription of the demand of this Other
whose original distance is never altogether surmounted."[2] The call from
the Other to which Ronell's writing responds traverses an irremediable
distance, coming through neither clearly nor cleanly. Whether AR figures
herself as an operator taking calls or a secretary taking dictation, the lines

1

of that communication are rattled by static and disruption and noise—onto which her ears remain sharply trained. Her transcriptions—what "you" are given to read—trace with exceptional precision the complex, and each time singular, trajectories of understanding's withdrawal. What AR addresses to "you," that is, are not simply identifying and identifiable appropriations but a sense of the inappropriability of meaning: what her writing gives you to read is already a *reading*, which by definition resists subsumption into a smooth interpretive scheme. So if "your mission" is to read Ronell, you will need first to perk up your ears, to adjust and hone what Derrida describes as "the most tendered and most open organ, the one that, as Freud reminds us, the infant cannot close."[3]

The tropological substitution, an ear for an eye, signals a shift from the relative security of that which can shut or turn away to the extreme vulnerability of that which cannot. Nietzsche's Zarathustra warns, for example, that the ear, a wide-open portal, can be invaded and taken over by the voice of the state through its educational systems, which take "you" by the ear, compelling it to grow disproportionately. "Having become all ears" for the state, ideological ears, Derrida writes in his reading of *Zarathustra*, "you transform yourself into a high-fidelity receiver, and the ear—your ear which is also the ear of the other—begins to occupy in your body the disproportionate place of the 'inverted cripple.'"[4] "Inverse cripples," Zarathustra explains, are human beings "who lack everything, except the thing of which they have too much—human beings who are nothing but a big eye or a big mouth or a big belly or anything at all that is big." In this case, at issue is "your" big ear—"An ear! An ear as big as a man!"[5]—which has morphed into a hi-fi receiver synced to an ideological machine, for which "you" become a loudspeaker. But this is not the ear you will need to read Ronell; this is not a *reading* ear.

"Your mission" will require an altogether different mode of reception and *another ear,* a trained and discriminating ear that has been finely tuned to what no ideological discourse—be it The State's or The Revolution's— can abide: "noise frequencies," "anticoding," "the inflated reserves of random indeterminateness." To "read with your ears": to attend to the static produced by "the contingencies of textual disturbance," to welcome the "rush of interference that produces gaps and unsettles cognition."[6] Indeed, "to read" already means "to read with your ears," to tune into that which thwarts interpretation's closural aims. In stark contrast to the comforting synthesis of interpretation, reading involves a trauma: "The possibility of a full reading without trauma," Ronell tells us, "is inconceivable."[7] Inasmuch as it requires remaining open to an unmasterable surplus irreducible to semantic appropriations, reading shatters prejudgment structures and overwhelms cognition, delivering no satisfying end-point, no refuge of mastery or payoff of certitude. Reading aims for a certain understand*ing*, of course, but according to Ronell, "having understood, or thinking one has understood, stands precisely on a refusal to read."[8] After her, there can be no past tense to understanding and so no end to reading: after her, that is, one can never *have read* anything. Snipping the presumed causal link between rigor and certitude, Ronell's exquisitely (and excruciatingly) meticulous readings orchestrate, each time, a depropriating encounter with the inassimilable—"the chasm of the real."[9] Reading at the extreme limits of responsibility (response-ability), Ronell enacts an ethics of reading that responds to the trace of the other while tirelessly demonstrating that there is no way, ultimately, to have understood (completely).

It was perhaps the fact that Ronell's extraordinary reading practice had not yet been taken up *for* her, in regard to her works, that the winter 1994 issue of *diacritics* devoted the first fifty pages to a "Special Section on the Work of Avital Ronell." Ronell's fourth book, *Finitude's Score: Essays for the End of the Millennium*, had just come out, and *diacritics* marked the event by publishing a "cluster of essays" that responded to an invitation to "take up her work," which at that point included *Dictations: On Haunted Writing* (1986), *The Telephone Book: Technology, Schizophrenia, Electric Speech* (1989), *Crack Wars: Literature, Addiction, Mania* (1992), and *Finitude's Score*. Then editor Jonathan Culler introduced the three review essays in a brief paragraph commenting not only on the remarkableness of Ronell's critical oeuvre thus far but also on the striking "response it evokes, as those who write about it seek to imitate or outdo her in discussing the texts she and they engage." There is something, it seems, about Ronell's style that inspires the sort of competitive mimesis that is fascinatingly displayed in this issue of *diacritics*.

Still, and despite Eduardo Cadava's luminous contribution to that issue, I was disappointed. The singular provocation of Ronell's "remarkable critical oeuvre"—the devastating insights, the unprecedented writing style, the relentless destabilizations—is a function of her ethics and practice of reading. So I had hoped for a more extensive and diverse assemblage of essays on this über-reader, an assemblage that would perhaps be less given to mimetic impulses and more interested in *reading with* Ronell: by reading Ronell reading, or by examining the ethico-political implications of her radical dislocations, or by carefully explicating, extending, and exploring the paraconcepts addressed in her works. I promised myself then that I would one day edit such a volume.

3

The essays gathered here were written in response to a letter of invitation I sent to each of the contributors in 2004, a decade after the *diacritics* issue first appeared: I invited them to participate in this project by engaging with or responding to some aspect of Ronell's work in writing. To avoid short-circuiting any potential approach or focus, I placed no further limits on the contributors. It was not my intention, in other words, to edit a volume that would claim to cover all aspects of Ronell's extensive oeuvre, nor one that would claim to address systematically each of her major works. Instead, my modest hope was to produce a collection of critical essays on Ronell's texts by a group of the most distinguished and innovative thinkers alive. And I must say that I received some delightfully surprising responses to my open-ended invitation.

Jean-Luc Nancy addressed his meditation on the subject of the address itself to "Avital" ("Avy") herself, frequently punning on her name (*à vie*, a-vital) and speaking both to and for her: "I am addressing to you, therefore, a few pages on the subject of the address, of this vital address without which between us—all of us, you and me, but everyone else, too—nothing would ever happen anywhere. . . . To you [*à toi*], therefore, Avital, it's your turn [*à toi*]." Pierre Alferi composed "Serial," a poem *for* Avital Ronell, in her honor, on what is known to be one of her issues: the series. Laurence Rickels produced a kind of tribute to analogy and the play of the pun, defending "Rickels and Ronell" against the violence of pun-controlling critics in the name of "an open reading, reading that opens." And Tom Cohen, Gil Anidjar, and Thomas Pepper all attend to Ronell's sustained meditations on war: Anidjar argues that "WAR for AR is primary," Cohen reminds us that in Ronell's work, "there are crack wars and drug wars, the tropes of Desert Gulf, war as illness," and the "warrior impulse," and Pepper reads the preface of *Finitude's Score* through a self-assembled constellation "*with* Ronell, Schmitt, and Heidegger," zooming in on the unparalleled devastation of air war.

Werner Hamacher responded to my invitation in the European tradition of the festschrift, honoring Ronell with his own approach to a text, Kafka's "The Test," of which her reading is well-known. In *The Test Drive*, Ronell exposes in Kafka's text a "double movement consisting of sheer being-called and being called upon to answer," noting that inasmuch as the protagonist is "singled out among the others by not being called up—he is on call, which is to say, permanently on duty (no schedule, no hours, finally, and logically no time off). Being off duty is his duty," Ronell writes, which is "[a] more relentless, imposing tour of duty than the fulfillment of a locatable task could measure."[10] In his contribution to this volume, which is entitled

"Uncalled," Hamacher offers another, altogether non-Heideggerian take on Kafka's short text, proposing that it operates as "an investigation of a world *without a call*—without determination or function, without profession or vocation and without work; without goal, and without guiding, claiming, or approval-granting authority."

Samuel Weber begins his essay in the tradition of the festschrift as well, but ends with an explicit response to Ronell's work. He zeroes in on two controversial phrases uttered by Heidegger: that "he is 'not convinced that democracy' is the political form best capable of responding to or confronting the challenges 'of modern technology'" and that "Nur noch ein Gott kann uns retten" [English: "Only a God can save us"; French: "Seulement un dieu peut encore nous sauver"]. Weber's careful analysis of the original German problematizes the oversimplified English and French translations, nudging their focus on "salvation" toward a hope for "salutation," and he closes with a reflection on Ronell's treatment of the greeting in her essay "On the Misery of Theory Without Poetry."[11]

Several contributions gathered here offer scrupulous readings of one of Ronell's books. Peter Fenves reads *Stupidity* from the perspective of Kant's "What is Enlightenment?," Hent de Vries performs a reading of *The Test Drive* across Deleuze's thoughts on testing, and Susan Bernstein, Elisabeth Weber, and Elissa Marder all offer provocative rereadings of *The Telephone Book*: Bernstein re-presents it as a triangulated conference call between Ronell, Heidegger, and George Oppen; Weber takes it up as a lens through which to begin to think the "space without an outside" that is produced by the cell phone; and Marder approaches it as an interrogation—continued in each of Ronell's later works—of "the ways in which technological objects come into being as symptomatic responses to certain conceptions and repressions of the body."

And finally, Shireen Patell and Judith Butler read Ronell reading. Patell unpacks the "illocutionary and ethical force" of Ronell's reading practice (her "abysstemology"), directing our attention to the "piano lesson" in the introduction to *Finitude's Score* and leaving us triply mise en abyme: she reads Ronell reading this *Urszene* of reading portrayed in Marguerite Duras's *Moderato Cantabile*. And Butler, in "Ronell as Gay Scientist," performs an exceptionally close reading of a section of *The Test Drive* in which Ronell is performing an exceptionally close reading of Nietzsche's *The Gay Science*: "I'm looking at her looking at him, and my reading is afflicted with the sense of humility that goes along with being cast to the spectatorial sidelines. I'd like to say that this is a complicated triangle, but that would be to overestimate my importance. Humor is thus required. I'll probably make myself known in the rendition I offer, but there is no guarantee that I could ever come between them."

This volume more than fulfills my now decade-and-a-half-old aspiration to edit a collection of critical essays by some of today's most important thinkers on the works of Avital Ronell. Nonetheless, I feel compelled to articulate one profound regret: that Jacques Derrida, who shared with me his delight that this volume was underway and his eagerness to participate in it, passed before he could complete his contribution. I assumed that he might contribute a lecture he had delivered at New York University in 2001 on hospitals and hospitality, which he had dedicated to Ronell's work on drugs and addiction. But Derrida had already begun a new essay that he hoped to devote to this volume: its focus was Ronell's groundbreaking book *Stupidity,* and I was fortunate enough to hear him deliver a part of it to students and faculty of the European Graduate School in Paris in April 2004. (Some of his last seminars were devoted to "stupidity," as well, and those lectures will be published in the near future.) At his home in Ris-Orangis one afternoon in late July 2005, when he was already quite ill, he again expressed to me his enthusiasm for this collection and his sincere hope to complete his contribution to it. I am extremely grateful to Derrida for his unwavering encouragement, and I want to mark his disseminated presence in these pages: though he could not complete his essay, he did contribute a great deal to this collection.

I would like to express my deepest gratitude to each of the other contributors as well, for their willing participation in this project, for their exhilarating engagements with Ronell's work, and for their patience and responsiveness as I pulled the volume together. I want to thank Saul Anton and Catharine Diehl for their respective scrupulous translations of the essays by Jean-Luc Nancy and Werner Hamacher; and I want to thank Willis Regier, director of the University of Illinois Press, for his impeccable advice and guidance throughout. And finally, most important, I would like to thank Avital Ronell, whose incomparable and ever-expanding oeuvre inspired this project and each of the contributions that follow.

6

NOTES

1. In *Dictations: On Haunted Writing* (Lincoln: University of Nebraska Press, 1993), Ronell writes: "A relation to alterity on the other side of the mathematical equation, Conversation necessarily resists appropriation or any subsumption of the other by the tyranny of the Same. The fundamental dissymmetry governing Conversation, the distance at the origin and the rule of non-requital—these are so many markers of the condition of separation that keeps it going" (xii).
2. Ibid., p. xiv.
3. Jacques Derrida. "Otobiographies," trans. Avital Ronell, in *The Ear of the Other*, trans. Peggy Kamuf, ed. Christie McDonald (Lincoln: University of Nebraska Press, 1985), p. 33. See also *The Telephone Book* (Lincoln: University of Nebraska Press, 1991), pp. 20–22.
4. Ibid., p. 35.
5. Friedrich Nietzsche, "On Redemption," in *Thus Spoke Zarathustra: A Book for None and All*, trans. Walter Kaufmann (New York: Penguin, 1978), p. 138.
6. Avital Ronell, *Stupidity* (Champaign: University of Illinois Press, 2002), pp. 103 and 101.
7. Avital Ronell. "On Hallucinogenres," interview with Gary Wolf, *Mondo* 2000 (v. 4): p. 68.
8. Ronell, *Stupidity*, p. 156.
9. Avital Ronell, *Crack Wars: Addiction Literature Mania* (Lincoln: University of Nebraska Press, 1992), p. 62.
10. Avital Ronell, *The Test Drive* (Champaign: University of Illinois Press, 2005), pp. 72–73.
11. In *PMLA* 120.1 (2005): 16–32.

Jean-Luc Nancy

Addressee: Avital

I address you, Avital. I address myself to you, the living, the vivacious, the vital. But I'm also addressing Abital, wife of David, mother of Shephatiah, whose name is also written as Avital, which is a man's name and which means "father of the dew." I address myself to the dew, which in Latin is also the drop, and thus also to the father, because what is a father if not a drop? What is a father if not the morning dewdrop clinging to a leaf or a flower that will exhale at sunrise?[1] I address myself to life, which is itself nothing other than address, because life says nothing but this, nothing other than "to life!"—as a dispatch, a call, an offering, a dedication. Life dedicates itself to life, and, of course, as a result, to the death that lives in and through it. Life addresses life to the death [à la vie à la mort] according to the formula of the most sacred sermons. Life addresses itself: that is what it does, and what it lives on. Life is neither produced nor reproduced, it is neither formative nor conservative; it aims at itself [s'adresse], and with this, it addresses [adresse] the living: it calls them, sends them, exposes, and ships them off to death for life [à la mort à la vie].

I am addressing myself to you first of all because it would be difficult for me to write "about you" here because my inadequate English prevents me from reading you in the way that would be necessary in order to respond to you properly. But also because the objects that you work—ghosts, telephones, addictive substances, tests, finitudes, and other stupidities—are transformed and appropriated by you to such an extent that they are rendered unrecognizable and thus impossible for me to consider approaching by their more common concepts. I am addressing myself to you, finally, and above all, because before and beyond all these books of which you are the author, you are the actress, and thus an incessant address: a call, an invitation, a challenge, a provocation, an invocation.

It is rare that you speak without also making a call, that is, without making your interlocutor show themselves in person, whether it is in the guise of a witness or a guilty party, a friend or an enemy, a suspect or a confidant. All your sentences silently say "to you": this is for you [*pour toi*], I am sending it to you, catch—*catch this as best you can*—and then, it's up to you [*à toi*], it's your turn, I'm awaiting your words, your answer, your refusal or your assent, but above all your humor and the tone of your voice right now.

I am addressing to you, therefore, a few pages on the subject of the address, of this vital address without which between us—between all of us, you and me, but everyone else as well—nothing would ever happen anywhere. And I begin by that which differentiates my language, French, from some of yours, English or German (because you certainly speak others, among them French): the two homonyms of—or in—the address: To you [*à toi*], therefore, Avital, it's your turn.

I.

There are two addresses in the French language. The first comes from *adrecer*, to set up [*dresser*], to raise, which led to the reflexive *s'adrecer*, to go toward, and *adrecer* in the sense of to direct. In 1177, an *adresse* is a direct road; in 1820, it is direction, the right way. In the fifteenth century, it becomes the action of calling upon someone for help. In the sixteenth and seventeenth centuries, one begins to see two words for *adresse*. The first still means a direction, but also "directions," that to which something leads: the place where someone is to be found. The second word is contaminated by *adroit*, which in 1559 means "able." *Adroit* comes from *dexter*, which means in Latin "to the right," "on the right side," but also "able." *Dexter* is opposed to *sinister*, the left side: the side of dexterity against the side of the sinister, the mortal, of missing (one's goal) and of unhappiness (happiness also means ability, address). This contamination results in address as ability. But the contamination of meanings here is even older and more complicated: in the vocabulary of medieval chivalry, "adroit" meant svelte, elegant, that is to say, thin, well planted on one's feet or on one's warhorse, but also "striking

10

one's target." The two *adresses* thus mix together to set up [*dresser*], to direct, and to attain (one's target). Behind this combination, there is a proximity and contagion between the two *droits,* one coming from *dexter,* the other from *directus:* at once the root *deks,* to the right, and the root *reg, straight ahead* [*tout droit*]. The ability that knows how to aim for and go straight attains its objective, accurately.

In German, it's different: the proximity of the two senses of *Geschick:* the outcome, or the destiny, and ability. Both come from the first sense of *schicken,* to send, to expedite. From this also come to prepare, to arrange, to make something happen, and the word *Schick,* which first designated form, manner, or usage before taking on the sense of the French *chic*—the origin of which we still do not know, whether, that is, it itself comes from the German word by way of Alsatian or Swiss German.

But in English, *to address* is first of all to speak to, to address oneself to, and also to speak of, to take up a question: for example, to address the question of address. In the plural, addresses can be good manners, attentions, those that one makes when one is courting someone. *May I address you, dear Avy?*

II.

What public am I addressing here? Which readers of essays devoted, dedicated, and addressed to Avital Ronell? How can one anticipate, discern, or transcendentally schematize such a public? And yet, I'm supposed to aim for this public, to go ably to it, to "target" my discourse for it. Or rather, to target this concept as necessary, the address, and to address myself to it in order to conceive it with precision, and to conceive it keeping in mind this public to whom I address myself in writing this. For this, someone addressed themselves to me; someone addressed themselves to the "philosopher." The assumption is that philosophy is the right address to send the message "how do you address Avital Ronell? (in English, how to address AR?)" or "how to address oneself to her?" Because I have been asked to read her, to do a "critical reading," which is supposed "to address her work" but which also implies, in the strong and Schlegelian sense of criticism, an address at her, that is, to target and hit the quality that is proper to her, her singularity—and I have already decided that it would be found in the address and that this is the concept I must unfold. I decided, I was obliged to decide that it had the character of address—to vital [*à vitale*].

The assumption is that the philosopher should have the address necessary to extract, analyze, or configure the concept: but this one not more so than another. He (or she) is asked for the conceptual address of the concept of address. However, what is address in this sense, if not the art and the manner—the savoir faire, the *know-how, technè*? It is necessary to understand that address itself, the concept as much as the thing, is of the order of technics, or art. It concerns the practice of arts: what, therefore, is a painter without address? An awkward dancer? Address is an element of the arts in all senses of the word, indeed the most general element—or even, the goal. The assumption is that the address is addressed to artists, or they to it. One assumes that it is a matter here neither of Avital's art nor her technique or techniques, abilities, resources, or ingenuity—which is inexhaustible—but rather of Avital herself as manner, turn, gift, address, as artist perhaps, as a manner of an artist to whom the philosopher addresses himself.

Or, on the other hand, no one has assumed anything. Someone addressed the word "address" to themselves without a specific goal in mind. They want to find the address of the address itself. Because they have put the address on the program, with the definite article: the absolute address, its essence. From where and to what does the address address itself? It's as if someone were asking themselves from where and to what is addressed the whole of language, the whole of thought, the whole of direction—all gathering, all sense of direction, all destination. It's an exorbitant, vertiginous request. Avital likes that.

III.

Let's decide, resolve, and address ourselves to one of the sides here supposed, between art and philosophy: to my side, the bank of the river from where I hail Avital on the other side. . . .

How and to what does philosophy address itself? One might think that it addresses itself first in the mode of exhortation, or incitation, between command and counsel: for example, know thyself. This is in some way the initial statement of philosophy, that of the oracle to Socrates, of Socrates to others. It's an address to the person, or to the subject, however one wants to describe it. It has a precise aim: it is not knowledge, it's not a matter so much of knowing what I am for knowledge, but rather of putting a wisdom to work. This address aims at wisdom. Wisdom is a *know-how* with myself: if I learn to know that I don't know anything, I will be wise. Not more knowledgeable, but knowing how to deal with myself, and with man in general, but with the man in general in me: able, therefore, to guide myself in my humanity in order to not be the victim of its desires, its agitations, and its sufferings. Capable of removing myself from humanity: at bottom, a betrayal.

One might also think that philosophy itself produces direction: the sure path of knowledge, *directio ingenii,* method, therefore, because this word signifies "the road." The general method of knowledge, which supposes that the idea itself of knowledge is given, and that one already knows something essential on the subject of knowledge itself. One is already in absolute knowledge, insofar as it well has to be knowledge-of-self, *selbtwissen,* originally and finally. The address is then only the address of knowledge to itself: at bottom, a manner of going in circles. (A kind of stupidity, she says.)

One can also think this differently. One can take up again the two preceding addresses and submit them to questioning. One will see that they still hide something, one and the other, and one like the other. They hide the same thing: what is outside the human and what relates only to itself, what is impassive and always there from beginning to end; why not give it its name, being? Philosophy brings itself into view under this invitation, under this call—indeed, under this intimation (which is also intimidating): to go right to being, insofar as it is.

Address: to being. Questions arise immediately: where? But there, everywhere, within hand's reach. How do we go there, then? In effect, there is perhaps no way. One is already at the address. What does "to be at" mean? Or rather: "to be there"? Are we there? What is the "there"? The place of being. But is there a place of being that is itself something other than being? There isn't, it is self-evident. Like all evidence, it grows obscure in the very moment one looks at it. No place for being, and being itself is not a place. It is not a space-time. How do we address ourselves to that which is nothing, nowhere, at no time? Philosophy begins with this vertigo: the disappearance of all address: no direction, nor even the ability to find the way or take aim. A worrying situation, without home or horizon.

IV.

What is it that one calls "art"? (By "one," I mean philosophy. There can only be a determination of art as such from philosophical conditions. As soon as one leaves these conditions, "philosophy" and "art" are together wiped away, dissolved into religion. The latter is no longer the business of address: it is the business of observance. For example, Avital has the religion of medicinal plants. Observance and address mutually exclude each other in principle. This does not mean that, from the heart of this mutual exclusion, they do not address each other in some manner, indeed in that they observe one another—but in what sense? That's another story.)

One calls "art" the know-how-to-take-place. Art is first and foremost a place. It exposes, it performs, it installs, it frames, it hangs, it poses. Art is always sedentary and local. Not only is this the case in general, it is true insofar as art never is "in general": It is always such and such art. Art, these are artistic places, taking-places of an "art in general" that has no place anywhere. It is called painting or music, sculpture or video, architecture or literature, a garden or cinema, and sometimes one doesn't even know what to call it. One says "intervention," "installation," "action," "work," and one even says nothing at all, and some take the opportunity to say that it's "whatever." Whatever, if you will, but not wherever or whenever, nor even however. Somewhere, sometime, it takes place, it performs. If not, there's nothing, no "artistic action." The artist himself does not much like to speak about art, nor call what he does "art." On the contrary, he quite likes to say "what I do"—which implies, for example, "I hope that what I do turns its back to 'ART.'"[2] The capital letters, obviously, are conceptual, and one can say that the concept of "art" is today always determined by the tone in which one utters the word, that is to say, by the nature and the aim of the address contained in the fact of using or not using it.

You, Avital, you hardly ever speak of "art." It's not your manner, it's not your way of doing things. Perhaps you are the one who has most spoken about art, or at least of artists, in speaking about addiction, in order to say that the practice of art supposes an addiction. Addiction or rather submission, receptivity, passivity, tolerability, susceptibility: it's always a matter of being receptive [*sensible*] to an address, of allowing oneself to be addressed by another, by others, from the outside, from a foreign country, from the foreign. It's a matter of finding oneself there where the address arrives, and to not impose upon its direction. To be at the place of address—that is what distinguishes "art" from knowledge or from calculation. (One can also speak of "faith.")

But this place of art that art is, this place of the address of art and this place from where it addresses itself (address as in a postal address), this location that is the gesture of the artist ("to praise," properly speaking, it is "to place," to situate) is not made to allay philosophical worry. It possesses neither a home nor a horizon. It does something else entirely. It tells us: your address is here. It's thus a place that addresses itself, and which thus gives itself as address. It tells us: this way, come this way, straight ahead, this is the place itself.

Therefore, the question is not that of being, but rather of being there [*y être*]—or of going there [*y aller*], coming there [*y venir*], going by there [*y passer*], and perhaps also of arriving there. And it's not a question. Just an address: go there [*allez-y*]. In familiar French: "Go on!" [*vas-y*] can signify "go to this place" or even "do it!" or "give it a shot!" Go on, try—try to see this shot, this turn, this address, this manner of going about it [*s'y prendre*] in order to be there [*y être*], to be somewhere—nothing but an instant, perhaps, but for this instant, to not be nowhere. Do nothing but pass by. A matter of the present. An artist's work always makes present a present (of eternity, if one wants to say it that way, or an instant).

V.

Philosophy is essentially employed in undoing the present, in throwing itself into its interval, which has neither place nor time, in disjoining it in order to let being be—never anywhere present.

From being to place: therein lies the tension.

There is the tension of which it is really a question of here, and that the words "art" and "philosophy" only cover very partially and very awkwardly. After all, one could invert the roles, or the places. One should not take the split [*partage*] I've just sketched too literally. I wanted to begin by playing out a sort of expected opposition, one that is supposedly understood—but, as Hegel says, what is "well known" is not known at all.

Nor must one presuppose what "art" and "philosophy" are, nor, consequently, what may allow them to address one another, or to address one against the other.

Rather, one must hold onto the following: from being to place, there lies the tension, and there is the address. Being is without place, even if it is the being of place. The place is without being, even if it is the place of being. It is therefore necessary to add that being is not "outside" of place, because this would still be in another place. And that the place is not "outside" of being, because there is no outside to what is without place. In a certain way, being and place are therefore the same thing. But the whole question lies in this "certain way."

Let's say again: being "contains" the place (but evidently in a nonspatial, nonlocal sense of the infinitive "to contain"). In effect, being = "that there is [there]" [*qu'il y a*]; the place is "contained" in the "there" [*y*], between the pronoun *il* and the verb *a* [to have].[3] And this distension between subject and verb, between *il* and *a,* is nothing other than the distension of an "it is" or a "that is." There is no "that is" (that is to say, nothing is) without the distension of the "there" between the subject (anonymous, indifferent, whoever, the thing itself) and the verb (*a* [to have], which does not have the sense of being, if it is not preceded by the *y*). (How will you write this in English?)

And again: the place contains being. In effect, everything only ever is "in" some place. The place seems thus to contain being in the proper sense of the infinitive "to contain." But one cannot rest content with this relation of container and contained, because if the place was the container of being, what then would be the being of place? Or rather, would one have to say that being is contained in a non-being?

Some probably think that I'm just amusing myself. And why not? There's an irresistible comedy around these limits, these extremities of possibility—and of necessity. Plato, first of all, was very sensitive to this kind of comedy—the irony or humor of the extremity of thinking, of experience, where extreme simplicity suddenly opens out onto vertigo and onto the inevitable appearance of a useless and exhausting intricacy. You, however, you're too familiar with these limits where exhaustion lies in wait for us to think that the game is not serious, but even more, much more, to think that the serious is not exhilarating, just like the laughter that in Hermann Broch paralyzes the windpipes of the Immortals in their knowledge of the inanity of knowledge, and "the laugh as end for the aborted flight into beauty" [*das Lachen als Ende für die abgebrochene Flucht in die Schönheit*].[3]

We recognize this interminable tension between an extreme gravity and an inextinguishable laughter right away as a tension between philosophy and art, even if only confusedly; we also recognize it simultaneously as a tension that is common to both, and that splits [*partage*] both one and the other. And even, in the way that we evoked with the *Geschick*, as the tragicomic tension between the two addresses of the *chic* and of destiny.

VI.

Let us start over and say things in another way.

Someone—Somewhere. In question here is the tension between one and the other. Someone is always somewhere. That's how a postal address is conceived: "AR This way, new place, some country." One can only address oneself to someone there in the place that they are. But how are they there? How do they address themselves in the place that they are? And reciprocally, one can address oneself to a place only for the possibilities of presence that it may hold—possibilities for being "inhabited" so to speak, or for "living" in the broad sense of the term.

For me, there are two symmetrical forms of what is probably a single obsessional structure: on the one hand, when someone close to me goes to live in a place that I don't know, I am discontent as long as I have not seen the place. I lose something of the person, and it bothers and frustrates me. I feel the abstraction that their postal address becomes for me in a very concrete way. On the other hand, when I am traveling by car, by train, or by plane, the brief sight of a place, of the corner of a farm, a barn, an old house with a fence, but also a tangle of highways, and so forth—all of this irresistibly makes me wonder: who lives there? Who is taking a walk over there? What singular history? What lifestyle?

(To amuse myself some more, the following comes to mind: perhaps I'm obsessed by these little obsessions because I myself have a name of a place, a city? It has already earned me several quid pro quos, misunderstandings, and jokes . . . Maybe I don't know if I'm someone or someplace. But let's put that aside. Let's hold onto only this: Avy, Nancy, *y, y.*)

The question is thus: how to address someone there where they are? But not abstractly there where they are: there where they are as they are. Or rather: how does one address oneself to a place as the place of someone who is there? How to address someone in a fashion that is not that of the abstraction of a postal address? Or rather, in a fashion that would play on the tension that the postal address inscribes as a gap between a name and a locality.

What gesture is needed so that it goes to someone there where they are—there where they "truly" are? What is the "true" address? It's a question about truth, in effect. It's a question even of the sense of truth.

If we say that there is a tension between being and place, it's a question of arriving at this tension—and neither exactly to being, nor exactly to place, but rather to what relates one to the other. I'll insist no further, but you know perfectly well how these kinds of questions are ready to suddenly spring up: questions of "habitation," "architecture," "urbanism," of "public or private space," questions of "borders," questions of "installation," "exposition," or of "the museum," questions on the possibility or the necessity of distinguishing between places of living and places of—and of what else—transit, haunting, surveillance, abandonment? Questions of the "landscape," of the "country," of "territory" and of "displacement," of "exile" or of "nomadism," and so forth. Questions of non-place, of displacement, of movement, of "homelessness," and I finally come to you: "Still, he is on the move again, and homelessness becomes an expression of renewed vitality, the overcoming of sterile destitution." (*The Test Drive,* 172). Vitality: this is your address. Vitality, avitality—ha, vitality!

VII.

I will now try to enumerate the characteristics of the gesture of address insofar as it must arrive at that which is in question here: being in its place, being-in-place, the place-of-being, or however one wishes to say it.

There are, it seems to me, at least five characteristics of address, that is to say, this time, of "dexterity," of address as the ability to handle address as the direction of a dispatch, or as the sending of sense.

1. Speed. There is no such thing as an instant transmission, or there wouldn't be any place that is distinct. If it's instant—or of infinite speed—then it's no longer "addressed" (I will not try here to decide if what is today called "real time," transmission that is said to be "instant," actually is so; it seems to me that it isn't, that it doesn't blur places one into another). There's always "from one to the other," and it's always a matter of a certain speed that is appropriate for this "to." High or low speed, that's exactly the affair of the address, of know-how. Someone who is showing a painting, or writing a book, or teaching—what speed of transmission are they counting on?

2. On what speed of transmission does. In order to arrive at the address, one cannot rest content with "precision," which admits a coefficient of imprecision, of approximation. As if it were indifferent whether a letter were addressed to me at number 8, 12, or at number 10, which is the correct one. (The postman knows, he reestablishes accuracy, but only if it's the regular postman of the street.) Accuracy is of an entirely different nature than precision: it's all or nothing. It superposes itself exactly over somewhere without remainder. It touches at its end, it touches at its heart. Of course, the question is: How does one take aim? As is well known, it's a question, or rather a non-question, for the art of Zen archery. It's also perhaps a question of the lucidity that only madness is capable of. But madness is not something one can aim for, or claim.

3. Touch. It's in fact a matter of touching. But touching does not only engage accuracy. It also engages "tactility," in every sense of the word. One of these senses is restraint, discretion, delicacy. In order to touch in the right way, one must handle something: one must handle, precisely, the very locus of the touch. One must not destroy it by pushing through it, crossing it, perforating it, or exploding it. In order to touch, one must also not attain to something. One has to restrain the touch in touching. This is still the art of Zen archery. One must retain something as much as one must send something—and it's perhaps the same thing—the same meditation, you say, of the same koan.

4. Retreat: one must retreat, to take a step back "to better jump," as some say. One must take off. This is to simultaneously prepare one's energy, gather up force into a ball or a package; it's the economic and energetic aspect of the thing, but one must also retreat—retreat from the very thing that it's a matter of doing: from the address. A step back, a retreat, a gap, in order to allow the address to go on its own, to deliver itself. It's a question of will. One must want to dissolve or distract the will, in order to leave room for surprise, which is at the very heart of will. I am thinking of this sentence by Seneca, which I find enchanting: "Do you know many people who know how they came to want what they want? It's not reflection that brought them to their desiring: it's with an élan that one comes to it." (Letters to Lucilius, 37:5).

5. Disappearance—or rather dissipation: address itself is not made to last. The envelope ends up in the paper bin. Or rather, it itself becomes part of the message, when it is kept with its content, as in these bunches of letters tied together with a ribbon, an image from old novels. As for dexterity, it must dissipate itself in its very execution. It must also welcome chance, luck—to the point of risking clumsiness.

But you already know all this, and you'll be able to crumple up my address and throw it in the trash. Just one more moment.

Clumsiness is the question—and it's not a question. It's not something one can thematize, and it's not a matter of organizing a dialectic, as subtle as it might be. Address can only be the movement of a loss of self—a loss of "Self" that addresses or is adroit, and of a loss of the address itself. It should neither save itself, nor make itself its own end. There are mishandlings that touch more than anything, and too much address repels us: too much ability, and too much intentionality. The truth is always beyond both one and the other. And it's perhaps exactly this, exactly this position of truth, that secretly organizes the permanent face-to-face of art and philosophy, I wanted to say you and me, but of you and yourself, of Avital in the face of Ronell, addressed one to the other, each inhabiting "an inside that is out of it" (*Finitude's Score*, ix). Sent one to the other, standing one against the other, slipping from one to the other and both from themselves. The father of the dew facing the Ronin, the samurai without master, without ties and without address.

NOTES

1. The verb Nancy uses here is *s'exhaler,* which would be correctly translated here as "evaporate." However, the French verb can also refer to something that arises and "exhales" itself from the throat. I have thus chosen to use the English *exhale,* despite its slight awkwardness in this context.
2. Toni Grand, cited by Wolfgang Becker, Vienna Exposition, catalog, 1994.
3. As should be clear from the indications in brackets, Nancy's commentary turns on the role of the locative pronoun "y" in the French expression *il y a,* which means "there is." To say *il y a* is to say, in effect, "there is there."

Judith Butler
Ronell as Gay Scientist

Of course, Ronell is reading Nietzsche throughout *The Test Drive,* so if we decide to focus on this reading, we will find that it defies our focus, because Nietzsche might be said to disperse himself throughout her text.[1] There is, however, a juncture in which it seems that she has a particular reason to follow him, but also to take her leave. It is this double-movement that I propose to trace, because it shows us something about how Ronell experiments and the kind of experiment her writing is. For instance, there are times when she seems very close to Nietzsche's cadence and voice. You will remember Nietzsche's way of disorienting his reader in *On the Genealogy of Morals* when he asks a question that was not supposed to be askable: "what is the origin of the value of good and evil?" His contemporary morality takes good and evil for granted as the oppositional and exclusive options for moral judgment. Given that this is true, he comes to ask: what is the origin of the value of morality? To ask this question is to already to scandalize those who are self-certain in their morality, because the question posits that there must be a value, a set of values, existing outside the framework of good and evil and that those values can and will be the ones by which the value of morality is adjudicated. It suggests further that whatever is meant by "origin" is itself a value, because we are only asking the question of the origin in order finally to understand the value of that morality based upon that distinction. The question does not so much *presuppose* as *posit* that

21

set of values, and so we come to understand the interrogative mode as a creative act: the question already introduces the possibility of new values, allegorizing the very means of its production.

Ronell has already introduced us to the multiple valences of science, testing our patience with a proliferating set of understandings for how science operates, how the hypothesis functions as a kind of constitutive wager in its method, and how testing itself is always conceding that there is something about the world that is not yet certainly known. Thus, Ronell brings science into the Nietzschean question about values, writing, "For different reasons, the worthiness of worth has been sidelined by science" (200). So in *The Test Drive,* we want to know how we begin to ask this question about "the worthiness of worth" in the context of science. It would seem that, through Nietzsche's *The Gay Science,* we arrive at the question of the worth of worth, the value of values, in relation to science through a procedure that is inarguably central to its own operation: *experiment.* Experiment is no simple exercise, and as we read along, it becomes clear that experiment is not only linked with life, but specifically a means for *affirming* life.

For Ronell, the experiment belongs to both science and art; it designates a procedure that works by way of hypothesis and requires testing in order to elaborate its conclusions as valid. But internal to the notion of the hypothesis and the test is precisely what is not known, and even unknowable, and in the face of which we can only form conjectures and guesses, that which defies any and all calculation. If we expected science to champion calculation and inference, we find central to the scientific method a conjecture and an affirmation of the unpredictability of outcomes that opens up a gap between method and result that no calculation can mend. The hypothesis conjectures a possible relation, and so is in that very business of "positing" that Nietzsche enacted for us with his disorienting question about morality. That question—what is the origin of the value of morality?— admits that we might be able to tell a story about the emergence of a particular morality, but this is a possibility that immediately undoes its claim to *a priori* truth. If the story we tell is a history, then it would seem that morality came into being, that it was not always there, and that some other configuration could have come into being, or will. Thus, if the inquiry into the origin of values is at once a way to probe new modes of valuation, then the very terms of the question introduce a new possibility or set of possibilities that point outside the already thinkable. Nietzsche's question, understood as a historical hypothesis, borrows its method from science. The result is curious, because the question could be read: "what would the world look like if we could find a way to establish the value of moral values, and so show that moral values are but one sort of value, and that value exceeds the domain of moral values that we currently take for granted?" That hypothesis introduces that notion of value and so performs and institutes a valuation becomes a discursive instance through which new values are posited. This positing is not the same as a thematic elaboration of new moral content, but a certain enactment of the question as the mode through which new values (which values?) are produced. This positing and producing are not just means to establish an end (new moral values) but are themselves modes of valuation; shifting "value" from a noun to a continuous verb, they entail a reconceptualization of values in terms of the posing of the question that is valuation itself.

The question is thus part of what is meant by "experiment," because established values are being tested through the question, and what was once taken to be a "ground" of moral life is exposed as a certain groundlessness. It then makes sense that Ronell elaborates on what experiment does by focusing on two of its most salient operations: "the opening of abysses" and the "the positing of values" (200).

Now this is not easy to do, reading Ronell reading Nietzsche, because I am having one set of relations with her text and she is having another set of relations to Nietzsche's. I am looking at her looking at him, and my reading is afflicted with the sense of humility that goes along with being cast to the spectatorial sidelines. I would like to say that this is a complicated triangle, but that would be to overestimate my importance. Humor is thus required. I will probably make myself known in the rendition I offer, but there is no guarantee that I could ever come between the two of them. How does she approach him? Ronell becomes something of a diagnostician after subjecting Nietzsche's text to close examination. She notes that, in Nietzsche's *The Gay Science*, "two essential desires motivate his text and pull it in different directions. . . . The experimental disposition offers him a way of articulating the doubling and division by which he proceeds" (205). How are we to understand this doubling and division? Even though his *The Gay Science* has something *fröhlich* or joyous about it, it makes a very grave claim to *Wissenschaft*. It would seem as well, according to Ronell, that the desires that motivate the text, that pull it in different directions, are not Nietzsche's own desires, the desires of the author. They are, rather, the desires "of" the text, understood as the ones that belong to it, that *motivate* it, and that tear it apart. We do not know where these desires come from, but we can read their textual trajectories. The desires are not "embedded" in the text but are themselves textual operations, and they seem to be emphatically non-teleological. Whatever the man Nietzsche may have intended, and however he was motivated by prior events to approach this writing, the motivations become something else when they assume a textual form. Whatever is happening is not just the result of Nietzsche's aims; the text also acts and transforms those aims, and we have to know how to read an aim in the text if we are to get anywhere at all. This moves us outside psychologism, but it also makes a different demand upon us: how do we understand the trajectories of desire and aim in and of the text? More specifically, how does Ronell explain this double directionality, the tearing apart, the doubling and division?

One directionality seems to consist in "active interpretation" and another in what is called "reactive," and these two are split apart. These line up with the notion of affirmation, or *affirming*—which inaugurates the new—over and against a defensive reaction, that "naysaying" activity that recoils from the obduracy of a countervailing world. This differentiation or splitting apart is not something that a subject controls or navigates, and here a figure emerges to do the work of clarification. Ronell makes clear that there is "no helmsman" who could control or predict the course of the ship (205). And the ship itself seems already shipwrecked, with different sections of the hull moving out in opposing directions upon the sea. So experiment would seem to imply a certain critique of the sovereign subject as well, because the ship is splitting in two, carrying no one very well, and its directions are unknown. Even as science would seem to prize predictability, it can only arrive at its predictions through the hypothesis, the experiment, and the test. A test is a test precisely because it is not known in advance what knowledge, if any, will be yielded by the test. Thus, the test presupposes an unknown future. And if there were no unknown future, there could be no test. Temporality is constitutive of the test, and if it were known in advance what knowledge a test would yield, it would be a fake test, even a nullification of the test itself. The future unknown is thus constitutive of the test itself, which means that experimentation is fundamentally linked up with a problem of temporality. The test, to be a test, must face and pass through what is unpredictable and, in that sense, unknown, and it cannot know in advance to what conclusions it will lead. This is not unlike a ship, equipped with working instruments, passing through a storm. The question of which direction will prevail, if any, is an open one, and cannot be known in advance even with the most precise instruments of calculation and prediction. Ronell writes, "the test is structurally staked. . . . Its performance cannot exhaust itself in some cognitive present but extends the terms of fulfillment to the future, which cannot, strictly speaking, be logically assured" (224).

So how are we to understand the duality of "opening abysses" and "positing values?" If these are trajectories that split the text apart, then they also refuse the text any final integrity. Of course, to author new values might seem, at first, to be a way of securing one's signature to a new mode of being, a flashy philosophical product newly arrived on the marketplace of ideas. Ronell is not tone-deaf here. She finds in Nietzsche's text both "'the desire for *being*,'" for immortalization, and "'the desire for destruction, change and becoming'" (205). The first would seem to correlate with the desire for certainty, results, even the monumentalization of results. The second suggests a countervailing desire for upheaval, for change and becoming that have no predictable closure. But how seriously are we to take the casting of these two desires as oppositional? Are we nearing a dialectical account of this opposition, perhaps a negative dialectic? What about the "value" of opposition itself? Does it commit us to a binary account of the desires in the text, the desires that belong to experiment, that would seem to be more Hegelian than Nietzschean?

We have seen that the experiment is a method and instrument that belongs to science and art alike. The two are conventionally contrasted but experiment cleaves them together, despite their ardent self-definitions. Thus experiment seems to mark the limit of an autonomous definition for either. Is this Ronell or is this Nietzsche? Nietzsche himself ends up sometimes overdrawing the distinction between science, on the one hand, and art, on the other. In the third section of *On the Genealogy of Morals,* he understands both science and art to be forms of sublimation, works that secure the passage to civilization. We know from his efforts to repudiate Wagner, and even the dialectical schemas that pervade *The Birth of Tragedy,* that Nietzsche sometimes moves beyond a certain oppositional thinking. And yet, he seems compelled to reestablish those oppositions as well. If he moves beyond good and evil, he seems to do so by introducing a new set of oppositions (slave morality and the morality of the nobles), or by establishing dialectical inversions (instinct turned against itself or instinct expressed outwardly). Here, however, is where Ronell might be said to track a certain division and splitting in Nietzsche that cannot be resolved logically into a problem of conceptual oppositions. It also begins to lay the groundwork for understanding how Ronell splits from him, taking another route than the one he could or would take.

If we imagine that affirming and negating are opposites, we have to think again, because there seems to be, *pace* the Deleuzian interpretation of late, a certain persistent negativity in the midst of affirmation. Ronell points out that "affirming" experiment, testing, and improvisation is *not* the expression of unmixed desire. She shows that the gay scientist cannot be gay without some pain: "the work of the gay scientist draws upon a history of suffering, exile, and pain, which necessarily becomes a measure of the field of discovery without erasing its more discursive requirements. The abundant personality inhabits suffering in a manner that proves difficult to share" (208). There is something both solitary and over-full for the gay scientist, a predicament difficult to convey effectively within the conventions of communication. No amount of sympathetic identification from our "dear pitying friends" seems to yield an adequate understanding of the suffering at issue (208). We are not referencing a common reality that language might name with ease. We are moving close to the question of the "opening abyss" even as it would seem that Ronell's text pushes us away precisely here. Can we be pushed away and still stay the course? At stake is an opening of *mixed* desire, and this gap—a gap without which there can be no test, no experiment—constitutes a break with communication and breaks apart those who would communicate. To say that this breaking or gap is essential to this mode of discovery is not to say that it constitutes the ground or condition for its operation. Rather, it is a breaking apart of the operation that turns out to be essential to the operation itself. Something opens up that is recalcitrant and not to be shared.

Hence, the "abysses that open" make it very difficult to sustain oppositions in the ways to which we might otherwise be drawn (if, for instance, we were in recovery from a certain Hegelianism). Can we still distinguish between "affirmative" and "reactive" with epistemological confidence? Are the two linked together precisely in the passage that marks the failure of communication itself? Indeed, those gaps seem to be bound up with a certain temporal predicament of probing, one that subtends all efforts at communication; it would seem that even in those contracts that belong to friendship, "an unnarratable story of distress" is presupposed. She writes, "a community of two, me and you, has a history hidden from almost everyone; it is bound by the incalculable risks and terrors, adventures and blunders (and so forth) constituting our scientific contract" (209). She upends us temporarily (or maybe fatally) by casting our friendship as a matter of science, but we forget to ask what worse damage she has done to a notion of science that would understand itself apart from the temporal predicaments of language.

We are asked to understand the gay scientist as a figure who is at once affirmative and in an isolated suffering, and this seems to follow from the protocols of experimentation itself. If there is no helmsman and, as Ronell puts it, the "strong personality involves the capacity to divest oneself constantly," then it follows that affirmation undoes the subject who performs it, and who undergoes a "self-submission to the radical deprogramming" that can hardly be a path without loss and pain (209). The desire for change and the desire to be are not precisely oppositional but locked in a complicated, if sometimes nasty, embrace. If what is affirmative is to be distinguished analytically from what is reactive, and if the extra-moral belongs to the sphere of affirmation (as instanced by the possibility of affirming a value outside moral values), then it would seem that morality has to be countered by something stronger than its own claims. If we think of the question, though, as instancing this positing of what is stronger than the claims of morality, we can see that the question must homeopathically enter into the moral domain to exemplify something of the testing procedure that turns out to be essential to the operation of morality itself.

I want to suggest that at this juncture, though, Nietzsche seems to take the bait too quickly, seeking recourse to "art" as a way of opposing the strictures of morality, a term that is nearly coextensive with that of "reaction." Morality arises, in his view, through several paths, but among the most prominent is the one that would denounce life itself. For Nietzsche, Ronell tells us "art introduces a vitality capable of hosing down the strictures of morality" (211). But how did morality put our vitality into jeopardy? And what is the link between morality and science? In *The Gay Science,* at least, Nietzsche affirms science and reads it as a mode of affirmation only to the extent that science proves to require art, and art proves to be more fundamental than science. The opposition is resolved, then, by making art primary.

Yet, if we link art with affirmation and understand affirmation to be the affirmation of life, there is no way around the problem of mixed desire that we have already considered. There can be no affirmation without the opening of a certain abyss, and affirmation, especially the kind involved in *amor fati,* requires a certain "yes" precisely to the sufferings that belong to life (221). I am not sure what the proposition finally is that life seeks to prove, although I am startled and engaged by the idea that there might be one. This "life" cannot be understood as a free-floating category, and Ronell directs us away from any resolution in vitalism. Indeed, she refers us back to the idea of the experiment, to the necessary collision between predictability and the future unknown, suggesting that this duality is what is meant by life, the thought that the proposition must somehow near.

The consideration of the experiment thus has implications for thinking about life, because the affirmation of life is at stake in this method whose outcomes are unpredictable. The abyss that opens up between hypothesis and result, the abyss that characterizes a path that cannot be known in advance, and so marks the limits of our knowing, is one that also threatens a certain nihilism, and so opens up the question of whether and how to affirm a life that cannot finally be mastered through knowledge or other forms of calculation and control. What happens to us cannot be known in advance, and no prediction can work without having to be repeated and retested. It is not just that we do not know future results of this test, but that this unknowing indicates a futurity that is in itself incalculable. Testing attests to this incalculability, to an abyss that opens without being able to close. We can become mad scientists, I suppose, and test infinitely in order to try and close the gap, but the gap would approximate that infinity with every step of the way, and so we would end up demonstrating, through showing the limits of all demonstration, the impossibility of ever collapsing futurity into demonstrability.

Every time there is a repetition and retesting, that abyss opens up again. If results must be repeatable to be accepted as valid, then they are subject precisely to a reiterated gap or difference between the instances of testing that opens up the abyssal conditions of experiment's own procedure. What follows is that even in the most reliably calculable of procedures, there is no way to avoid the iterability of the test, and no way to overcome that difference that is required for certainty itself. That difference, however, cannot precisely be known or thematized, because it constitutes the abyssal condition of knowing and thematizing. And it has certain consequences for the problem of how to affirm life. There is no affirmation of life without the affirmation of this abyss (the abyss is central to the affirmation itself), and because affirmation cannot take place in a singular instance, because it must be temporal, hence, iterable, the abyss yawns in the difference that establishes every iteration and so functions as a precondition of affirmation itself. The mixed feelings we spoke of earlier turn out to be a function of the structure of affirmation.

If we track this "opening of abysses" and "positing of values" in Ronell, we find a certain dedication to Nietzsche, but also a way of tracking a different path that establishes the difference that makes her own reading possible. She is indebted in all the right ways to Nietzsche's thinking of *amor fati*, of the difficult thought that "everything that happens to us turns out to have been meant for us, addressed to us" (221–22). Of course, this does not mean that there is a divinely intending subject who has sent events our way; rather, *precisely because* there is no divine sender of that kind, events are "addressed" to us. The sender is lost, but the message makes its way, and we read it not for meaning as such but because it arrives as that which is yet to be read, as a challenge and prompt for reading. Thus, if a message is intended for us in this way, it is accidental, but it turns out that everything accidental "has profound use and significance precisely for us" (222).

There is no single declaration that proves that *amor fati* has been achieved or that, in turn, shows that all that has happened was a matter of necessity. To affirm the accidents that are addressed to us, that have significance for us, is not something that can be done at once. It has to be "proven again and again" (223). One can neither fully refute determinism nor fully embrace arbitrariness ("believing in chance"), because we are up against an epistemological limit here with the question of what has happened. Thus, it is interesting to me that on page 223 of Ronell's text there is a space between paragraphs that separates the discussion of *amor fati* from the excursus on irony. I want to suggest that this is the moment where Ronell distinguished herself from Nietzsche, though plying his text for the resources to cut her own path. Nietzsche moves to the affirmation of "art," and Ronell characterizes that move this way: "Thanks to art, Nietzsche suggests, we can now genuinely welcome science the way one welcomes the future" (212). Ronell does not move in such unbridled ways, though, and the very conundrum of affirmation turns out to draw upon another strain in Nietzsche's text.

Nietzsche's welcome presupposes a certain facing forward toward the future, but Ronell's suggests something different. She refers to the "trope of irony and the high velocities of rhetorical deviations that dominate the Gay Sci" (223). And she moves to consider the relation between the scientific project and "irony's particular temporality as a structure of the instant." This last move extends her reflections on *amor fati* and identifies the trope of irony as that feature of experiment linking science and art despite themselves. This is clearly not the same as showing that science depends upon art and that art is primary. Rather, the effort to "link the scientific project, its many and diverse aspects, with irony's particular temporality as a structure of the instant" (223) discloses something about "occurrence" itself, the structure of the event, and the way in which there can be no event without a temporality that sidetracks desire itself, or what we have been calling the "aims" in and of the text. Ronell refuses the expressive affirmation of art in favor of the mixed feelings articulated in irony. The point is not to face the future with welcoming arms but to undergo an invariable and ironic dislocation of aim by virtue of the structure of testing. Ronell replaces art with irony and finds irony in the resemblance between testing and anacoluthon. She welcomes de Man into the text, thus spoiling something of Nietzsche's plan for welcoming the future. She writes, "anacoluthon is more often used in terms of syntactical patterns of tropes, or periodic sentences, where the syntax of a sentence that raises certain expectations is 'suddenly interrupted and, instead of getting what you would expect to get, you get something completely different, a break in the syntactical expectations of the pattern'" (224). De Man breaks into Ronell's text, a text that has already established an unexpected break between the discussion of *amor fati*, which we expected to lead to a revaluation of "art" in Nietzsche's sense, and a discussion of irony in de Man's work. We get what we do not expect, and so anacoluthon works to structure this text. But does it also work to give an ironic structure to scientific explanation that rests upon the experiment?

Every experiment must posit a hypothesis, must articulate a conjecture and submit that positing to a temporal process. Of course, that positing already takes place in time, in an instant, and the instant is possible only by virtue of the structure of the instant. Irony is thus at work here, because what is posited is separated from what is posited next, and the "abyss" that opens precisely here, an abyss without which there can be no positing, is precisely what binds positing to the problematic of destruction. As a result, we may seek to welcome a future, posit the future in a welcoming way, but what will come our way is in no sense known at the time of the positing. This is not just an epistemological limit that afflicts all acts of welcome but a structural one that establishes the possibility of the radically unexpected as the abyssal basis of all prediction. The "sudden interruption" and "break in syntactical expectation" characterizes not only the figure of anacoluthon but the "procedure" of Ronell's text, a text that shows us that all procedure is bound up with this irony. The abyss that opens up between instances of positing is the condition and undoing of predictability. The different path that Ronell takes is precisely the path of difference: gay, difficult, affirmative, ironic.

NOTE

1.   Avital Ronell, *The Test Drive* (Champaign: University of Illinois Press, 2005). All future references to this text are cited parenthetically.

Peter Fenves
The Courage of the Critic: Avital Ronell and the Idea of Emergence

I.

Few propositions of modern philosophy are as famous or memorable as the one with which Kant begins his "Answer to the Question: What is Enlightenment?" This proposition contains *in nuce* the answer to the question: "Enlightenment is the emergence of human beings from the nonage for which they are themselves responsible."[1] Enough said, one might say; but Kant does not simply stop. As if driven by a fear that his answer is insufficiently clear, he proceeds to explain two of the terms in which it is formulated: "nonage" (*Unmündigkeit*) consists in an inability to use one's own understanding without the guidance of someone else; "for which they are themselves responsible" (*verschuldet*) rests on a distinction between those who are capable of understanding and those who, as Kant writes, exhibit a total "lack of understanding." What Kant fails to clarify—and this failure cannot be altogether distinguished from the threat of this "lack"— are the other two terms on which he draws: "human being" (*Mensch*) and "emergence" (*Ausgang*). About the former term, Kant is famously hesitant. As he indicates in a representative discussion of "philosophy in general," all of what is called by this august title "in its cosmopolitan sense" revolves around this question: "What is the human being?"[2] With respect to *emergence,* however, there is no similar hesitation—and this despite the fact that the "cosmopolitan sense" of any term, including *Mensch,* can itself emerge only in light of the "emergence" in question.

Instead of making sure that all of his readers understand what he means by *emergence,* Kant asks them something akin to a "test question": identify the condition under which it can take place. The answer to *this* question can be found in a schoolboy exercise—specifically, that of translating a line from a Latin poem. Its author is Horace, who provides the "motto" of enlightenment: *sapere aude.* Although it is unlikely that anyone who came across this "motto" in the pages of the *Berlinische Monatsschrift* would fail to understand it—under the presumption, of course, that "understanding" here means devising an adequate German equivalent—Kant provides a translation of his own: "Habe Mut, dich deines *eigenen* Verstandes zu bedienen." This can be then translated into English as "Have the courage to use your *own* understanding." With his own translation, emphasis included, Kant encourages his readers to emerge from the nonage for which they can be held responsible without having himself discussed what it means for them "to emerge." This much is certain, however: "emergence" *must* be dangerous; otherwise, it would not require courage. And the *other* condition under which emergence is possible—other than the ambiguous virtue of courage—is that an answer be found to the question of the human being, an answer that rules out, once and for all, the possibility that this being is constitutively lacking in understanding.

This possibility *almost* enters into Kant's subsequent commentary on his one-sentence response to the question of enlightenment, however, when he writes, apropos of the self-serving "guardians" of the status quo, that they impress upon "the greater part of the human race (including the entire fair sex)" how difficult and dangerous it is for them to emerge out of their self-imposed nonage. It is not as though, for Kant, as opposed to the "guardians," there is no difficulty or danger in emerging—only that the dangers and difficulties are not the ones that the "guardians" seek to conjure into existence. Courage, then, is required of Kant's readers to identify the *real* danger, which consists, above all, in discerning and therefore opposing the guardians' pretense of danger, and this courage to the second degree—which comes very close to a second "nonage," as it were, whatever it may be called—goes a long way to answering the "test question" Kant poses at the opening of his "Answer to the Question."

II.

One of the very few inquiries into *this* question—the "test question"—can be found in Avital Ronell's *Stupidity.* The aim of this inquiry can be briefly summarized as follows: *stupidity* is the name of the second-order courage that is the condition under which "emergence" can take place. Few proponents of enlightenment philosophy that developed during the eighteenth century would have agreed with this proposition. As Ronell writes in the introduction to *Stupidity*, "The expectation that philosophy can train thought to detach from stupidity has its source in the Enlightenment."[3] It could be said that the proponents of enlightenment are equally committed to the program of wiping out addictions and drives as well—all in the name of "freedom," understood as the capacity to choose whatever one wants, under the condition that these wants are themselves rational and can therefore be wanted by everyone in general and therefore perhaps by no one in particular. Ronell's *Crack Wars* analyzes the idea of unfree aims, and *The Test Drive* the ascription of enthralled motives. In this regard, *Stupidity* represents something of a middle term, especially in the section devoted to "The Rhetoric of Testing," for stupidity both contributes to addiction and keeps drives from being recognized for what they are. If stupidity can be eliminated, so goes the argument of those who argue for the virtues of enlightenment, addiction would be amendable to effective treatment and drives would be effectively tamed, if not entirely squelched. The question, then, is how this task of elimination can be carried out. A respite from drives and addictions—this is what the detachment from stupidity promises and what the proponents of enlightenment, as Ronell emphasizes, went so far as to expect of philosophy. Emphasis should be placed on *expectation*. At issue in the program of enlightenment, as it is often proposed, is not so much the possibility or even only the promise of distinguishing between the capacity for understanding and an irreparable "lack of understanding" as the expectation—grounded in the knowledge of an insuperable distinction between the capacity and the incapacity for knowledge—that philosophy can someday secure this distinction. *Stupidity* begins by putting an end to this expectation, and it does by affirming, from the outset, that we know only one thing in advance about stupidity, to wit, that it "does not allow itself to be opposed to knowledge in any simple way, nor is it the other of thought."[4]

Despite the fact, then, that *Stupidity* does not explicitly discuss Kant's "Answer to the Question," this affirmation—once again, that negative knowledge is the beginning of a certain wisdom—can be understood as an altercation with its opening gesture. To be more precise: a reading of *Stupidity* discloses the extent to which Kant, unknowingly perhaps, disengages himself from any version of enlightenment philosophy that assigns itself the role of "train[ing] thought to detach from stupidity." For Kant shows something at the opening of this essay that runs counter to what he says: he says that "emergence" is possible; but he shows that it may not be so. The showing proceeds in the following manner: it may be impossible, after all, to fulfill the demand that you use your *own* understanding, for, if you use your own understanding, you are not really using your own understanding but are, instead, only following Kant's orders; if, however, you do not use your own understanding, you are not using your own understanding either, because you are being led by a "guardian." In general, then, you cannot use your own understanding as soon as it is demanded—by the "guardian" of philosophical norms, say, who draws on the "guardian" of poetic standards—that you do so. In order for there to be room for "own-ness" in "your own understanding," a certain stupefaction must interfere with procedures by which the "motto" of enlightenment is understood as such. And this stupefaction is legible in the words Kant chooses for his "motto": the Roman poet says nothing about "ownness" when he writes "*sapere aude.*" This is Kant's "own" choice, which at once clarifies the words of the poet and puts into question the very coherence of his "Answer to the Question." Its possible incoherence, however, contrasts with the coherence of what the "guardians" say: namely, be afraid.

III.

This is a lesson drawn straight from *Stupidity*: the very formulation in which programs for the overcoming of stupidity succumb to a kind of stupefac-tion that traverses the distinction between a failure for which one can be held responsible and a failure for which one cannot. Just as Kant demands of his readers that they emerge from their self-incurred nonage, Ronell demands of hers that they work themselves out of the conviction that this emergence can occur—which does not mean, however, that it is therefore impossible, a "pipe dream" from which we should awaken ourselves, just as Kant awakens himself from the "dogmatic slumbers." The problem is not so much the idea of a world without stupidity as the *project* of making it so. Indeed, the problem is not so much the project per se as its *beginning,* the initial answer to the question under discussion from which further answers are derived. For Kant, the initial step of getting human beings set on the proper course, in which they use their "own" understanding, is doubtless paradoxical, for the one who speaks in the name of enlightenment must assume for a moment the dubious position of the "guardian." Similarly paradoxical—but in a reverse direction—is the step Ronell takes at the opening of *Stupidity,* in which she must occupy for a moment the position of one who is immune from the quality she is naming. Just as Kant turns to a "motto" in order to enact the paradox—and thereby overcome it, to a certain extent—so, too, does Ronell. The only difference: Kant calls his "motto" (*Wahlspruch*) by name; Ronell chooses an utterance (*Spruch*) that repudiates the very idea of "choice" (*Wahl*). Kant turns toward a Latin poet for his "motto," Ronell toward a German one, namely Friedrich Hölderlin, who modeled the metrical form of his odes on the very poet whom Kant had chosen. Among Hölderlin's Horatian odes is "Dichtermut," which can be effortlessly translated as "Courage of the Poet." Another is "Blödigkeit," the title of which cannot be so easily translated. These two poems not only occupy the opening pages of the introduction to *Stupidity;* in combination with each other, they can be read as the unchosen—or fated—"motto" of stupidity under the condition that it is no longer understood as either the opposite of knowledge or as the other of thought.

Using her own understanding, leaving aside the guardians of the German tradition in English, Ronell courageously translates "Blödigkeit" as *stupidity.* Previous translators of Hölderlin's poetry, a number of whom are very good, have not been so bold; they generally preferred to see the later poem as the revision, repudiation, and ultimate reversal of "Dichtermut." The opposite of courage is diffidence or timidity, and these terms therefore would serve as translations of "Blödigkeit." Both diffidence and timidity share something in common with courage: the atmosphere of danger. Whereas those who are courageous allow themselves to enter into the field of danger, those who are diffident or timid do not. As for the nature of the atmosphere in which the poet emerges as a poet—in contrast to a farmer, say—one can readily refer to one of the first of Hölderlin's supposedly "late" poems, "Wie wenn am Feiertage" ("As When on a Holiday"), which presents the danger as a bolt of fire from the heavens. Standing out in the open, "denuded" (*entblößt*), poets are exposed to the threat of the heaven-sent lightning bolt. Heidegger, for one, is emphatic about the importance of this passage, so much so that it can be seen as the base note in his "soundings"(*Erläuterungen*) of Hölderlin's poetry. For Heidegger, it goes without saying that those who expose themselves to lightning are heroic. Not for Ronell, and her inquiry of what might be called "poetic heroism" represents the opening step of *Stupidity*: those who stand in the open, "denuded" in the midst of electrical storms, could *also* be considered stupid—and with equal justice. In general terms, however, courage and stupidity are not opposites; they are mutually exclusive. If you are too stupid to recognize a threat, or if, conversely, you are stupid enough to make up a threat when there is none, you cannot be called "courageous," regardless of the dangers you may endure. Ronell's decision to translate "Blödigkeit" as *stupidity* at the opening of *Stupidity* is, for this reason, a telling departure from a tradition that represents the actions of the poet either in terms of heroism or timidity—the heroism of a revolutionary, for instance, or the timidity of the social conservative, which a heroic critic then uncovers. *Stupidity* bypasses these reversible formulae by insisting that two poems of Hölderlin, "The Courage of the Poet" and "Stupidity," are bound together.

IV.

The alteration in the translation of a poem's title—even if the poem is Hölderlin's—is doubtless a minor affair; but the stakes of this alteration are nevertheless immense, for it begins to cast doubt on the martial ethos that is preserved by those who directly oppose this ethos and proclaim, in whatever form, their allegiance to the project of perpetual peace. This later transformation is already evident in Kant's "Answer to the Question," especially in its final paragraphs, which equate the "age of enlightenment" with the "age of Frederick II" and applaud this king for both his negative courage—"fearing no shadows"—*and* his "well-disciplined and numerous army," which allows him to make others fear him.[5] To be sure, the association of courage with stupidity does not, of itself, spell the end of a martial ethos, for stupidity can always be understood as a kind of "natural grace" that overcomes those who enter into battle and allows them to dampen cowardly voices of conscience; but this manner of allying stupidity with courage can only be taken so far. If stupidity precludes *any* awareness of danger, if, more exactly, stupidity means, at least in part, obliviousness to danger, then it cannot be squared with the idea of courage that arises from martial contexts. A rigorous association of stupidity with courage, which does not shy away from the suggestion that the two are equivalent in the end, cuts far deeper into the martial ethos than any self-consciously heroic critique of war or self-endangering project for perpetual peace. Such an association can be discerned in Hölderlin's two poems, as Ronell reads them in tandem. And for this reason alone these two odes can be read as the "motto" that is destined for *Stupidity*.

Ronell does not say this. She never says that her discussion stands under the sign of Hölderlin's two poems, which, taken together, represent an "a-heroic" assault on the martial ethos. Still, she comes very close to doing so: "'Dichtermut' (the poet's courage)," she writes early in the introduction to *Stupidity*, "has been widely considered the blueprint for the poem on which *my discussion* centers."[6] Of course, "my discussion" in this context can be easily understood as a reference to the following two or three paragraphs, which are largely concerned with "Blödigkeit." But no such limits are stated, and for good reason: the import of Ronell's remark is to cast doubt on the idea that the poem in question is only *one* poem, isolated from its putative predecessor. If "Blödigkeit" is not simply one poem among others, if it cannot be simply understood as *a* poem that derives—and departs—from an earlier one, which would be its supposed "blueprint," then it can continue to be at the "center" of her discussion even if it is no longer under discussion. All of *Stupidity*, if not all of Ronell's other readings, can then be understood as the referent of "my discussion." This makes discussion of her work difficult. For nothing can be said to follow anything else. It is not as though everything happens "all at once," but the happening of things, their event-character, cannot be understood along the lines of a sequence. If understanding is understood as the ability to follow a rule—and this is what Kant himself asserts when he represents concepts as rules and identifies the origin of their applicability in their corresponding schemata—then the absence of this ability amounts to stupidity: instead of being able to say "this follows that according to such-and-such a rule," those who exhibit a "lack of understanding" are fixated on singular occurrences, none of which "follows" from the other. In the introduction to *Stupidity*, Ronell introduces a term for this version of anacoluthon or non sequitur: "co-emergence." With this word she describes the relations between the two poems under discussion: they "co-emerge, one giving birth to the other."[7]

Not only does the "later" poem of Hölderlin emerge from the earlier one, according to Ronell, the "earlier" poem emerges from the later one, such that there could be no "courage of the poet" without "stupidity," and no "stupidity" without a certain courage—the courage, more exactly, to be transfixed by singular occurrences, such that they digress from the series of which they are nevertheless also a part. Nothing, not even a writing implement, *begets* either poem. Ronell's refusal to give priority to one poem over the other does not derive from philological skepticism, which would suggest that literary-historical scholarship is incapable of determining which poem came first. The point is, rather, that any determination of this kind rests on the principle that there can be no such thing as "co-emergence." Granting room for "co-emergence" is by no means a simple feat, however, as Ronell's discussion emphasizes: it requires that the critic be attentive to an occurrence or event that—because of *another* occurrence or event—can no longer be *called* either an occurrence or an event. The two poems of Hölderlin, taken together, constitute such an occurrence or event. We stumble in speaking about them as what they are: "We can no longer say in Heideggarian tonalities that when Nietzsche fought with Wagner (or so-and-so said this or that) it was an historial event. Yet we can still intimate the gravity of an emergence, no matter how complicated, when Hölderlin welds 'Blödigkeit' to 'Dichtermut.'"[8]

Ronell does not say why it is no longer possible to speak of certain occurrences as "historial events." It is by no means difficult, however, to identify at least one reason for this delicate situation: "Heideggerian tonalities" are unacceptable to the extent they suggest that the horrific stuff of history— death and poverty—are mere phenomena, whereas historial events themselves are accessible only to a mode of thinking that is attuned to something equivalent to the death of thinking or poverty of philosophy. With this rebuke in mind, it takes courage to say that, nevertheless, something does happen, an event does take place when Hölderlin "welds" one of his poems onto another. Added to this rebuke is the fact that a statement to this effect runs counter to the dense and astonishing analysis Walter Benjamin proposes in his "Two Poems of Friedrich Hölderlin," which was written at the beginning of the First World War—long before Heidegger had tested out the tonalities with which his name would be associated. Whatever else can be said of Benjamin's essay from late 1914 or early 1915, this much is certain: it presents the mythos of "Blödigkeit" as a decisive advance over the mythology of "Dichtermut." Not only is there, for Benjamin, no "welding" of one poem onto the other, the "poetized" of "Blödigkeit" approaches the ideal of "aesthetic commentary" in general—an ideal that he calls, following the lead of certain neo-Kantians, "the pure poetized." To the extent that the "poetized" approaches the ideal of its purity, the corresponding poem renounces any efforts, including that of the poet, to mingle it with any other poem. Departing from both Heidegger and Benjamin, Ronell asserts that the two odes of Hölderlin, welded together, make us aware not so much of a "historial event" but of a certain force—she calls it "gravity"—that corresponds to "emergence."

V.

Among the recent assertions reverberating in "Heideggerian tonalities," none is perhaps more important for the inquiries undertaken in *Stupidity* than the following remarks of Paul de Man, which appear in a posthumously published lecture entitled "Kant and Schiller":

> History, the sense of the notion of history as the historicity a priori of this type of textual model which I have been suggesting here, there history is not thought of as a progression or a regression, but is thought of as an event, as an occurrence. There is history from the moment that words such as 'power' and 'battle' and so on emerge from the scene. At that moment

things *happen,* there is *occurrence,* there is *event.* History is therefore not a temporal notion, it has nothing to do with temporality, but it is the emergence of a language of power out of a language of cognition. An emergence which is, however, not itself either a dialectical movement or any kind of continuum, any kind of continuum that would be accessible to a cognition, however much it may be conceived of, as would be the case in a Hegelian dialectic, as a negation.[9]

The discussion of history as emergence in de Man's lecture on Kant and Schiller develops out of his reading of Kant's critical program, especially its crowning achievement, the *Critique of Judgment,* and more exactly still, the following passage from an appendix to the Analytic of the Dynamically Sublime, which de Man first analyzes in "Phenomenality and Materiality in Kant": "To find the ocean nevertheless sublime we must regard it as poets do [*wie die Dichter tun*], merely by what the eye reveals [*was der Augenschein zeigt*]—if it is at rest, as a clear mirror of water only bounded by the heavens; if it is stormy, as an abyss threatening to overwhelm everything."[10] This curious passage, made famous by de Man's reading, could be called Kant's version of either poetic courage or stupidity—or a kind of nonendangering courage welded to a form of willed stupidity. Ronell, for her part, detects a pattern at work in de Man's analysis: "The only point I wish to urge at this time, without engaging the many heuristic demands of 'Phenomenality and Materiality in Kant,' concerns de Man's consistent investment in figures of stupefaction, mindlessness, dumbness, even where Kant went elsewhere."[11] By leaving aside these "heuristic demands," which would perhaps require a "return to Kant," Ronell goes straight to the question of what de Man's "consistent investment in figures of stupefaction, mindless, and dumbness" means. The answer, in shorthand, runs as follows: de Man is "already" Schlegelian, even though he, of course, came "after" Schlegel; more generally—with the understanding that generalization is problematic—the various terms in question ("stupefaction," "mindlessness," "dumbness") refer to something prior to understanding, but this priority cannot be understood in terms of either a temporal or conceptual continuum. This means, in Kantian terms, that the power of judgment cannot successfully subsume the faculty of intuition under the faculty of the understanding, with the result that *every* schematization must be considered only provisional, so much so that the term *provisional* must itself be considered only a provisional schematization of the priority under investigation: "Already Schlegelian, de Man considers these terms [*stupefaction, mindlessness, dumbness*] to mark a place prior to understanding. Yet, we show (though, in keeping with Kant, we understand such showing to remain a questionable endeavor) the extent to which the determinations, 'before and after' understanding, cannot be seen as temporal categories, for the provisional is final and the 'fore-' lies' in the future."[12]

A slight difference—here marked by *yet*—thus emerges between de Man and Ronell. The difference can*not* be captured by the following formulation: for de Man, stupefaction precedes understanding in terms of a temporal continuum, whereas Ronell shows that the precedence of stupefaction over understanding is not temporal. Ronell's deviation from the line of argument pursued by de Man appears, rather, in the parentheses: "(though, in keeping with Kant, we understand such showing to remain a questionable endeavor)." What we understand, in other words, is the questionable character of what we show—including the difference between showing something that is "there" to be shown and putting on a show in which there is nothing but this very showing. It is questionable in the case of de Man's reading of *Augenschein* in the *Critique of Judgment,* for example, whether or not de Man understands that his reading is questionable. In Ronell's discussion of this reading, by contrast, there is no question that her reading is questionable. Not by accident does this discussion appear under a title that welds enlightenment and mystification: "Ghosts (The *Schein*ing)." By keeping with Kant, Ronell foregoes the chance of demonstrating, once and for all, that stupefaction precedes understanding and the precedence of stupefaction over understanding reflects the precedence of history, or the historial event, over time, or the temporal continuum. For de Man, the following summary is probably accurate. To an *event,* an *occurrence,* or—as de Man writes, once again in "Kant and Schiller," to an *emergence*—there corresponds stupefaction; to progress as well as to regress and therefore to everything that is reversible and for this reason "unhistorial," there corresponds the dialectic of understanding and misunderstanding. The second does not follow the first; rather, there is only the first, the first alone *happens,* and in this regard it is "prior" without there being a temporal continuum that would represent this event as a sequence. Understanding, then—and least of all, the use of one's "own understanding"—is never historial; it is never a matter of emergence.

For Ronell, by contrast, who keeps with Kant, all of this may be true; it may even participate in "the true," as in the famous line of Hölderlin's "Mnemosyne," which de Man quotes in "Kant and Schiller" immediately before his characterization of history as emergence. But its demonstration is nevertheless objectively or constitutively problematic. In schematic terms, this means that "Blödigkeit" should *not* be taken for an historial event, whereas its Schillerian counterpart—and this is a fitting characterization of "Dichtermut," with its image of the poet as doomed swimmer—would be "ideological" or, in Benjamin's terms, "mythological." Rather, for Ronell, the historial event would consist in the "welding" of the two poems, "The Courage of the Poet" and "Stupidity." This metallurgical event gives an intimation of an "emergence"—but only an intimation. "There is history," de Man writes, once again, "from the moment that words such as 'power' and 'battle' and so on emerge from the scene. At that moment things *happen*, there is *occurrence*, there is *event*. History is therefore not a temporal notion, it has nothing to do with temporality, but it is the emergence of a language of power out of a language of cognition." *This* emergence is accessible only to the stupid—or better yet, the courageously stupid, whose "seeing" of the "emergence" is the very emergence they "see." A word such as "battle" enters into a cognitive discourse. Conversely, Ronell's "emergence"— which *we* intimate without thereby showing ourselves as courageous—keeps with Kant's *Ausgang*: it is not the heroic emergence of human beings, who, using their own understanding, are in a position to take a step on their own; rather, it is the an-heroic emergence of a peace that—to quote an old saw—"passeth understanding." This peace should probably be called a "stupid" peace, which stands in stark contrast to the perpetual peace Kant discusses in the famous "philosophical project" he proposes under this title: a "race of devils," Kant avers, could institute and maintain this peace under the sole condition that the members of this accursed race, certain of their powers and cognizant of their vulnerabilities, fully understood and acted on the basis of their own interests.

VI.

Peace is not among the major terms Ronell discusses in *Stupidity*. In its introduction she briefly describes the trajectory of her project in specifically nonpacific terms: "We go first to the poets, and to war."[13] There is no indication that the movement from poetry to warfare ever touches on—much less, leads to—peace. On the contrary, this one-sentence paragraph leads into her analysis of the relation between "Dichtermut" and "Blödigkeit." Instead of discussing peace, she writes of a certain linguistic passivity, more exactly, the passive voice, which, in the hands of Benjamin, corresponds to the hyperbolic passivity into which Hölderlin's "Stupidity" issues: "formless being, utter passivity ('das regellose Dasein, die völlige Passivität')."[14] So little does this passivity have to do with peace, however— or so it appears—that Ronell detects a "warlike beat" in the rhythm of the poem: "an order issued from another topos of the self."[15] The sounds of

Hölderlin's "Friedensfeier" ("Celebration of Peace") do not make themselves known at the level of theme. As Ronell notes, Benjamin's discourse of "utter passivity" can be understood as a gloss on the following image, which occurs only in "Blödigkeit": poets are "Drawn erect on golden / Leading strings, like children." This image represents a reversal and revision of the one through which Kant explains his answer to the question of enlightenment and begins the project of nondiplomatic peacemaking that would culminate in *Toward Perpetual Peace* some ten years later. At issue is the rhetoric of the "guardians" who maintain their guardianship by stupefying the herd into seeing them forever in this leading role: "Having first made their domestic animals stupid and having carefully made sure these passive creatures will not take a single step without the go-cart to which they are tethered, these guardians then show them the danger that threatens them if they sought to walk alone."[16]

Whereas "Answer to the Question" asks of its readers that they break free from all "leading strings," Hölderlin's poem asks of the poet that they see themselves as guided by golden ones. As Ronell emphasizes, quoting Benjamin, this upright position is the "authentic disposition of the poet." Being restrained by strings, which would prevent the "emergence" of which Kant speaks, the poet "has nothing left, no core, no boundary other than formless being, utter passivity."[17] Inasmuch as "Stupidity" is welded onto "Courage of the Poet," this passivity must be understood as a certain form of heroism—but precisely not that of the "action hero." Ronell then specifies the character of what might be called the "passion hero" who is constitutively incapable of triumphing, even in the end: "The gesture of traversing peril and running a risk—a risk that does not know and cannot tell where it's going—points in these poems not to a morph of the action hero, quick and present to the task, sure of aim, but to the depleted being, held back by fear or indifference (we are never sure which), a being from the start stupefied, nonpresent—'not all there.' No one has been able to account for that which is missing, not there, in poetic origination, but the poets have in their way avowed the secret experience of stupidity."[18] For Kant, *experience* and *knowledge* are equivalent terms; here, however, the two terms part ways, such that the "secret experience" that the poets avow departs from the order of knowledge without, for this reason, being consigned to a sphere of mere ignorance. The analysis of Kant from the perspective of de Man here imposes a question: Does this departure mean, using de Man's term, that stupefaction marks the emergence of a "language of power out of a language of cognition," which would be the "emergence" *tout court*, the "event" or "occurrence," perhaps even the "event" or "occurrence" of "the true," which, according to the lines of Hölderlin quoted by de Man, takes a long time, or even makes time long, but nevertheless "appropriates itself" or "takes place" ("ereignet sich") as well?

VII.

The answer to this question is probably "No." A language of power does not emerge; history—understood in this manner—does not occur. There is, for Ronell, "emergence" neither in the Kantian nor in the de Manian sense: neither the emergence of a humanity that, regardless of its devilishness, has enough "good sense" to institute peace among its kind, nor the emergence of a language of power, even if only in the negative mode of impotence. To be sure, as Ronell indicates, attuned to the characteristic sound of Hölderlin's poetry and not simply bent on deciphering them for their putative "content," the rhythm of the two poems under discussion is warlike; but because these poems are Hölderlin's, after all, and Hölderlin had proposed in painstaking detail a doctrine of tonal alteration, this beat can be heard only under the condition that it give evidence of an opposing tendency, which, in this case, would be the syncopation of a peace that "passeth understanding."[19] Whether or not this syncopation is thematically associated with stupidity is of little importance. More important than the question posed by such a thematization is the image of what runs counter to the warlike beat. *Stupidity* revolves around just such an image. And this is nowhere more so than in the last of the "satellites" of stupidity Ronell launches, a "satellite" that begins with late Kant and turns into an exposition of what might be called "the co-passions of Sarah and Isaac." Even if this label is misleading, the relation of God to Abraham and then again of Abraham to Isaac can be described with a certain degree of exactness in terms drawn from the penultimate stanza of "Stupidity," as Ronell translates it: "Drawn by golden strings."

Even the word *golden* in this line corresponds to the argument pursued in "Kant Satellite." Gold resonates with money (*Geld*). Apropos of those whom he associates with a fixation on gold and *Geld,* namely the "Palestinians who live among us,"[20] Kant denies that they are capable of enlightenment. With acute philological rigor Ronell analyzes a complicated and disturbing note in the *Anthropology from a Pragmatic Perspective,* one of those apparently offhand notes that "Kant scholars" generally ignore because it is only a satellite of his larger philosophical project, far removed from its weighty and lofty "critical" center. Despite the complexity of this note, however, its point is unmistakable: there can and will be no program of enlightenment for the aforementioned "Palestinians who live among [*unter*] us." On the contrary, they will be forever distinguished from—more exactly *below*—us, whoever "we" may be. Not allowing this understated *unter* to pass without notice, Ronell emphasizes the untrainable, more exactly, the *intractable* character of the ever-roaming "Palestinians" who, as a purely trading people, are strangely unfamiliar with the idea of freedom. Their intractability represents a limit to the cosmopolitan program of enlightenment. The source of this limit is a desire—on Kant's part, to begin with—not to be cheated. But this desire is only a desire not to be, or be considered, stupid. For anyone who lets him- or herself be cheated is self-evidently stupid. The way to prevent oneself from being cheated by those who are cheaters by nature is to withdraw from any dealings with them. Not to be drawn into dealings—this is, for Kant, an imperative of a very peculiar sort, as Ronell shows: it is his *own* imperative, in which the difference between "us" and the "Palestinians" both consolidates and repudiates the "motto" of enlightenment:

> Rather than talk to them [the Palestinians living among Kant's own people], he will seek understanding for himself, he will take recourse to reason and history, powerful allies in reckoning the deficit by which they are recounted. The final contradiction, of which there are numerous other examples, concerns the curse that Kant turns at the end of the note into a blessing. ["So it appears that their dispersion throughout the world, with their unity of a religion and language, can by no means be counted as evidence of a curse pronounced on these people, but must rather be regarded as a blessing, especially since their wealth, in personal property, probably now exceeds that of any other people of like numbers."— Kant]. It is not certain whom the philosopher addresses in this instance or whose perspective he appropriates in order to make his point, and to what end. The point gives the appearance of a conciliatory gesture but is not one. For if the Jews regarded their fated wealth as a curse, this must be due to the fact they do not regard money as a blessing—it is Kant who does.[21]

At this point in her discussion Ronell adds a sign: * * *. This sign, the penultimate of its kind, introduces the end of the "Kant Satellite" and, with it, the final remarks of *Stupidity* as a whole. Of course, it is perfectly legitimate to read * * * as the conventional indication of a break in the train of the argument; it says nothing more than "I'm done with this thought and am moving onto another." In this case, however, and in view of a typographer as careful as Ronell, there is good reason to think that the series of five-pointed stars indicates something else as well. It may even be the schema of the enigmatic emergence she discusses in the introduction. Nothing can be seen to emerge from this series of asterisks; but the emergence that Hölderlin's two poems, "welded" together, allow us to intimate, was never supposed to be understood as an alteration of something hitherto in existence. For this reason at least—a wholly negative one, to be sure—the series of equivalent asterisks almost demands to be read as a schema of emergence. The very senselessness of the asterisks in abstraction from the series they form makes them "comprehensible" as the insignia of stupidity that refrains from assigning itself a more appropriate, cleverer, or smarter word for itself. And in addition, as a bonus, the series can be read as a "string" that is supremely valuable ("golden") because its breaks represent the results of a "higher" kind of pulling, a pulling that does not need to demonstrate its strength by making one thing follow after another. This kind of pulling, this drive without a regiment of drafting, finds expression in the image through which Ronell begins to read—with and against both Benjamin and Heidegger—the two poems of Friedrich Hölderlin: "*gravity of an emergence.*"

VIII.

In schematic terms, in which nouns and names such as *God, Abraham, Sarah,* and *Isaac* are made into variables, the final paragraphs of *Stupidity* issue into the following question, which resonates with that of enlightenment: how can one resist the *other* kind of pull, the "normal" pull, so to speak, the pull that puts one (called either "Abraham" or "Isaac") in line with another (called either "God" or "Abraham")? The draft goes both ways, such that those who pull also find themselves pulled: "Since He got drawn into economy," Ronell writes of God, "it is a matter of survival for Him as well, for there remains the possibility that he would not have survived the offering, that He could not have founded the primal father to guarantee His survival, and in this regard He is Abraham's son and creation."[22] The laughter of "Sarah" is the image of a counter-pull that responds to the "gravity of an emergence": "The economy of cheating was there from the start, which is why Sarah laughed," Ronell writes, and then adds, "Abraham was too old." To the dotage of Abraham there corresponds the nonage of Isaac: he is there to be drawn to the sacrificial mountain. It even goes without saying that he is to be drawn to the site of sacrifice, for the concept of draft, as Kant would say—although not with regard to this example—contains that of being susceptible to sacrifice. The "guardians," in Kant's term, have those whom they draw at their disposal, to use as they see fit. Abraham is the first of the "guardians" who threaten anyone who falls under their charge. The question, then, is how one can say "no" to the pull that mediates both dotage and nonage into a "maturity" that takes responsibility for itself (*selbstverschuldet*) and recognizes the scales of credit or faith (*Glauben*) and guilt or debt (*Schulden*)as a result. Not by simply saying "no" to this pull can this be done, for the enunciation of a "no"— which may very well require courage—is the sign of an exit from both nonage and dotage. Sarah does not say "no"; she laughs. As for Isaac, he, too, refuses to say "no"; instead, according to Ronell's reading, he *digs:* "Isaac, knowing what he cannot say, keeps on digging holes into the old story, preparing new plots."[23]

With this sentence, marked by a final series of asterisks, *Stupidity* almost comes to an end. To say that this sentence contains Ronell's *reading* requires that the concept of reading be dissociated from the following image: one term in the relation, the reader, is pulled along the other term, specifically the text. Kant, for his part, understood enlightenment as emancipation from the leading strings of the book as well as the priest: "If I have a book that has understanding for me . . . I don't need to make any efforts of my own."[24] In the case of *this* reading—Isaac digging holes "*into the old story, preparing new plots*"—nothing in *the* book, the first of the Bible, could be identified as its authorization. It would be a mistake, however, to say that Ronell makes all of this up. There is, after all, Genesis 26, in which Isaac is said to dig; but he digs only wells. More exactly, he re-digs his father's wells, which had been covered up after his death. Instead of interpreting this re-digging as something like an homage to the dead father—which also serves the eminently practical function of making the promised land arable during times of extreme drought—Ronell reads Isaac's digging-complex as a nonpurposive and perhaps even as a "stupid" inscription of the event about which God himself speaks at the beginning of Genesis 26: "Abraham obeyed Me and kept My charge: My commandments, My laws, and My teachings."

Instead of responding to this speech, Isaac digs. This digging, in Ronell's reading, runs counter to being drawn; but the countermovement is not so much an expression of "freedom" as an exercise in reading—specifically, in reading old stories, so that they are made new. Such as, for instance, the old story of Isaac re-digging Abraham's old wells. Here, however, for me, is the most interesting question raised by Ronell's reading of Isaac as reader of the land promised to his father: if the wells had indeed been covered up—by the Philistines, no less—how could Isaac have found them, so that he could re-dig them? The old wells emerge only when the newly dug ones do. This is, so to speak, the very principle of "co-emergence," as it is introduced at the beginning of *Stupidity*: the new does not follow the old but, rather, emerges with it. Or in this case, co-submerges with it. In any case, by the end of *Stupidity,* the two names, *Isaac* and *Sarah,* come to represent the countermovement to the act of being drawn that is not itself in the train of any project of enlightenment. The emergence in which they emerge as paradoxical "leaders" owes little to the image, borrowed from Plato, of the philosopher coming out of a cave into the blinding light of day. The familiarity of this image is probably the reason Kant took it for granted that his readers would understand when he defines enlightenment by way of a certain *Ausgang* ("exit"). The underlying assumption is that the way out is already there, waiting to be found, so that one can then "emerge." But if this way out is not already there—and this, too, seems an assumption any self-proclaimed enlightener must accept—then there is only one thing to do: dig, or re-dig. And this re-digging must be accompanied by laughter, which enacts, again and again, this "understanding": by re-digging what has been thoroughly covered up, one only gets deeper into the hole. Ronell's readings are this combination of laughter and re-digging: a "welding" of Sarah and Isaac into an uneasy alliance against the lineage that leads Abraham, for one, into his experience with the "test drive."

NOTES

1. Immanuel Kant, *Gesammelte Schriften,* ed. Königlich Preußische [later Deutsche] Akademie der Wissenschaften (Berlin: Reimer; later, De Gruyter, 1900–), 8: 35.
2. Kant, *Gesammelte Schriften,* 9: 35.
3. Avital Ronell, *Stupidity* (Champaign: University of Illinois Press, 2002), 23.
4. Ronell, *Stupidity,* 5.
5. Kant, *Gesammelte Schriften,* 8: 41.
6. Ronell, *Stupidity,* 5; italics added.
7. Ronell, *Stupidity,* 5.
8. Ronell, *Stupidity,* 6.
9. Paul de Man, *Aesthetic Ideology,* ed. Andrzej Warminski (Minneapolis: University of Minnesota Press, 1996), 133.
10. Quoted by de Man on the basis of Bernard's translation, *Aesthetic Ideology,* 80; Kant, *Gesammelte Schriften,* 5: 270.
11. Ronell, *Stupidity,* 114.
12. Ronell, *Stupidity,* 114.
13. Ronell, *Stupidity,* 5.
14. Ronell, *Stupidity,* 8.
15. Ronell, *Stupidity,* 9.
16. Kant, *Gesammelte Schriften,* 8: 35.
17. Ronell, *Stupidity,* 8.

18. Ronell, *Stupidity*, 8.
19. On the idea of syncopation, see the following work, which is very much in evidence in Ronell's own: Jean-Luc Nancy, *Le Discours de la syncope, 1. Logodaedalus* (Paris: Aubier-Flammarion, 1976).
20. Quoted by Ronell, *Stupidity*, 303–4.
21. Ronell, *Stupidity*, 306.
22. Ronell, *Stupidity*, 307.
23. Ronell, *Stupidity*, 310.
24. Kant, *Gesammelte Schriften*, 9: 35.

Susan Bernstein
Conference Call:
Ronell, Heidegger, Oppen

I do not understand *The Telephone Book*. But how could one understand it? It begins:

> Warning: *The Telephone Book* is going to resist you. Dealing with a logic and topos of the switchboard, it engages the destabilization of the addressee. Your mission, should you choose to accept it, is to learn how to read with your ears. In addition to listening for the telephone, you are being asked to tune your ears to noise frequencies, to anticoding, to the inflated reserves of random indeterminateness—in a word, you are expected to stay open to the static and interference that will occupy these lines. We have attempted to install a switchboard which, vibrating a continuous current of electricity, also replicates the effects of scrambling.[1]

The Telephone Book cannot call for understanding the way a clearly delineated object might ask for it. But this much I can glean: Heidegger answered a (telephone) call that involved him in Nazism. As we know, he never clarified or theorized how this involvement might be related to his thinking and thus closed off the passageway from history to philosophy. In the same way, he denies the apparatus of the telephone—that is, the imbrication of the technological device of the telephone in the ontological investigation of "receiving the call of conscience" in *Being and Time*, for example (*The Telephone Book*, 5–6). Without going into an in-depth analysis of these particular issues and questions, I want to focus on the telephone. "Why the telephone?" *The Telephone Book* asks. "In some ways it was the cleanest way to reach the regime of any number of metaphysical certitudes. It destabilizes the identity of self and other, subject and thing, it abolishes the originariness of site; in undermines the authority of the Book and constantly menaces the existence of literature. It is itself unsure of its identity as object, thing, piece of equipment, perlocutionary intensity or artwork . . ." (9). The telephone connects yet separates its two ends, just as it connects the ontic and the ontological in the question of the "call" in Ronell's treatment of Heidegger. *The Telephone Book* is a network, held together not by its binding but by its switchboard: that is to say, ALSO by its binding, its binding that is the telephone. *The Telephone Book* is and is not about the telephone. "To trace these calls, the condition of a long distance that speaks, and the many toxic invasions waged by telephone, it seemed necessary to start with the absolute priority of the Other to the self, and to acknowledge the constitutive impurity that obliges a self to respond to its calling . . ." (10). The apparatus ensures impurity; the ontic priority of the telephone call taints the ontological call of conscience, or the transcendent call to make philosophy.

These are conjectures, messages I thought I heard while attempting to read *The Telephone Book*. Most important, as I pick up the receiver I acknowledge the priority of the other and am indebted—to Ronell, the telephone, and *the Telephone Book*. What is reading Ronell? *The Telephone Book* is barely "legible" but sets up an infinitely complex interworking of texts, problems, questions, readings, and so forth. I heard a telephone ringing and the call of conscience, the strange connection and dehiscence between these two things, solidified in the classically black apparatus that used to be the telephone. I heard a double sense of telephone, a synecdoche, Ronell writes, always more and less than itself. I strained to trace immense and vast readings of Heidegger's text that came to serve as a condition of possibility for further readings. Among the most obvious, I came across Heidegger in the neighborhood of someone on the telephone—this time a poet.

To reconfigure the relation between the telephone and the call, the ontic and the ontological, perhaps to do so it is necessary to look beyond the bounds of Heidegger himself to a poetic interlocutor. *Dichten* and *Denken*, we know, form a pair that are "the same," yet dwell in their difference. Ronell has written about this beautifully in her article, "On the Misery of Theory without Poetry: Heidegger's Reading of Hölderlin's 'Andenken'": "When he attempted to give a face to the cobelonging of poetry and thought," she writes, "Heidegger said that poetry stretched upward, toward evanescent heights, while thought reached into abysses, gaining depth. Elsewhere he figures poetry and thought as twin summits."[2]

Heidegger writes:

> Das Dichten und das Denken begegnen sich nur dann und nur so lange im selben, als sie entschieden in der Verschiedenheit ihres Wesens bleiben. Das selbe deckt sich nie mit dem gleichen, auch nicht mit dem leeren Einerlei des bloss Identischen. Das gleiche verlegt sich stets auf das Unterschiedlose, damit alles darin übereinkomme. Das selbe ist dagegen das Zusammengehören des Verschiedenen aus der Versammlung durch den Unterschied. Das Selbe läßt sich nur sagen, wenn der Unterschied gedacht wird. Im Austrag des Unterschiedenen kommt das versammelnde Wesen des selben zum Leuchten. Das selbe verbannt jeden Eifer, das Verschiedene immer nur in das gleiche auszugleichen. [Poetizing and thinking encounter each other in the same only when, and only as long as they remain decisively in the difference of their essence. The same never overlaps with the equivalent, nor with the empty sameness of the merely identical. The equivalent refers to the lack of all difference so that everything comes into agreement there. In contrast, the same is the belonging together of what is different through the gathering by means of difference. The same can only be said when the difference is thought. In the struggling of what is different, the gathering essence of the same comes to shine. The same exiles all eagerness to even out what is different in equivalence.][3]

The relationship between thinking and poetry allows for a connection that brings up all the issues of priority and origination invoked by the problem of the telephone: the absolute priority of the Other, the ontic priority of the telephone call.

I would like to attend here to another call and name the call George Oppen, American poet and Pulitzer Prize winner. This call inscribes Heidegger in the poetic program not of a proto-fascist, right-wing high modernist, as we might expect, but of a committed leftist who lived in Mexico during the McCarthy era. Oppen gave up writing for twenty-five years because he found political activism and poetry incompatible, but began to write again in the 1960s. Oppen was clearly opposed to tendentious political writing and his poetry is in no way socialist-realist, but there are many political strands throughout it. He also worked as a carpenter.

Oppen refers directly to Heidegger in a couple of places in his poetry. I am concerned here with a more or less direct quote that appears in the long poem "Route" in the book *Of Being Numerous* (1968), for which Oppen won the Pulitzer Prize. It would be difficult to offer a totalizing interpretation of this text, ten pages long and spanning fourteen numbered sections. But the poem clearly takes up questions of the sense and possibility of poetry in a war-driven and technological world with direct references to World War II, in which Oppen fought in France.

In section 13, Oppen shares with Heidegger concerns about technology. It presents the image of a broken-down world—clearly one in which dwelling, in Heidegger's sense, is not possible:

> Department of Plants and Structures———obsolete, the old name
> In this city, of the public works
> Tho we mean to entangle ourselves in the roots of the world
> An unexpected and forgotten spoor, all but indestructible
> Shards
>
> To owe nothing to fortune, to chance, nor by the power of
> his heart
>
> Or her heart to have made these things sing
> But the benevolence of the real
>
> Tho there is no longer shelter in the earth, round helpless belly
> Or hope among the pipes and broken works
> "Substance itself which is the subject of all our planning"
> And by this we are carried into the incalculable.[4]

The perspective of this section steps beyond the availability of the objective—the *Bestand,* standing reading to be ordered up and used—because the plants and works are broken down, the operativity of the technical still legible as a trace, but reduced to fragments. In stepping beyond the technical to the *Ge-stell,* the human subject is no longer the master of these materials—"nor by the power of his heart, Or her heart to have made these things sing"—that is, the poet cannot resuscitate or reanimate this, but rather it is Being itself—what Oppen calls "the benevolence of the real"— that summons both voice and things into singing. Twice the poem seemingly denounces its own poetic capacity: "All this is reportage," a merely repetitive activity. Yet when the "I" is released, the world still can reveal something (section 11):

> Tell of the life of the mind, the mind creates the finite.
> All punishes him. I stumble over these stories—
> Progeny, the possibility of progeny, continuity
>
> Or love that tempted him
>
> He is punished by place, by scene, by all the holds
> all he has found, this pavement, the silent symbols

> Of it, the word it, never more powerful than in this
> moment. Well, hardly as epiphany, but there the thing
> is all the same
>
> All this is reportage (199–200)

Reminiscent of Baudelaire's stumbling on the pavement bricks of poetry, as the "I" is turned over to the third person, the "silent symbols" yield up something after all, revealing "it." The "small word," for which Oppen is famous, points to a minimal ability of language to point, to call attention to itself.[5] "In this moment"—the very slight interruption of the "mere reportage" that activates the performativity of language and draws it out of the broken rubble of plants and works. Similarly, following the quote from Heidegger, "Substance itself which is the subject of all our planning," Oppen's text breaks out of repetition and reportage, of the calculability of the technical: "And by this we are carried into the incalculable"—again by the very small performative presencing of "this," by this something happens in the present that interrupts the manipulation and calculation of the technical. This, the poetic, interrupts it.

However, in some sense the interruption is no interruption. If we look in Heidegger's *Identity and Difference,* the text that Oppen was reading at the time of writing this poem, we find first of all the second clause, not in quotation marks, is also in Heidegger's text: "Im selben Maße wie das Sein ist der Mensch herausgefordert, d.h. gestellt, das ihn angehende Seiende als den Bestand seines Planens und Rechnens sicherzustellen und dieses Bestellen ins Unabsehbare zu treiben" (23). The translation, which was all Oppen knew, poses problems: "To the same degree that Being is challenged, man, too, is challenged, that is, forced to secure all beings that are his concern as the substance for his planning and calculating; and to carry this manipulation on past all bounds" (35). The word Oppen especially noted as one he would not have used—substance—is lacking in the Heidegger's German. It translates the equally strange *Bestand*. It also suggests that calculation itself is driven beyond the calculable, through which the *Ge-stell*—the essence of the technical, which is itself nothing technical—is glimpsed. In some sense, perhaps Oppen and Heidegger are saying "the same."

Oppen is himself extremely concerned with his use of Heidegger's line. In a note to himself dated June 1, 1966, Oppen elaborates upon the importance of his experience with Heidegger's text, and also relates a set of confusing circumstances around his borrowing of the phrase. After reading *Identity and Difference,* Oppen sleeps in the afternoon and has "confused and elaborate dreams." In his dream, Oppen receives a call: "At one time in the dream—the only section I was able to remember clearly—I was sitting in a chair near a group of people gathered around a small card-table at a sort of conference. The phone had rung, and I had answered—there seemed to be a small telephone table at my left . . ."[6]

Already the message is double—Heidegger's voice on the line and the strange conference table. Oppen's body itself reaches from the factical—the conference room scene—to the ontological, the call out of the *Un-zuhause* that calls, like anxiety, and awakens *das Man* into his *Unheimlichkeit.* The dream/call follows Oppen's reading of *Identity and Difference.* Oppen describes: "That night I sat up very late, very carefully reading the essay, and after many hours felt I had understood it—It was very difficult for me to grasp the extreme Idealist assumption on which it was based. When I had grasped it, I turned it over and over in my mind for a long time, unable to accept the assumption, but convinced that a part of the statement was of crucial importance to me, of such importance as to alter the subjective conditions of my life, the conditions of my thinking, from that point in time" (135).

This is quite a testimonial. The dream/call suggests basically a profound confusion between what has been invented and what has been received: whether the statement in question belongs to Heidegger or to Oppen. Convinced he has plagiarized the phrase, Oppen reads and rereads Heidegger, yet cannot find the stolen phrase: "'Substance itself which is the subject of all our planning'/ And by this we are carried into the incalculable' " (*NCP* 201). Oppen agonizes about whether to place the words in quotes, whether to use it as the climax of the poem, as he considers it "plagiarized," but then reaches the conclusion: "I have not been able to find it, tho the essay is only 19 pages long . . . ——It seems necessarily true that I did not read those sentences." (*SL* 136). In another letter (p. 157), Oppen reiterates that the sentence is not in Heidegger. Yet in the translation of Heidegger's essay, we find: "Is it that Being itself is faced with the challenge of letting beings appear within the horizon of what is calculable? Indeed. And not only this. To the same degree that Being is challenged, man, too, is challenged, that is, forced to secure all beings that are his concern as the substance for his planning and calculating; and to carry this manipulation on past all bounds."[7] The lines conclude a paragraph introducing the notion of the *Ge-stell* as that which challenges or sets forth (*heraustellt*) man and Being to face each other in the relation of calculation and manipulability—that is, no longer where man is viewed as the master-subject who manipulates, but where the relation of technology is viewed in terms of a characteristic

54

of Being itself—where even calculation and technics will reveal something of the true call of being.

Oppen loses both himself and Heidegger in this situation of citation. Feeling at first he is simply "using" a phrase of Heidegger's, it then becomes impossible to "calculate" the order of priority or to clearly set up an instrumentalization of Heidegger's text. This might be possible if Oppen had simply read the text and then incorporated the line in his own poem. But strangely, Oppen and Heidegger relate in a kind of syncopation that allows neither to be originary, and neither to be simply used or appropriated by the other. Instead, Oppen's reading is elaborated by his dream experience, which opens up a double reception. This double reception begins in a house: "And I told Mary," Oppen writes, "the one thing I could remember out of what seemed to have been a long and complex dream. Mary and I were in a large country house. . . . I don't remember ever having seen that house before, and yet it was a kind of house very familiar to me, a large, light wooden house, a very large sitting room, very lightly and casually furnished; I have an impression of chintz-covered wicker chairs, and a vague familiarity about the carpet, for which reason I didn't visualize it clearly, and probably French windows—certainly not any other kind of window— an openness" (*SL* 134). While filled with domestic detail, the room here is characterized by openness—open/Oppen—as are many building structures and elements throughout Oppen's poetry. Thanks to this openness, two inputs are opened up: the surrounding conversation (ontic) and the call through the telephone line—Heidegger on the ontological connection. Interestingly, even the transcendent line is punctuated, alternating between language and silence:

> I . . . was listening with the receiver held between my chin and shoulder and I was taking notes either of the telephone conversation—in which there were, for some reason, very long silence [sic] broken by short sentences in a rather low and rather rasping masculine voice— . . . —or I was taking notes on the decisions at the table—I don't know which. I was surprised that I could listen to two conversations at once, and pointed out to myself that the phone conversation contained those long silences. Explaining to myself that that made it possible. (134)

The two discourses are intercalated in a way that allows Oppen not just to *hear* (*hören*) Heidegger, but for them to *belong together* (*zusammengehören*). The line from Heidegger is interrupted and repeated through its interconnection with the surrounding world—the conversation at the table and the house in which it takes place. Because the house opens outward, it allows this connection to take place. The house does not hold fast, but opens. (Here we might note that the interest in the house does not in fact lead to a vocabulary of the homeland—and notice too Oppen's family name was originally *Oppenheimer;* his father dropped the second half.)

The opening of the house and the entrance of Heidegger take place in another confusion of Oppen and Heidegger. Consider this very early poem of Oppen's, written in 1929:

> The knowledge not of sorrow, you were
> saying, but of boredom
> Is——aside from reading speaking
> smoking——
> Of what, Maude Blessingbourne it was,
> wished to know when, having risen,
> "approached the window as if to see
> what really was going on";
> And saw rain falling, in the distance
> more slowly,
> The road clear from her past the window—
> glass——
> Of the world, weather-swept, with which one shared the century.
> (*NCP* 5)

Borrowing on the force of a semi-citation from Henry James, Oppen has the woman look outward; the house opens out to connect with the world in its boredom. Reading Heidegger in the 1960s, Oppen discovered and became touched by Heidegger's use of the term "boredom":

> . . . I have a superstition concerning my relation to H. The poem which happens to be printed as the first poem in *Discrete Series*—my first book— was written in 1929. That, I've learned, was the year in which H. was giving his Inauguration Speech in which he spoke of the mood of boredom (in the translation I have) which leads, again in the translation I have, to 'the knowledge of what-is." The poem . . . begins with the "knowledge of boredom." . . . And boredom was an odd word to use. I am touched by superstition remembering my hesitation over that word and the sense of having been given it. (*SL* 156)

Oppen contrasts this "giving," which never "took place" but was perhaps an "event" in Heidegger's sense, with what he believes is the mistaken giving of the later phrase. Thus he accepts the gift where there could have been no literal giving, and denies it where there in fact is an actual borrowing.

Thus there is a knowing and borrowing here that is neither actual nor non-actual, for it takes place not in a simple repetition but in a re-saying of the same, in a relatedness: as Oppen says: "Not truth but each other" (*NCP* 183). This dissolution of subject-object poles and confusion of identities takes place through the window. The lines from Oppen's early poem are revised in "Route" to read: "... approached the window as if to see... / The boredom which disclosed/Everything——" (*NCP* 186).

The quotation this time could be seen as a self-quotation, thus a self-differing within the author himself.

To treat the confusion of transmission in "Route," Oppen returns to the ending of Heidegger's *Identity and Difference*. "Whatever and however we may think, we will think in the context of tradition. Tradition preponderates if we are liberated from afterthinking into anticipatory thinking which is no longer a planning. Not until we turn our thoughts toward what had already been thought, shall we be employed for what has yet to be thought" (136). What may at first appear to be a kind of "anxiety of influence" scenario actually pierces right to the center of one of Heidegger's most important thoughts: that of the undoing of linear temporality through the thinking of the unthought. This kind of reading undoes arithmetical ordering; the turn into the unthought of what is thought also enacts the critique of the instrumental structure of language, and no longer allows it to be seen as a vehicle that "contains" or "transmits" meaning. This structure, too, would order signifier and signified along the same lines as text and reader. The turn into the "unthought," or a certain kind of repetition that implies no originality or priority, overlaps with what Heidegger calls the *Einkehr* [turn inward] or *Sprung* [leap] in this essay. These both express the vibrating or humming—or for Oppen: "It is true the great mineral silence/ Vibrates, hums, a process/ Completing itself" (*NCP* 179) of the difference crossed with no bridge. Trying once more to account for his "invention" of Heidegger's phrase in "Route," Oppen writes: "Reacting with shock to what he had written, my mind went on and said the rest, and I thought that he had said it ? But the name of the essay is Identity and Difference
a thought which has not been greatly simplified by the event" (*SL* 137).

The event is itself the vibrating, the "verging on vertigo," the "dizzy incredulity" (*SL* 156) that connects and destabilizes *Identity and Difference*. With the destabilizing of the event, the house shakes and opens up. Housing elements remain as the very medium for this exchange between finitudes that opens a glimpse beyond the merely technical relationship between entities. Housing is itself the *Ge-stell* insofar as it has both the potential to obscure what lies beyond the relationships among *Seiendes* and to *reveal* the belonging together of man and being in the relation of the technical—*something that is itself not technical*. This latter is building.

Building, in a positive sense, would be a taking off from the technical that opens up onto something other than the technical. In this sense, too, it remains grounded in the finite, the everyday, the ontic; yet it operates in such a way as to create and reveal crevices in its own structuring. Let us return for a moment to this passage from *Identität und Differenz*:

> Das Ereignis als Er-eignis denken, heißt, am Bau dieses in sich schwingenden Bereiches bauen. Das Bauzeug zu diesem in sich shwebenden Bau empfängt das Denken aus der Sprache. Denn die Sprache ist die zerteste, aber auch die anfälligste, alles nervaltende Schwingung im schwebenden Bau des Ereignisses. (102)
>
> [To think of appropriating as the event of appropriation means to contribute [bauen] to this self-vibrating realm. Thinking receives the tools [Bauzeug] for this self-suspended structure from language. For language is the most delicate and thus the most susceptible vibration holding everything within the suspended structure of the appropriation. We dwell in the appropriation inasmuch as our active nature is given over to language. (37–38)]

The phrase "am Bau bauen" (to build on the building, translated as "contributing to the realm") seems to describe a kind of linguistic thinking that can be reduced neither to the visible nor the invisible, the present or absent, but is characterized by an alternation, a syncopation, a cooperation, between both, with no finality. This kind of language would participate in truth not as a concept or a proposition but as aletheia, a kind of revealing. Oppen writes: "I think that poetry which is of any value is *always* revelatory. Not that it reveals or could reveal Everything, but it must reveal something . . . and for the first time."

The confusion of "must not mean but be" comes from this: it is a knowledge that is hard to hold, it is held in the poem, a meaning grasped again on re-reading—"The holding that cannot be held is building, or sometimes a house, a house whose window opens up upon re-reading, or reading the un-thought." Oppen continues: "One can seldom describe this meaning—but sometimes one has stumbled on the statement made in another way. As Parmenides' 'The Same' is to think and to be is Charles Reznikoff's " . . . 'the girder,' still itself among the rubble" (*SL* 133).[8] Oppen makes a kind of simile—"as . . . [so] is . . ." between Parmenides' fragment and a fragment of a poem that itself holds a fragmentary building element, ready to construct—holding itself—even when being lost among the rubble.

NOTES

1. Avital Ronell, *The Telephone Book* (Lincoln: University of Nebraska Press, 1989).
2. Avital Ronell, "On the Misery of Theory," *PMLA* 120, no. 1 (January 2005): 17.
3. Martin Heidegger, " . . . Dichterisch wohnet der Mensch . . ." in *Vorträge und Aufsätze* (Stuttgart: Neske, 1954), 187.
4. George Oppen, *New Collected Poems* (New York: New Directions, 2002), 200–201.
5. Thanks to Forrest Gander for this attention to the "small word." I am generally indebted to him for my reading of Oppen. See his "Finding the Phenomenal Oppen" in *A Faithful Existence: Reading, Memory, and Transcendence* (Emeryville, Calif.: Shoemaker and Hoard, 2005). For an analysis of the relation between Heidegger and Oppen and further readings of Oppen, see also Susan Thackery, *George Oppen: A Radical Practice* (San Francisco: O Books and the Poetry Center & American Poetry Archive, 2001).
6. George Oppen, *The Selected Letters of George Oppen,* ed. Rachel Blau duPlessis (Durham and London: Duke University Press, 1990), 134.
7. Martin Heidegger, *Identity and Difference.* Trans. Joan Stambaugh (New York: Harper and Row, 1969), 35.
8. Heidegger discusses this fragment in *Identity and Difference,* 27.

Laurence A. Rickels
Take Me to Your Reader

At some mid-career point in the series of my horror film class at UC Santa Barbara, I thought it was time to check out the current scholarship. Because cultural studies had started running its commentary all over the place abandoned by Marxist sociology, there was an outside chance that there would be a compatible reading out there of the mass socius in terms of the mass of murder. I, too, was more interested in the overlaps (and gaps) between slasher or splatter movies and off-screen violence than in another film-studies interpretation of "his" and "her" pleasures as closely read and embedded in discrete cinematic works. It was 1999, the year in which I had made a popularity-testing commitment to mass cultural studies with the publication of *The Vampire Lectures*. (Immersion of theory in mass culture holds interchangeable places with the allegorical immersion of eternity in finitude.) There were in fact three or four new books (all of them by academics) on both the horror genre and our mass-murder culture, which aimed to swim up the mainstream (but were deadbeat in the backwater of academe). In one of these compromise formations, the 1998 study titled *Serial Killers: Death and Life in America's Wound Culture*, the index entry "Ronell" seemed to signify that dissociation in this case might have preserved its better half. One out of two references was to a footnote, from which I quote the second paragraph:

More locally, the tendency to proceed by way of analogy or pun in some recent work on the technology question—for instance, the work of Ronell and Rickels—has the effect of invoking without specifying the relays between persons, bodies, and forms of technology. That is, analogizing or punning into relation persons and machines, insides and outsides, bypasses the articulation of the relays between inside and outside (what Freud called "the system between the outside and the inside"). Hence the equivalences posited by pun and analogy bypass articulation of the work of making-equivalent and in effect bypass technological differences generally. Such work puts in place of such an articulation of relays, resistances, and differences that make a difference a sort of black box. Proceeding by way of analogies immune to differences is troubling not least because it's precisely the violence-inducing tensions between analogy and cause that traverse these cases of murder and machine culture. It's troubling, also, because such black-box accounts are remarkably inattentive to what I take to be two of the governing premises of the *cultural logistics* I mean to instance here: that things are in part what they appear to be, and that nothing is simply reducible to anything else.

In the pun-free or -pure discourse above, the recourse to "logistics" serves as placeholder for a whole jargon of "utilization." In the culture industry, the intellectualization of ordinary thought meets the momentum of "dumbing down" more than halfway. But that is just another way of saying that the footnote is more theoretical in its formulation than what one tends to encounter up in the main text. When an author stakes untenable claims to originality, he or she will regularly try to off the more original competition in a footnote. I remember coming across an article in a nearly *New Yorker*–type academic journal once upon a time in which all the materials of my reading of the Frankfurt School's reading of Mickey Mouse had been resituated within the prose of someone who clearly knew how to write the good grant proposal. Then I found the footnote to *The Case of California.* The book was acknowledged and dismissed as not on the theoretical level of the sudden upsurge of deconstructive reading of the "break" Mickey Mouse does not get because the proposal author was pulling it on me in the mode of emergency (restricted, thus, to a footnote).

Before the collapse of pun onto analogy (a confusion as jarring or jarheaded as that between unconscious and conscious thought), one might consider, if only because *Serial Killers* claims that Freud is on its side, the pervasive momentum of analogization in Freud's thought. Freud raises two series of analogization of psychic processes—with haunting and with technical media—to the status of endopsychic perception. It is true that

Freud first encounters these reinscribed analogies as props in delusional systems. But as documented at the close of Freud's reading of Daniel Paul Schreber's *Memoirs of My Nervous Illness,* they are also the properties of Freud's own theorization of the psychic apparatus. It is possible to argue that the work of analogy in Freud's discourse occupies interchangeable places with the work of mourning (or with melancholic unmourning, which is work, too). *Serial Killers* is not interested in mourning, not interested in the dead, but is overdetermined by Death and its personalization as murder (which subsumes perpetrator and victim). What allows *Serial Killers* just the same to skip the beat of retraumatization and related cheap thrills and shots is its quasi-theoretical frame-up of the murders as among the many manifestations of addiction, even addiction to addiction. Instead it is the discourse of collapsed difference in the absence of pun control that sparks the real violence. In the footnote underworld "Ronell and Rickels" are the serial killers in *Serial Killers.*

Puns, resisted in particular by the academic, as Ronell demonstrated in her essay on puns ("The Sujet Suppositaire") because they park in the rear, are the accessories of analogies (and not accessories to their merger, according to *Serial Killers*). Puns encode latent text as decodable up to a certain point within the manifest (which belongs to the black box, which is an analogy). "The Black Box" that serves as section title in Avital Ronell's *The Telephone Book* is committed to this sense of "black-box accounts" as being in the service of survival guidance. In "TraumaTV," an essay that revisits addiction as analyzed earlier in *Crack Wars* in new media settings, Ronell again uses this specific sense of "black box." The surviving crashed manifest or black box offers feedback aiding future survival via an evolutionary adaptation of technologies to the fit with catastrophe's containment.

Serial Killers, which never strays far from a current-edition dictionary, seems to mean by "black box" any device to which we relate via its input and output functions without knowing its internal constitution and means of operation. This use arose during World War II when a certain device added to a fighter plane improved function but remained a mystery. By the 1950s at the latest, this black box came to signify the bypass operation of behavioral psychology with regard to the area between (brain, nervous system) stimulus and response. Behaviorism bracketed out the happy medium between stimulus and response as unknowable. Freud's psychic apparatus functions not unlike the box in behaviorism. Rather than stimulus/response, however, the relationship to the apparatus involves the medium of transference, which by analogy is not only compatible or continuous with the apparatus but is also transmitting through it.

"Black box" also referred, in the 1960s, to a specific device whereby so-called phone phreaks blocked the supervision signal sent by the receiving phone handset when the call was answered. The box kept up the appearance that no one answered at the receiving end, which meant that billing was never started on the call. In the theater world, a "black box" is a basic space, basically a movie theater without screen and projector, that fits or foots the bill of low-budget and/or experimental dramatic art. "Black box" also signifies a label of extreme warning on medications. Marconi's radio was referred to as a "black box," and the legendary off-the-map quadrant in Nevada, Area 51, set aside for military innovation and hallucinatory metabolization of the technofuture, is known now as "Dreamland," now as "The Black Box." Before the semantic sprawl of "black box" from bracketed-out apparatus to the container and conveyor of undead or live testimony to the causes of an otherwise annihilating catastrophe (and back again), "black box" was originally located, as analogy, between the photographic apparatus and the coffin (for which black box was already in the baroque synonym and symptom). The camera qualifies as the first candidate for this version of the black box, but only at the remove of analogy. The coffin boxes in a more perfect union. What is in the box is the missing body and its projections, ego and company. Every apparatus belongs to the same lineage of projection or reproduction as the psychic apparatus, which, within its egoic span, contains what it projects, the body as missing body. All instruction manuals to the contrary, it is the missing (the dead or undead) who are inside the apparatus.

In *Toward a Philosophy of Photography,* Vilem Flusser refers to the photographic apparatus as "black box" (in English in the German text) that, as foreign body to its own history as analogy, serves as placeholder for a whole relay of apparatuses, the inner workings of which withdraw from the outside chance of our knowing them from the inside. And yet Flusser's book was composed, in a sense, *inside* a black box, since written in willed isolation from the words of every history, philosophy, or genealogy of media he had read over the years. Thinking inside the box, he summons his own theory or philosophy of media out of his synthetic mix of innovation with whatever he can remember from his many sources, without looking back at the books. These are the black box accounts we routinely come up with whenever we teach.

By virtue of its topological structure, the apparatus that transmits or produces meaning makes no sense in itself as apparatus. But this need not paralyze or even render us passive. The input-output control panel is not a barrier to knowledge of or in technology: it is where it all begins, even in the mode of excess. Developments currently culminating via digitization as open-and-shut access via input to throwaway machines were already discernible to Walter Benjamin in his analyses of the gadget zone of technologization.

The second page reference under "Ronell" in *Serial Killers* is summoned by citation from *Crack Wars*, which gets pressed into the service of personalizing abyssal addiction (in the setting of "a general process of substitution") as "'serial indifference' whereby 'structures of repetition and substitution take precedence over the "real" qualities of the other.'" On location with Ronell, however, we find that the summons was issued to reformulations and revalorizations of Michael Riffaterre's symptomatic diagnosis of Madame Bovary (as over-reading hausfrau), which make room for the following affirmation of an ethics of "pathivity" embodied by Madame:

> Passive but on the way, she exposes herself to a sort of foreign aggression (so much is foreign to this woman: everything "active" belongs to a foreign currency . . .). Inactive living is another way of saying active destruction—a woman finds a substitute. In this case, she consumes novels. The solitary experiment of eluding a politics of community (by choice or by imposition) frees her into a domain of precarious pleasure, as it detaches her from active or responsible living. On the side of the letter, wearing shades to shield her from the blazing living logos, she is a reader of epitaphs, in exile from living reality. (101–2)

Madame thus becomes the heroin/e of a radical passivity as deconstruction (which I will be considering down these pages as deconstruction's "supplemental synthesis," emplaced with regard to the "synthesis at a standstill" back in the Frankfurt School, and to be taken like energy supplements that boost reading). But we are still in the phase and phrases of recovery from Riffaterre's profiling of Madame—until we reach the end of the quotation and begin to read the epitaphs within addiction. In the pages that follow the showdown above with a certain putting down of *Madame Bovary* (as one of the unread), the analysis of addiction is always in cite-specific proximity to Flaubert's text. I would like to distill from this analysis just the same a potion that can pass as joint appointment of readings of addiction in different settings. The span of its ingredients reaches the heights of super vision and the depths of an original poisoning. A symptomatic strain in *Madame Bovary*, even though it does not attain to "the level of Dr. Schreber's *Memoirs*," is nevertheless followed out via a "clandestine rapport to machinery for which paranoid strategists are famous. Surveillance apparatuses, the listening device, and the magnifying glass all belong to its narratology" (108). On the down side, what lies literally buried in *Madame Bovary* is an encrypted transmission passing through so many corpuses of addiction, namely what Ronell designates the "*toxic maternal*": "this body continues to transmit through Emma the persecutory rules that govern her habits, and hence rule her out. The toxic maternal means that while mother's milk is poison, it still supplies the crucial nourishment that the subject seeks. It suggests, moreover, that the maternal is too close, invading the orifices and skin with no screen protection, as it were, no intervening law to sever the ever-pumping umbilicus" (118–19).

Goethe's *Faust,* injected in *Crack Wars* as Junker-junk by one of the eternal feminines, saw super-vision and super-humanity come to grief over a series of potions of varying dosages of toxicity. Goethe's *Faust* has the bad rep of assembling lines of toxic concepts marching as to war and mass murder. Take "Superhuman," for example, which is a good enough translation of *Übermensch,* the term or concept we saw first in Goethe's *Faust.* The Earth Spirit Faust conjures expects to meet in him match and maker, in other words an *Übermensch.* But the term comes up as a put-down: The Earth Spirit declares that Faust is no *Übermensch,* and must go elsewhere to meet his *Ebenbild,* or double. Though *Übermensch* can be found in use around the time of Luther, but to signify the superiority of the especially good Christian, or also already in Herder's lexicon, but linked and limited to superiority on the sliding scale of existing humanity, it was in Goethe's *Faust* that *Übermensch* came to mean, via the rebound of negation, a human being equal to divinity, which is up for grabs or, in Faust's case, just out of reach.

As we first encounter Faust, he is a mood swinger. Even after the songs of his childhood reopen a future of possibilities coming toward him and stay the mirroring merger with the poison in his father's cup, he still dips into depression. But this lack can find compensation, he announces, as he turns to the New Testament to translate into German the word or logos that was in the beginning. The German word for translation, *Übersetzen,* points toward a translation of *Übermensch* as "transhuman," a translation grounded in ambiguities inherent in the related words or prefixes "over" and *über.* The "over" or *über*—human has crossed over to one in a series of stations of the crossing but also or alternatively as crossed out: man as over, over and out. Certainly that is how Faust starts out.

In the course of the translation attempts that usher in the performative word as deed or act, as the push-button temporality or technology that Faust will in deed receive, the poodle reveals the Devil in the tails, who as Faust's split-off double will administer Faust's wishes as commands. Thus the "act" of Faust's translation is picked up, literalized, and administered by the Devil.

Faust's striving, which the Devil mediates as a series of self-realizing acts of murder and merger, is on its own not so much active as radically passive. If Faust is bracketed out of this infernal culture industry of technologization and administration of wish or desire, then it is not only to relieve Faust of any responsibility precisely through this dissociation with the Devil. It is also because the Faustian striving that takes over where the suicidal depression left off, or where it begins to defer the suicide itself, runs counter to the Devil's nihilism. Faustian striving can't get no satisfaction, in fact craves incompletion, and thus performs the superhuman as trans-human. Should Faust ever decide that he is fully himself in the moment—a whole in one—then he belongs to the Devil. Thus he performs a more Nietzsche-compatible understanding of the superhuman as process or transition and as irreducibly future goal, as the future of the future.

In the context or contest of World War II propaganda or mass psychology, American interpretations and embodiments of the superhuman as transhuman (notably the comics figures Superman and Wonder Woman and the movie hero Tarzan as played by Johnny Weismuller) struggled against fully realized supermen of Nazi Germany who, by all accounts, were ready, set, to go win the master race. Between Goethe and Nietzsche, the figure of the "superhuman" or "transhuman" raised the stakes of reading and misreading to life or death. Because one man's future is the next generation's present, Freud rescheduled the superman (in *Group Psychology and the Analysis of the Ego*) as belonging not to Nietzsche's future but resolutely in the past as the primal father, from whose superiority we are still in recovery in the mode of mourning. But we find in Freud another trajectory taking off from this living dead end of the superhuman. In his essay "The 'Uncanny,'" Freud interpreted the two souls in Faust's breast, one aspiring upward and the other clinging to the earth, as a doubling of the ego whereby what would soon go by the name superego keeps ego under surveillance. "The fact that an agency of this kind exists, which is able to treat the rest of the ego like an object—the fact, that is, that man is capable of self-observation—renders it possible to invest the old idea of a 'double' with a new meaning." This new meaning was introduced via the evidence of "delusions of being watched." In such pathological cases, "this mental agency becomes isolated, dissociated from the ego, and discernible to the physician's eye." What immediately follows the "new meaning" is the reference to *Faust* down in the footnote underworld: "I believe that when poets complain that two souls dwell in the human breast . . . what they are thinking of is this division . . . between the critical agency and the rest of the ego" (*SE* 17: 235–36).

Thus surveillance as super-vision appears between the lines of Freud and Goethe as our inner-world connection with the dead or Dad as wholly other—who watches us, observes us. But what comes out in the watch is that there is no looking back for us. We observe in the sense of follow: we observe the law of mourning. Primal repression, which fills out the mother's missing person report in everyone's development and is legislated according to Freud's mythic history in the aftermath of the primal father's murder, guarantees, as Freud argues in *Beyond the Pleasure Principle,* that there can be no perfectibility drive for humanity. There is always something missing in the past that keeps us striving onward toward the unattainable. Or in other words, which can be found among the closing words of Goethe's *Faust,* the eternal or internal feminine, as principle of mourning and guarantor of self-difference, drives us onward. But there is also always the uncanny underside of all of the above. The uncanny gaze of the primal father is back, Freud allowed, when we are mediatized as in hypnosis. And one leftover or hangover of the mother's missing body is the "libido toxin," which, according to Freud, is the unattainable high that sets us up for addiction. What fits this frame of inter-reference, including the phantasm of super vision, the structure of addiction, and Goethe's *Faust,* is Philip K. Dick's *A Scanner Darkly,* which updates or upgrades the mirror or glass in St. Paul's famous image of our skewed vision that at the end of time will be all clear. But already at his end of time, protagonist Bob Arctor reflects, the mirror reflection that St. Paul contemplated as "his own face reflected back up at him, reversed—pulled through infinity" was at least at last reversed and thus cleared with the onset of visual mediation (212). It is within this series of reflections that Arctor learns that what has happened to his brain on the drug Substance D, otherwise known as Death, restores this reversal as irreducible. The attending psychologist explains: "*It is as if one hemisphere of your brain is perceiving the world as reflected in a mirror.* Through a mirror. See? So left becomes right, and all that that implies. And we don't know yet what that does imply, to see the world reversed like that. Topologically speaking, a left-hand glove is a right-hand glove pulled through infinity." " 'Through a mirror,'" Arctor responds; "A darkened mirror, he thought; a darkened scanner. . . . I have seen myself backward. I have in a sense begun to see the entire universe backward. With the other side of my brain!" (212).

Before the drug-induced brain damage is introduced or diagnosed, however, Arctor is doubled via surveillance. Arctor reports back as undercover agent Fred when he is not hanging out as part of the drug-taking milieu he is spying on. His superior suddenly assigns Fred to keep close tabs on

Arctor, on himself, to which end video surveillance is secretly installed throughout his house. "To himself, Bob Arctor thought, *How many Bob Arctors are there?* . . . Two that I can think of, he thought. The one called Fred, who will be watching the other one, called Bob. The same person. Or is it? . . . *Which of them is me?*" (96). But the tabs he keeps end up subsumed by the tabs he has already taken. Or in other words or images from the book, where the hallucinated aphid bugs that a drug addict whose receptor sites in the brain are irreversibly gone leaves off, the bugging of surveillance picks up and switches delusion channels via what is referred to as "cerebral lateralization" (113). Arctor, under his own surveillance, becomes an actor (134), while the wasting of the one side of the brain otherwise responsible for language prompts the surviving side to find linguistic compensation or translation. This compensation, which proceeds as lateralization, opens wide the alternate worlds or self-reflexive interiorities of delusion, for example via acting. Is the subject of surveillance acting, is he pretending not to know that he is under surveillance? These questions rise up for Fred even or especially as he watches himself as Arctor on tape. "Each day the experience of the scanners had grown. . . . Like an actor before a movie camera, he decided, you act like the camera doesn't exist or else you blow it. It's all over" (184). "But—you can't be sure. There are shucks on top of shucks. Layers and Layers" (191).

A Scanner Darkly is a novel as much about surveillance as it is, up front and at first, about drug culture. In chapter 11, moreover, there are five untranslated quotes from Goethe's *Faust,* including the one double-featuring the two souls in one breast. Fragments, translations, repetitions of this material are scattered throughout the pages that follow chapter 11. The chapter ends on the suicide notes and plans of one of the druggies. He leaves Ayn Rand's *The Fountainhead* lying around to prove that he was a misunderstood "superman." But this time he was sold hallucinogens instead of the suffocating downers he was counting on, and so he trips out, not unlike Faust, to a transcendent realm where a creature with compound eyes reads out his sins for all eternity. Dying in Goethe's *Faust* takes all the time in the world, all the time Faust invested in the world, all the time in the world he consumed, all the time it takes to rewind in order to erase or dematerialize the ego's span of retention of the world.

The stations of Arctor's crossing are allegorical, as in Goethe's *Faust II,* and as elaborated by Walter Benjamin in *Origin of the German Mourning Play.* Thus Dick does not replace metaphysical frames of reference via the new and improved but maintains them, but as ruins or condemned sites; he rescues them without getting back their redemption value. Thus Christian views of life and death flash before our eyes but ultimately as more shucks upon shucks. After one of the police psychologists proclaims that "the infinity of time . . . is expressed as eternity, as a loop! Like the loop of cassette tape!" (215), Fred or Arctor flashes on this timeline: "In time—maybe the Crucifixion lies ahead of us as we all sail along, thinking it's back east. . . . The First and Second Coming of Christ the same event, he thought; time a cassette loop. No wonder they were sure it'd happen, He'd be back" (216). But what he is left with is the emptied-out shell of this transcendent loop, which he nonetheless struggles to maintain: "Keep surveillance alive, as I've been doing. For a while at least. But I mean, everything in life is just for a while" (220). Or again: "Otherwise, he thought, they could die and no one would be the wiser. Know or even fucking care. In wretched little lives like that, someone must intervene. Or at least mark their sad comings and goings. Mark and if possible permanently record, so they'll be remembered." (221). Surveillance as a functioning technology that keeps a permanent record of witnessed existence is a belief system. But the lateralized alternative realities come to another rescue by fixing the focus on the technological condition, with an unprotected clarity reminiscent of certain psychotic delusions, reminiscent in fact of many of Dick's earlier works characterized by smart appreciation for the schizophrenic perspective. As a kind of prologue to the Faust chapter, we are given an inside view of the exchange between the two souls in Arctor's one brain. The lateralized view sees the doubles as fully inhabiting the tape medium. "But now Fred is here, too. But all Fred's got is hindsight. Unless, he thought, unless maybe if I run the holo-tapes backward. Then I'd be there first, before Barris. What I do would precede what Barris does. If with me first he gets to do anything at all. And then the other side of his head opened up and spoke to him more calmly, like another self with a simpler message flashed to him as to how to handle it" (171). But following this restoration of the connection to the sane brain, which leads Arctor to go in person and replace the bad check he assumes Barris forged and passed just to mess with him, the alternation between sides or doubles, substantially mediated by the foreign-body quotations from *Faust,* begins to turn over rapidly. Now he is not sure, for example, whether he did not write the check after all and then forget about it (178). Lateralization from the remaining side of his brain presses Arctor into closed circuit encounter with the technology of the seeing I or ego: "Which may just be my imagination, the 'they' watching me. Paranoia. Or rather the 'it.' . . . Whatever it is that's watching, it is not a human. . . . Something is being done to me and by a mere thing, here in my own house. Before my very eyes. Within *something's* very eyes; within the sight of some *thing.* Which, unlike little dark-eyed Donna, does not ever blink. What does a scanner see? he asked himself. . . . I hope it does, he thought, see clearly, because I can't any longer these days see into myself. I see only murk. Murk outside; murk inside. I hope, for everyone's sake, the scanners do better. Because, he thought, if the scanner sees only darkly, the way I myself do, then we are cursed . . . and we'll wind up dead this way, knowing very little and getting that little fragment wrong too" (185). They do wind up or rewind dead this way. A burned-out addict fits the span of doubling between insect bugs and surveillance bugs: "Until it clicked and clacked like an insect, repeating one sentence again and again. A recording. A closed loop of tape" (66). In sum, "Every junkie, he thought, is a recording." (159). In the closing chapters that describe the new path through recovery that Arctor/Fred, now named Bruce, undergoes, the encounter group works through these connections between life and death. To be dead is to be an unmoving camera: not to be able to stop looking at whatever is in front of you. One of the supervisors at an occupational therapy farm for recovering addicts concludes: "But the dead—he glanced at Bruce, the empty shape beside him—should, if possible, serve the purposes of the living. . . . The dead . . . who can still see, even if they can't understand: they are our camera" (266).

A belated discovery in my case, Philip K. Dick is nonetheless the poster boy of *The Case of California*. He reads California as the tech-no-future within a lexicon heavily mediated by the foreign body of Germanicity. In *Martian Time Slip,* for example, the housing projects on Earth form a corporation called Amweb, which is the acronym for *Alle Menschen werden Brüder.* The German intertexts or introjects remain largely untranslated and decontextualized. (Indeed it is only in *A Scanner Darkly* that the main text begins to metabolize and even integrate the German passages.) In Dick's corpus we are thus back at the face-off or interface between Horkheimer/ Adorno and Benjamin over the unread body of the culture industry, a concept or condition that critical theory saw first in or as California.

In *Dialectic of Enlightenment,* Horkheimer and Adorno argue that civilized man attains self-identity by being the image of the invisible power. It is an identity that cannot disappear through identification with another but instead takes possession of itself once and for all as an impenetrable mask (10). The magician, in contrast, did not interpret himself as the image of the invisible power. In "The Work of Art in the Age of Its Technical Reproducibility," Benjamin contrasts the magician, as mascot of the former work of art as totality, with the surgeon, as slasher mascot of the work of art transformed—disseminated, fragmented, recombined—via the reproduction, recording, and reception of the apparatus. Recording and reception, which are both signified by the one German word, *Aufnehmen,* in Benjamin's essay, thus double back on one another as loop. Dick's concluding depiction of a society dominated by recovery—it turns out that the occupational therapy laborers tend fields of Substance D grown for the consumers at the other end of yet another loop—meets three phrases or phases in *Dialectic of Enlightenment* more than halfway. Narcotic intoxication self-medicates the strain of holding the ego together, the strain that adheres to the ego in all stages of its development and well being. The temptation to lose the ego has always been there with the blind determination to maintain it. But the balancing act narcotic intoxication attains is doomed, just as sublimation, according to Freud's essay on Leonardo da Vinci, is doomed to lose the speed race against repression. Sickness thus becomes a symptom of recovery (113). Dick's culture industry of recovery can also be seen to take up the two positions Horkheimer and Adorno found readymade in Odysseus's encounter with the Sirens. To survive the temptation of that which is unrepeatable—of that which calls for abandonment of the ego—one can, like Odysseus's rowers, not hear or receive it. This applies to those in recovery, too, who are the only laborers in Dick's novel. Or one can go ahead and listen or receive the song of the Sirens, but only while tied to the mast. For the operators of the seeing-eye drug world, the temptation is also neutralized, ultimately as literature.

Derrida often identified the computer as the enabling context or condition of deconstruction. Though the nonlinearity of the connections and clicks might come to mind in this setting, it is also the case that digitization has not so much introduced more new media as it has served as a supplemental synthesis that allows for exchange between media where before conflicts, like that between the projective and the live media, had seemed without end or issue. The particular conflict between film and tape has been displaced with regard to the digital processes of development and editing where all visual media meet and now, in theory, can cross over. Deconstruction also serves as supplemental synthesis whereby Adorno and Benjamin, for example, can be read together without taking sides or falling for opposition. To this opening, deconstruction brought Freud back from the returns to him.

Ronell distinguishes her reading of TV, which signs up with the Benjamin of "Toward a Critique of Violence," from the monolithic mass media of the Frankfurt School reception. And yet the Frankfurt School (or Adorno) squeaks back every time one again finds "TraumaTV" reduced, in art journalism for example, to postulation of a fateful interchangeability between serial murder and serial TV. If *Dialectic of Enlightenment* crosses the back of one's mind as laugh track while reading Benjamin's media essays, then there is still synthesis at a standstill or dialectics still standing. But the supplemental point I am after, what Ronell contemplates as an ethics of radical passivity or pathivity, opens up the following negative charge (from *Dialectic of Enlightenment*) to reading of both Benjamin's "The Work of Art in the Age of Its Technical Reproducibility" and Ronell's *Stupidity* as on one (dis)continuum: "The enjoyment of the violence suffered by the movie actor turns into violence against the spectator, and distraction into exertion. Nothing that the experts have devised as a stimulant must escape the weary eye; no stupidity is allowed in the face of all the trickery; one has to follow everything and even display the smart responses shown and recommended in the film" (139). That no stupidity is allowed by the culture industry places the call: "I am stupid before the other" (the bottom line of *Stupidity*). The opening I am after here coincides with a certain shutting down of media differentiations as will follow, in the near future, from the monopoly of one monitor for and over all media options and outlets. But will not renewal of our vows with interactive relations be along for the ride into virtual reality? Turn on the laugh track and start reading for the silver lining up every dead end with an affirmation beyond hope.

What Ronell and Rickels inherit from Derrida is open reading, reading that opens. Benjamin offers opening in reading as maintenance via his conception of allegory (and all that follows from this rereading in his media essays). When Adorno identified immediacy as the object of his critique, it was not in order to dismiss it as delusion. In his writing he tries to bring back the mediations, even or especially the untenable ones (like the notion of subjectivity for example), which the new and improved has streamlined out of existence. This is an allegorical practice. When Hannah Arendt refers to Adorno as Benjamin's only student, she is right to the extent that the good student or reader often knows the teacher's former work better than the author himself in the midst of new reformulations. In their correspondence Adorno only criticizes Benjamin's writing in the name of *Origin of the German Mourning Play*. When Adorno joined the graduate faculty at the postwar university in Frankfurt, his first seminar was dedicated to Benjamin's Origin book. But Adorno still took sides, against Brecht, against Heidegger, in the name of those mediations or allegories brand-new discourses render illegible in their newfound originality and perfection. Adorno neglected to recognize the larger opening of thinking, in which Heidegger's language does not even try to escape the untenability of metaphysical systems, and which deconstruction remetabolized, reallegorized, reopened. I am reader before the other. *Aberrations of Mourning* was a reading of Ronell's *Dictations, The Case of California* and *Nazi Psycho-analysis* were readings of *The Telephone Book.* It looks like the book I am working on now, on the corpus of Philip K. Dick within a setting established or symptomatized by modern Spiritualism and in which Benjamin, Freud, and Schreber are equal sharers, is reading *Crack Wars.*

While playing himself in the film *Ghostdance,* Derrida observes: "Psychoanalysis plus film equals a science of ghosts." Derrida's understanding of trace structure promotes a reading of aura (in Adorno and Benjamin) that goes beyond the short *Schrift* it is given as eliminated but then also on occasion as retrenched. According to Derrida, the media image is always spectral; it is of the visible, but of the invisible visible; it is a trace that marks the present with its absence in advance. Aura's decline is also not imposed from without. Aura's bottom line is departure, taking leave. Like the eternal/internal feminine it delivers the beat of mourning, a beat that cannot be policed, not even as surveillance. It is true that aura under techno conditions is no longer interpersonal or reciprocal. Mediatic aura does not return our glance, does not look at us. As Samuel Weber carefully showed via his reading of Benjamin's media essays ("Mass Mediauras, or: Art, Aura and Media in the Work of Walter Benjamin"), mutated aura looks upward, opens a look so close and yet so far away, like the reproduction you hold in your hands. Aura is still the singular leave-taking of the singular, but the singularity is no longer uniquely that of an original moment but, as Benjamin writes of photography's impact on the moment (in "Some Motifs in Baudelaire"), that of its posthumous shock. For Derrida and Dick (as for Ronell and Rickels) mourning raises the question (like a ghost): Where are the dead *here,* where are they housed, installed, included? The dead or undead take leave as aura indwelling the double loop of addiction or surveillance. In *A Scanner Darkly,* the dead are our cameras; they fill in the blank of that something that looks without blinking and before which or whom we are recorded and received.

Werner Hamacher

Uncalled:
A Commentary on
Kafka's "The Test"

The philosophical and religious texts of the European tradition know only a world that follows a call, a world called forth and called on to do something, in which everything has a vocation and everything is addressed as that which it is. They declare, either explicitly or implicitly, every other to be impossible. A short text by Franz Kafka from "Convolute 1920" with notes from the fall of that year, published by Max Brod under the title "The Test," can be read as an investigation of a world without call—without determination or function, without profession or vocation and without work; without goal and without guiding, claiming, or approval-granting authority. This text, in which nothing indicates that it reaches a "conclusion," and nothing that it is a "fragment," begins with the sentence: "I am a servant, but there is no work for me." It ends with the lines: "That was only a test. He who does not answer the questions, has passed the test."[1]

The *I*, who introduces himself as a *servant* in Kafka's study, suggests many "causes" for there being no work for him. "I am anxious and don't push myself forward, indeed I don't even push myself into a line with the others, but that is only one reason for my inoccupation, it's also possible that it has nothing at all to do with my inoccupation, the main cause in any case is that I am not called upon to serve . . ." As the first *cause* for his *inoccupation,* the servant names his anxiousness, which prevents him from competing with the others, but he immediately concedes: "it is also possible

    TRANSLATED BY CATHARINE DIEHL

that it has nothing at all to do with my inoccupation." Thus, not only is the servant without work, without employment, and inactive, also the *cause* that he names for this possibly has "nothing at all to do" with his inactivity. A cause that—if only possibly—does nothing, has nothing to do, does not affect the "effect" it should ground; such a cause does not only not have the explanatory function, it also does not have the foundational meaning of a cause. It is, of course, still called "cause," "but there is no work for it." A cause without foundational force, it is merely a possibility that is possibly none at all and therefore ceases to be in force as a possibility. A cause, which might not be one; a possibility, which perhaps does not offer the possibility of a foundation of reality; a vocation, which is not linked to any activity, occupation, or function—Kafka's text speaks of a de-causalized world by speaking a de-causalized language. This language seems to withdraw the ground tendentially from all its statements and attests that it perhaps "has nothing at all to do" with that which it says and nothing to do with the fact that it says it. Benjamin remarked that the law in Kafka's writings is a mere decoy [*Attrappe*], but each individual word in these writings is used as a trap for an attention that can find no support in the word.[2] None of these words designates a "thing," a "cause," or an object, and none presents itself as an objectively justified statement. If it is a vacancy of causality that speaks in Kafka's text, then the *I* with which it begins also cannot be the subject that grounds the construction of a secure linguistic world. The *I* does not speak as the representative of an authority that this *I* would help to express; the *I* is a helper who helps no one, a *servant* without work, without its own voice and without the voice of an other, for whom it could serve as a mediator. Neither master over itself nor servant of a master, the *I* is the figure of a speaking without task and thus not a figure of something that could claim, either behind or above it, a secured authority, be it of sense or of function. *I* is a word without the call, without the capacity, and without the *work,* to speak in the name of an other, a personal pronoun, but only as the pro- of a *persona* without noun and without a tone that could ring forth through it. An anonymous formula, a decoy, a *scandalon,* in whose trap nothing is contained or held.

Whatever the derivative and secondary causes for the lack of work may be, it is said: "the main cause in any case is that I am not called upon to serve"—thus it lies in the fact that a cause is lacking. Work is not there because the call to it, which alone could be its cause, is missing. The existence of work—but just as much of a working language that works out its own meaningfulness, and of a subject that could communicate itself in this language—would be being-called, being-called-to-serve. Where there is no call to work, there is no work; for, work would be—this is implied as obvious—work for a call that demands, claims, and guides it. The call—whatever its content, form, and register may be—would be that which could induce service, namely service on this call. The call would give work. It would lead toward a goal, provide a meaning and a sense of direction, and the work would lie in hearing the call, in answering it, and in corresponding to its paradigm [*Vorgabe*]. The call would be the gift pure and simple: paradigm [*Vorgabe*], task [*Aufgabe*], gift of meaning [*Sinngabe*]. Being-called would be being. And being-at-call—the hearing, to which the call gives itself and through which the call would come back to itself—would be service on call. Whoever hears the call serves it and works. Calling always means calling-to-work. Even before it is a call to a particular activity, the call is the first, the proper, the appropriating employer [*Arbeit-Geber*]: the giver of work as being-to-the-call.

The call thus would be the unavoidable condition of a world held together by meaningfulness and work, a linguistic world that determines itself as working world. Where no call, no demand, neither an appeal nor a request or invitation is heard, there may still be a world—and perhaps none other than this world, but it is not there as given, not as given by something other or by someone other, and not as a world ordered by a founding claim and the work corresponding to it. Kafka's world is such an un-given, un-conditioned world; a world in its absolute worldliness. It is a world in which not even the possibility of transcendence through language and work is secured but that, precisely because of this, knows the wish—admittedly only the intermittent, inconstant, and for itself non-constitutive wish—for this. It is characterized by Kafka as a world that very well may wish to hear, but hears only that it does not hear: "Others have been called and have not applied themselves to it more than I, indeed have perhaps not even once had the wish to be called, while I at least have it sometimes very strongly."

Not to be called—that means not to belong to the receivers of a message, which, simply in virtue of being a message, would be a joyous message. The call would be the gospel for a being whose sense is work. This call would be not only messianic; it would be the Messiah himself. It becomes clear through an allusion to the Christian Gospel that the call, concerning whose failure Kafka's text speaks, is in the horizon of a salvational history directed toward the kingdom of heaven, its householder, and the messianic call emitted by him. In the sentence speaking of the "main cause," of un-calledness, the sententious formula, "others were called" evokes—whether it was consciously cited by Kafka or whether it merely imposed itself upon him—the maxim from the Gospel of Matthew: "For many be called but few chosen."[3] This maxim concludes the parable of the workers in the vineyard with which Jesus answers a morose remark by Peter. The parable begins with the sentence: "For the kingdom of heaven is like a householder (*oíkodespótes, pater familias*) who went out early in the morning to hire laborers (*èrgátas, operarios*) for his vineyard" (Matthew 20:1). Those standing idle are hired as day laborers. Because they begin their work in the vineyard at different times, thus working for different durations, but all receiving the same payment, they complain at the end of the day about the injustice of the householder. He insists that the payment is just, because it was agreed upon with each individual worker, with the first as well as the last to come: "So the last will be first, and the first last." They are all equal in a time that is not the comparative time of private interests but is the time—the time of work—of a kingdom of heaven, which is common to all of them, if also for each in his own particular manner. The last quoted sentence is then followed by the one that resonates in Kafka's text: "For many be called (*kletoi, vocati*), but few chosen (*èklektoi, electi*)" (Matthew 20:16). The elliptical, and incidentally dubious for editorial philologists, conclusion to the parable allows for multiple interpretations of the maxim; the one most plausible for the context may be that many are called (*kletoi*)—namely all those to whom the householder offers work in the vineyard—but that among these, only a few are chosen (*èklektoi*) to begin their work early. But all of them, thus the many called as well as the few chosen among them, receive the same wage from the householder, the kingdom of heaven. For no distinction shall be tolerated between the first and the last, the called and the chosen. Therein lies the not comparative but absolute justice of this householder who grants his wages equally to all.

This divine justice may of course be granted to all, but only to all those who are called. Godly, kingly, or householderly justice does not reach the uncalled. Kafka's prose, however, dwells on the uncalled. It speaks of those who receive no call, not of those who, according to the representation of the biblical texts, are condemned by a judgment or turned away by it. The Gospel of Matthew offers, not far from the parable of the vineyard, another parable in which the maxim of the many called and few chosen is repeated in a hardly Christian sense. In this parable, the kingdom of heaven is compared to a king who has the guests called (*kalésai*) to his son's wedding celebration. Because the called refuse the invitation—they have to work—he lets those who are found idle on the streets be called to the feast; however, he examines those who have come and expels from the house one who has appeared at the feast without festive clothing: "'Bind him hand and foot, and cast him into the outer darkness; there men will weep and gnash their teeth.' For many are called (*kletoi*), but few are chosen (*èklektoi*)" (Matthew 22:13–14). The difference between the called and the chosen, denied in the vineyard parable, stands in the center of the wedding parable: although they are called not to work but to celebrate, not only the chosen belong to the called; also called is the one who is ultimately bound and cast into the outermost darkness. He did receive the call, but because he is not commensurate with it, he remains within the bounds of the call, excluded from its enjoyment.

The joyous message in both parables is the message of the message itself; it is the message of the call that extends to the inactive, the idle, the unemployed and unoccupied on the street; it calls them from the street into the house or into the cultivated field, under the rule of an *oíkodespótes* or *basileus,* and offers the idlers either work or a feast, both of which would follow the same script. The parable of the Christian Messiah does not only concern this call; the parable is itself a call and an appeal to the idlers to follow it to work or to the feast of the kingdom of God. A call to the call itself that speaks of nothing other than the call, the Gospel presents itself as theology of the *klesis*, as *kleseological*—and only therefore ecclesiological— theology, as kleseo-tautology and theo-tautology; it calls to the call as the sole guarantor of its truth, the truth of its *klesis,* its *logos,* its *theos.* The messianism of the Gospels knows only the call and the called who serve the call; it knows only those called by the call to work on the call and among them the chosen and the cast away, both of whom hear it equally and answer it, even if in different ways. This messianism does not know the uncalled.[4]

The messianism of the Old Testament writings does not function differently. Kafka's intensive study of Kierkegaard, from at least 1918, has been documented, in particular with respect to the interpretation Kierkegaard develops in *Fear and Trembling* of the founding episode of Israel, the test of Abraham through the demand that he sacrifice his son. The relevant biblical text begins with a call of Elohim, a call that has been the topic since Genesis 1:3, where it is said that Elohim called (*wayyomer*) "let there be light"; called (*wayyomer*) "let there be a firmament," and carried on the whole process of creation through a sequence of calls of becoming, dividing, and naming. The text introduces Abraham's test as follows: "After these things God tested (*nissa*) Abraham, and called (*wayyomer*) to him, 'Abraham!' And he called (*wayyomer*) 'Here am I.' He called (*wayyomer*) 'Take your son, your only son Isaac, whom you love, and go to the land of Mori'ah, and offer him there as a burnt offering upon one of the mountains of which I shall tell you'" (Genesis 22:1–2). Abraham follows this call of his God without the slightest hesitation and becomes, after he has passed the test in this way, the father of an endless line of future generations, the father of the future and of the Messiah who is supposed to approach with this future. Kafka remarked in June 1921—thus two years after beginning his reading of Kierkegaard and approximately a half year after the composition of "The Test"—in a highly polemical letter to Robert Klopstock that this biblical Abraham follows the demand to sacrifice, "ready to serve like a waiter." His reflections on "another Abraham" culminate in the following observation: "But another Abraham. One who quite wants to sacrifice correctly . ., but cannot believe that he is intended. . . . He fears that although he will ride out as Abraham with his son, he will be transformed on the way into Don Quixote. The world would have been shocked then about Abraham if it had watched, but this one fears that the world would laugh itself to death at the sight of him. . . . An Abraham who comes uncalled! It is as if at the end of the year, the best pupil were to receive a prize and in the expectant silence the worst pupil, because he misheard, came forward from his dirty, last bench and the whole class burst out laughing. And it is perhaps not even a mishearing, his name was really named, the reward of the best was supposed to be, the teacher intended, at the same time a punishment of the worst."[5] An Abraham who comes uncalled or one who cannot believe that he and no other is intended by the godly call, but follows the call nonetheless and becomes thereby the ridiculous erring knight: for such an Abraham, the call of God has divided into a demand that reaches him and another demand that is not meant for him, or not for him in the sense of an award, appointment, or choosing. The call that Abraham answers like an echo in the biblical text, and which only thereby forges the bond between Elohim and Abraham, has divided for Kafka into a call and a faux call emptied of its intention and therefore, at best, only claiming to call. A call that does not call, be it only because it is missing the correlate of a faithful hearing—a call, which is not a call but only pretends to be one, can, however, be only the tale, only the legend, the fiction or the rumor of a call, a call-decoy, which, pretending to be absolutely powerful, is powerless to ground or put to work a bond, whether a linguistic bond or a bond of faith, and powerless to give a promise for the future. Unlike the call of Elohim in the biblical story of Abraham, the unheard call devised by Kafka is nothing other than a parody of itself, its self-erasure, and the de-powering of the claim that it raises. No one is called by it, the uncalled call. "Another Abraham" comes—even if to no predetermined place—"uncalled."[6]

Kafka's hypothesis of an uncalled Abraham is not, above all, a blasphemous fabulation about the unsoundness of the Jewish foundational story, of the religion of the covenant and of monotheism, but the sober demonstration of the internal decomposition of the structure of the call in general. If Abraham, the called *kat' exochen,* he whose essence lies in being called, in hearing his call, and in corresponding to it in the work of sacrifice; if this Abraham, among all the called, is the one whom Kafka can assume is not called, then it is only because the call itself—and, that is, each call insofar as it is a call—includes the possibility to be directed to another than to the one who hears it, and can never exclude the possibility not to be heard by the one to whom it is offered and not to be heard *as* call by the one who hears it. The structure of the call always implies the possibility of never being that which it is itself called upon to be. Not from the call "itself," but from the split in the call—from that which is uncalled within it—is the call to be thought. The thought of an uncalled Abraham is the thought of someone not called in the call itself: the thought that every call, even the highest, must be able, through its mere relation to an other, to one called by it, to distance itself from itself without mediation and therefore at the same time from this very relation and therefore to be exposed to the possibility not to be a call. The structural depotentiation of every call—not its self-*re*vocation from its power over itself, but its *de*vocation from its powerlessness to be itself—opens the space within it for that which must remain uncalled by it. This uncalled is not that other that does not yet or no longer stands in the call-relation; it is not the recipient of a diminished call or of a call in a deficient mode, but it is that which cannot stand in any relation to a call because structurally a call must be exposed to that which does not belong to its intention, that which does not hear it, or which does not hear it as call. The uncalled is the ir-relational in the call-relation itself and thereby the opening in the call onto that which can neither belong to it nor hear or fulfill it. It is other than that other to the call that could be its answer; other than that which could be its revocation or its refusal; the uncalled in the call is not *its* other; it "is" that other-than-the-other in which the call suspends itself, in which it does not merely silently and therefore misapprehensibly signify, but in which it falls silent, incapable of signification. Though the foundational stories of messianic religions and religions of the covenant suggest the internal coherence of the call and its prestabilized consonance with every answer of every possible other, Kafka turns in his letter and his notes to the one who cannot be reached by their call and who cannot answer it, to the uncalled.

Kafka's prose speaks of the ones—and is spoken by those—whom no message, neither happy nor unhappy, reaches. It speaks of the uninvited, the unbidden, and the not even discarded who do not come into question for service or feast; it speaks of the unaddressed, those forgotten by the messianic religions, by their call, by their language, their *logos,* and its parables. It speaks of those to whom God and his Messiah cannot turn with a call—it speaks of an incapacity in God. Kafka's text cannot, however, be understood for this reason as counter-parable of a counter-Gospel from which, upon the right occasion, a new religion, more encompassing than those previously announced, could arise. In his great essay on Kafka, Benjamin made the observation that Kafka "was not tempted to become the founder of a religion"—this temptation must have remained foreign to him precisely because he had dedicated himself to an experience that must be on systematic grounds foreclosed by religions of whatever type.[7] For the minimal condition of every religion lies in a relation—in the, it is believed, most common, most presuppositionless, and indestructible relation—between an addressor and an addressee in which both simultaneously acknowledge and recognize each other. Kafka's text flatly states that this absolute minimum is missing: that indeed an *I* may be posited that hears but that the call remains absent through which this *I* could become a real hearer, one who knows itself to be called and in knowing professes to have a vocation. Kafka's language is that of the unaddressed; it is irreligious. It is not antireligious; it contests no God, no householder, and not even the possibility of a theological economy for others; it least of all contests the wish—a wish that *sometimes* appears, if only irregularly—for such an economy, such a law of the house, of the householder and his call; but this language remains with the wish as mere wish, with the uncalledness of this wish—its unserviceability, unrelatedness, and unconditionality. It remains with a wish that does not itself have the messianic power to create or to hear what is wished for, an extra-messianic wish that knows no expectation or even simple waiting. Nowhere in Kafka's text is waiting mentioned: even waiting would be in the service of the expected, and an attentional tension is, like every other intentional relation, impossible outside of stable salvational economies; every salvational economy is, however, an economy of calling and vocation. The coming of the messianic—of the call, of vocation, of work, of exchange, of recognition in the medium of language—is not anticipated by a single word in Kafka's text and not announced by any promise: a promise would already be an answer to a call; it would be the authentic labor of language.

Kafka's linguistic world is not in any inherited sense messianic: it is absolutely a-messianic. "The main cause in any case is that I am not called upon to serve"; thus it is stated in a grammatical present that stretches into the past as well as the future, a diffuse present that does not wait in view of another time and therefore is not in any traditional sense time at all—not a time of protention, production, or work, but also not a time of celebration, collection, recollection, or retention—but the idleness of time, fallow time. In the present tense of "that I am not called upon to serve," the unusedness, perhaps the unusableness, of time spreads throughout all its dimensions. This unusedness is just as much forgotten by philosophy, which is devoted to that which is used in knowledge and action and is in its service, as the uncalled must be forgotten by religion. The un-time of Kafka's story is that of the surplus, the unutilizable remnant that has never lain within the realm or the calling-range of a philosophy or religion. Fallow time, fallow language, it lies outside the course of history, not on a path and especially not on a high road of the experience of reason, which is always a reason of hearing a call and always a reason of the use and usefulness in principle of time, language, and world. This reason lies fallow in Kafka. It is not redeemed from its unappointedness and is not employed by his texts for any cognitive, moral, or even aesthetic use but presented as the primary fact of an experience—laid bare—with which nothing can begin and cannot end. Kafka's prose does not only speak from a world promising redemption to nothing but from a non-world into which no call of creation reaches. It is therefore prosaic like no other—a prose of bare lying—horizontal without a horizon, evocative without voice—a description of that which absorbs every writing.

"So I lie on the plank bed in the servants' hall, stare at the beams in the ceiling, fall asleep, wake up and soon fall asleep again. Sometimes I walk over to the tavern where a sour beer is served, sometimes I have even poured out a glass in disgust, but then I drink it again."

The rhythm of naming and negation, evocation and devocation, which begins with the first sentence of Kafka's text and keeps the following ones in motion, is the rhythm of the evacuation of functional language through its de-functionalization, of the language of action through its deactivation; it is, however, also the rhythm in which the emptying out of language is still brought to language—to a neither working nor celebrating language. This aporetic motion without beginning or goal leads from call-lessness into call-lessness; it leads—also where it encounters an other, whether a glass of beer or a likewise unemployed servant—back to itself, a *vox inanis*. This reduction to itself, itself a *reductio inanis,* is made clear in the sole narrative passage of the text. "Once," it says there, "when I arrived at the tavern, a guest was sitting at my observation post. I did not dare look at him closely and was about to turn around and leave. The guest, however, called me over, and it turned out that he too was a servant whom I had once seen somewhere before, but without having spoken to him." The site where this meeting takes place is a site neither of work nor of celebration but of inaction and observation, thus the same site spoken of in the whole text. The call—"the guest called me over" [*der Gast rief mich zu sich*]—is the call of a substitute of the *I*—"he was sitting at my observation post"—of a doppelgänger and usurper, not the call of a master but of a servant and guest—and even of a guest of the guest who takes on with his invitation the role of a host. It is a call from servant to servant, from an idler to another, from an uncalled to an uncalled. The change of positions between guest and host, inviter and invitee, as well as the verbal exchange between them, happens in the milieu and in the medium of servicelessness, of call-lessness. The call of the second workless servant is thus the call not only of one who is uncalled to another; it is a call into uncalledness and out of it. The call in the Elohistic story of Abraham and the evangelical call of the parables of the Christian Messiah move in a vertical direction from a master, king, or householder to those who are unpropertied and idle; the call in Kafka's story moves horizontally from an uncalled servant to a second, and nothing suggests that a task would thereby be fulfilled or a message delivered from a higher authority. This call exists only among the inactive and unpropertied whose position can be occupied by others at any time, because they have nothing that they could pass along and nothing whose communication would pay, enrich, or return a profit. What belongs to the one, be it only out of banal custom, just as much belongs to the other, because it is proper to neither. And in the same way, they hear each other and adhere to each other: as those who belong to no one, who are in no one's service, who are needed by no one.

The communication among those who find no acknowledgment in the call, no support or address [*Zuspruch*] in language, and no use in work to which they appear, however, to be appointed, is the communication among those who do not even possess a common medium of communication: "He asked me several things, but I couldn't answer, indeed I didn't even understand the questions."[8] The question and questioning, in the philosophical as well as the literary tradition from Antiquity (Oedipus, Plato) through the most recent modernity (Heidegger, Lévinas), is not only the dominant figure of the opening and directing of conversations but it is the very beginning of thought, the form of the investigation of the uncertain, the ground of cognition and of action directed by knowledge. All movements of searching—of *quaerere*—are initiated in this tradition by explicit or implicit questions and are maintained by them. What one understands by cognition and practical action follows the guiding thread of the question in order to reach thereby the goal of the answer. In the beginning is the call

of the question; at the end is supposed to be the symmetrically corresponding answer. Whether in the form of *quaestiones,* with the help of juridical
inquisition, of technical and pedagogical testing, or of police investigation,
it is always questioning that is supposed to lead out of unclear or dilemmatic
relations into philosophical, religious, or political clarity. However open
a question may be, it is always also an instrument of binding, of framing
and fitting of something hitherto unknown or elusive into controllable
contexts. The triviality that questioning is not understood as such or that
its content remains incomprehensible is, of course, familiar to everyone, but
this could only detract from the philosophical and institutional privilege
of questioning where the power of the quotidian and of its institutions was
suspended anyway: only in literature—even in the literatures of *quests* for
an answer, for a grail, a ground, or a self—is the question not the first and
not the last word of thought and of action. Kafka's *I* abrogates the pathos
for questioning of a whole culture in the most laconic manner; it poses no
questions but reports what "someone . . . once, without my having asked
him, said"; it does not oppose the appeal of questions, does not evade it, asks
nothing back, is fascinated neither by questioning nor by its own inability
to correspond to it. And this *I* remarks, disengaged as from the absent call,
that it has not understood and cannot answer. The claim, plea, or appeal
of the question may be made, but because it cannot be understood, the
one who is asked also cannot understand himself as the one intended by
the appeal. Kafka's prosaic handling of the question differs most starkly in
its very capacity not to find itself intended from Kant's manner of dealing
with the question. Kant begins the *Critique of Pure Reason* with the remark:
"Human reason has the peculiar fate in one species of its cognitions that it
is burdened with questions which it cannot dismiss, since they are given
to it by the nature of reason itself, but which it also cannot answer, since
they exceed every capacity of human reason."[9] Kafka's prose abrogates the
critical task of the self-limitation of reason in finding the questions that
force themselves upon it merely incomprehensible—and therefore hardly
"given to it through the nature of reason itself." Of course, there are questions,
but there are none that could say something to the one questioned—and
thus no questions for him; of course there may be a call, but no one who
would be called—and thus no call, which could mean something to him
as call; of course a servant, but not one who concerns himself with the
Oedipal work of solving riddles—and therefore not one who serves. If the
questioner, guest and host of the *I,* encounters the *I* only as the reverse
and double [*Doublette*] of himself, then the *I* does not understand itself
in the questioner; it is for itself an indifferent someone, a redundant third

whose call presents to him nothing other than the meaninglessness of the call. Kafka´s prose inconspicuously and unassumingly lays bare that the unintelligible cannot be reduced or retraced to an intelligible substratum, where it would find its cause, its reason and justification. It spells out the experience of being left—and left free—from all possibilities of invocation, convocation, and vocation, and therein the experience of transcendence into a world that is divested of all conditions transcendent to it. No care about the call of care. No *I* that would be master in his house or even only an occupied servant in it. No dialectic of master and slave. No hierarchy, no economy, no kleseonomy.

"So I said: 'Perhaps you are sorry now that you invited me, then I'll go,' and I was about to get up. But he stretched his hand out over the table and pressed me down. 'Stay,' he said, 'that was only a test. He who does not answer the questions has passed the test.'" One may see in this sentence, with which the text breaks off or concludes, a paradox, for it is not the one who answers the questions who passes the test but the one who does not even understand them. The one who fails passes the test. But what appears as an inversion of the norm and therefore paradoxical is only the consequence of its never being beyond doubt that there can be a call—a questioning call or a question that calls for an answer. A question is always an appeal to answer it, but it is a call only for one who recognizes himself as intended, and in fact as recognized, in this question and, as both recognizing and recognized, holds himself already in the horizon of the call. The parable of the workers in the vineyard lets the call reach only those who are thereby already chosen and who fulfill the call. There is no servant who is not put to work by the call, no idler who has not by following or refusing the call already submitted to its power and, having become a *subjectum,* has fulfilled its intention. Whoever has heard and understood a call has already, like the biblical Abraham, confirmed it as call and closed its horizon. For the religions of the call, thus for all religions, a hearer without understanding is mere nonsense, because call and the one called are the same for them and only in this sameness fulfill their sense—and the sense of every possible sense. The only question that is an actual question in this tradition is one that is understood as a question and precisely through this is answered, regardless of whether rightly or wrongly; the only call that is a call is one that through its understanding leads back into itself and comes to self-understanding. And like the Elohimian and the Paulinian, so the call of conscience for Heidegger: as the call of care, it is the summoning of *Dasein* to its ownmost, insurpassable possibility, call out of the uncanniness into the uncanniness of *Dasein* and thus the call to the call itself. While Kafka speaks, probably following upon Kierkegaard, of "anxiousness" as one possible *cause* of the uncalledness, in *Being and Time,* Heidegger—also with Kierkegaard as a starting-point—characterizes the call as one of silence from its connection with anxiety: "The call discourses in the uncanny mode of keeping silent. . . . The 'it calls me' [*es ruft mich*] is a distinct kind of discourse for Dasein. The call whose mood has been attuned by anxiety, is what makes it possible first and foremost for Dasein to project itself upon its ownmost *potentiality-for-Being.*"[10] But must it as call into the uncanniness not also be a call into the uncalledness of the call and must it not therefore cease even to speak in the *mode* of keeping silent as a *distinctive* kind of discourse? Can being-there as being-to-the-uncanniness-of-being still retain the distinction between silence and muteness, between *distinctive discourse* and none at all? Must it not be *un*attuned and must not being-there, if truly uncanny, be exposed to its being-mute? And can that to which it is called still be termed its *ownmost potentiality-for-Being?* Despite the dramatic differences between the biblical and the existential-ontological call-structure, the call in the purview of the tradition between both of these extremes is always that which leads from the same into the same and in the economy of its circularity ensures that the call is saturated in those who hear it. A call that is not issued to one's own [*an das Seine*] and least of all to one's own self is unexperienceable in this structure of the call. In it, there is only such a call that fulfills itself—and therefore none that could leave itself and the sphere of the self. Yet precisely because it always already fulfills itself in those who are called and in its fulfillment is annulled, can it, in its barren self-sufficiency, only become noticeable for those for whom it remains foreign in its incomprehensibility? Their position, their exoklesical exposition is adopted by Kafka's prose.

In it, the uncalled understands only that he does not understand, hears only that he is not called, and experiences that he is exposed to the experience of the inexperienceability of a call. He speaks out of this experience, and he only communicates within it. Like his hearing, his speaking is a passage into what remains impassable and nevertheless unavoidable: transcending into a world without transcendence without *causa* and grounding claim. If he passes the test to which he is submitted, then it is because it is a test of his uncallability [*Unrufbarkeit*] and his untestability. It is the initiation into a world *ante initionem*, an absolutely anarchic world, before the beginning of the world of the call. The anarchistic joke of this text lies in the fact that it bespeaks a world before that world which could be reached by a call of creation, election, or redemption: it denies the fundamental, the fundamental logical and fundamental ontological claim that there be

86

only such a world as originates from a claim—from the claim to be a claim at all, however sublime or banal it might be: in the final instance, from the determining claim of language—and from the claim that there be only such a world as satisfies this claim of language. Kafka's prose is just as little an *ancilla theologiae* as an *ancilla vocationis;* it is, however, also not an *ancilla linguae,* which would be concerned with the meaningfulness or even only the logical coherence of that which is said in it. Whatever is said to be call or question, certainty or judgment, turns in this prose to an uncertainty about which no judgment is possible and which makes none. It may in any event still be a servant—but a servant without work for language and without any vocation other than to uncalledness. It is, in a rigorously critical sense, mere means without end. It can therefore not be interpreted but only clarified.

Now, the objection could be made to Kafka's text that it contests the evident fact that the experience of something is articulated in it—the experience of a particular historical, psychical, social, or linguistic situation—and that it contests with its discourse of the uncalledness of its protagonist that it may itself already represent the answer to a demand, a question, or a call. This reservation is understandable, but it employs a shortcut. Namely, it narrows the horizon of experience that it calls upon to a given world, while for Kafka the horizon of the world and the manner of its givenness themselves are in question. This is clearer in the following both chronologically and thematically closely related note than it is in the text of "The Test": "It is a mandate. I can by my nature only take up a mandate that no one has given to me. In this contradiction, always only in a contradiction, can I live. But probably everyone, for one dies living and lives dying."[11] If it is said here of the mandate—of a given, given to the hand—that "no one" has "given" it, then it is because life is not a given, but rather that which is withdrawn from death, and death in turn not a given, but the very withdrawal of givenness; both thus stand in *contradiction* with another and with themselves insofar as they refuse themselves to that which they should be. The mandate is therefore not only given by *no one,* it is not given at all, but merely the acceptance of that which refuses every acceptation. In the same sense as there is for the mandate no mandater, so there is for the servant no call. What he could possibly receive, hear, and understand would have to present itself to him within a horizon of givenness and as a self-given horizon; because, however, such a horizon never presents itself without withdrawing in this presentation; because it always only presents itself in a *contradiction,* and indeed in a contradiction of language with itself, only the un-given allows itself to be received and only the contra-dictory [*das Widersprachliche*], the mute, allows itself to be heard. The horizon of the "obviously" given is for Kafka a-horizontal. Therefore, only a servant without work and a hearing without call can be "given," and therefore even their givenness must adopt the character of a contradictory mandate. In Kafka's prose, there is hearing without something heard, and speaking without something said. It does not move within a given horizon, but circumscribes the structure of withdrawal of every horizon that could be given. Only thus does it do justice to hearing and speaking. For if the mandate of hearing is taken seriously, then it cannot be implemented as a well-rehearsed routine but as a hearing of that which was never before to be heard. Whoever begins to hear has not yet heard, and, in order to remain a hearer, cannot stop not being able to hear. Not to hear is thus not a preliminary stage to hearing but its unconditioned—ungiven—precondition and accompaniment. A call in turn can only then be made if it does not speak as the repetition or variation of a preceding one but begins where there was none before it; a call is always made *ex nihilo vocationis* and thus out of that which remains, as uncalled and uncallable, the resistance against which it must rebound or repel itself.

A reflection of Kafka's, which may have been written a short time after the text about the impossible test, counters the objection that a call comes out of that which it was not to that which is entirely itself and that hearing leaves non-hearing behind it in order to be entirely hearing. In it is stated: "I can swim like the others, only I have a better memory than the others, I have not forgotten the erstwhile not-being-able-to-swim. Since I have, however, not forgotten it, the being-able-to-swim does not help me at all, and I still cannot swim."[12] If the former not-being-able-to remains unforgotten, then also the former not-being-able-to-hear and the not-being-called; then also the former not-being.[13] The better memory of Kafka's prose returns this forgotten pre-world of the non-given, of not-being-able-to and not-being. It can speak like the others, but this does not help at all; since it has emerged out of the not-being-able-to-speak, it can still not speak, and it says only that it cannot. As the swimmer swims his not-being-able-to-swim, so the hearer hears his not-being-able-to-hear and speaks his not-being-able-to-speak. Whoever is, is his not-being-able-to. "The word 'Sein' [to be]," according to a succinct note, which was important enough to Kafka to write down twice, "means in German both: being-there and belonging-to-him. [*Das Wort "sein" bedeutet im Deutschen beides: Da-sein und Ihm-gehören.*]"[14] Who, however, does not hear, adheres to no *him*, and as little as he stands in a possessive relation to someone who calls him into his service, so little can being-there be ascribed to him. Being would be being-there in the call, a possessive relation to a caller that expresses itself as work and reproduces itself through work, an ergo-ontological, a kleseo-ontological relation—because the call is absent, so is work; because work is absent, so is the relation of possession, and so is being [*Sein*]. If there is still work, then in the not-being-able-to-work; if something is still heard and adheres, then in the not-adhering of a not-being [*Sein*].

Kafka repeatedly took up and then abandoned his reflections on work, on the anxiety of working, the inhibition regarding work, and the incapacity to work, which were closely connected to his function as a lawyer for the Prague Worker's Accident Insurance Institute, but even more closely to his interest in a syndicalistic reform of labor. These reflections do not culminate in his sketch titled "The Propertyless Workers," where it is planned: "Possess or accept no money, no valuables. Only the following property is permitted: the most simple dress . ., what is necessary for work, books, groceries for one's own use. Everything else belongs to the poor."[15] This almost Franciscan reform for the propertylessness of the workers is far surpassed by the Franciskafkian reform for call-lessness and unemployment sketched in his text on the impossible test. In a countermove to the Protestant Reformation, which promulgated the absolute ethics of vocation and work of all those called and elected to faith, it is a reform for an unchosenness, for an un-called—and vocationlessness, which precedes every form of work and every form of religious or secular organization, but which must accompany—for a better memory—every such form as its pre-world [*Vor-Welt*]. Kafka's text is, however, just as little a socio-technical declaration as a playful fabulation on unoccupied workers. It is the investigation of a language of the call, of the claim, of the address and demand, and of the simple naming that leads to the demonstration that these minima of the world of language, work, and life are nothing other than the forms of articulation of its insistent lack: of a lack that cannot cease distorting, making indeterminate, and anarchizing the forms of linguistic life and with them the forms of societal work. The ideal of Kafka's prose is the empty page before writing: *lingua rasa*. The world out of which it speaks—one completely other than ideal—is that in which only the not-being-able-to-speak is spoken, the not-being-able-to-hear is heard, and the not-being-able-to-work is done: *opus inanis*. With this, the ground of every language and of its world is disclosed: *factum infactum* of a not-being-able to be.

The Old Testament, like the apostolic and evangelical writings and the Koran—"Koran" means "Call"—know no one who is not called. Adam and Abraham are called; Moses and Jonah, the idlers are called, and even Lazarus answers to *"veni foras."* They are all used and set to service and work in order to correspond to a call that leads back through all resistances and rejections into itself. This call is the telos of all actions and expectations in history since. The Messiah is, therefore, in this Abrahamic tradition—whether he is introduced as political, historical, or intimately personal—not only the caller and the called; he is also, publicly announced or silently sensed, the call itself. Even for Walter Benjamin, the "weak messianic power," which "is given with us," lies in the "claim" [*Anspruch*] that the past has on us and in the "secret agreement" between past races and ours.[16] Not so for Kafka. Just as he conceives of the father of messianism as an "uncalled Abraham," so he thinks of the Messiah as an uncalled Messiah. In Kafka's world without call, the coming of the Messiah is neither an eschatological nor a kleseological event. Kafka notes about him: "The Messiah will only come when he is no longer necessary, he will only come after his arrival, he will not come on the last day, but on the very last."[17] A Messiah who would come when he was needed would be a necessitated Messiah, a needed and used, a working, functional, and instrumental Messiah; he would be the Messiah of the circumstances in which he intervenes, a Messiah of the call that summoned him, a Messiah who would be homogenous with the well-rehearsed and named world of the call and of work and therefore would be without the slightest chance to bring about a world of justice and peace. Only he or it can come as Messiah, who or which "will no longer be necessary," not needed, not used, and not called. He can only be one without work, belonging to no one, and even dispossessed of every *being*. And thus one who could never be named as himself, never be hoped for or expected under his name, neither corresponding to his call nor to his *being*. This one who is uncalled, unused, and belongs to no one could only "come after his arrival," for he would have to miss, like his "self," also his "own" time: it would be solely the not-being-able-to-come that comes in him.

The Messiah can only be the one for whom there is no Messiah. The Messiah is, in this sense and thus in every sense, un-savable. He is the most desolate of all figures who have been conceived by religions and their appended philosophies, and he is the most uncalled-for and unclaimed figure, who could never be conceived by them. Kafka's uncalled servant, forgotten by every historical messianism, is the sole possible Messiah, the unnecessary, un-arriving, unable, impossible. It is he who in the prose of the after-last and the pre-first day writes: "I am a servant, but there is no work for me."

NOTES

1. [Transator's note: Franz Kafka, *Description of a Struggle*, trans. Tania and James Stern (New York: Schocken Books, 1958), 207–9. In what follows, I cite published English translations of the texts whenever possible. The translations I provide in the text have been modified and often differ significantly from the published versions.] Concerning Kafka's text, there are, as far as I see, two commentaries worth mentioning: the first is "Phénoménologie de Kafka" by Bernhard Groethuysens in his book, *Mythes et Portraits* (Paris: Gallimard, 1947); the other in Avital Ronell's *The Test Drive* (Champaign: University of Illinois Press 2005), 71–74.

2. Walter Benjamin, *The Correspondence 1910–1940*, ed. Gerschom Scholem and T. W. Adorno, trans. Manfred R. Jacobson and Evelyn M. Jacobson (Chicago: University of Chicago Press, 1994), 463.

3. [Translator's note: translation from the King James Version, Matthew 20:16. This line is not found in the Revised Standard Version. Where not otherwise noted, English translations will be taken from the Revised Standard Version.]

4. In the third chapter, "Luther's Conception of the Calling," of *The Protestant Ethic and the Spirit of Capitalism,* published for the first time in 1905 (thus about fifteen years before the writing of Kafka's text) in the *Archiv für Sozialwissenschaft und Sozialpolitik*, Max Weber traces the history of translations of the concepts *klesis* and *vocatio* and the history of development of the New-High-German concept *Beruf*—compare, in particular, the short disquisition contained in the third footnote of this study (Max Weber, *The Protestant Work Ethic and the Spirit of Capitalism,* trans. Talcott Parsons [London: Routledge Classics, 2001], 158–63]). Kafka was, so far as I know, not familiar with the reflections of Weber; he knew, however, the essay published in 1917 by Ernst Troeltsch in the second volume of the *Neue Rundschau* with the title "Luther und der Protestantismus" ["Luther and Protestantism"], which displays clearly enough the ethos of the calling, vocation, and chosenness in Protestantism.

   In *The Call and the Response,* trans. Anne A. Davenport (New York: Fordham University Press, 2004), Jean-Louis Chrétien has provided a rich survey of the theology and philosophy of *klesis* between Plato, Heidegger, and Lévinas, which, however, itself remains committed in every regard to the founding premises of kleseology. Giorgio Agamben has attempted in his commentary on the Letter to the Romans, *The Time That Remains,* trans. Patricia Dailey (Stanford, Calif.: Stanford University Press, 2005), to make more precise the concept of *klesis* through the Paulinian *hos me* interpreted as revocation. The interpretation of Paulinian messianism he proposes seems to remain equally within the boundaries of a logic of the call that is suspended by Kafka's prose.

5. Franz Kafka, *Letters to Friends, Family, and Editors,* trans. Richard and Clara Winston (London: John Calder, 1958), 285–86.

6. In a text, which I only encountered after composing these reflections, Jacques Derrida writes, under the title "Abraham, l'autre," about the passage from Kaf-

ka's letter to Robert Klopstock discussed here, that the structure of the call is of a kind that a decision whether it really takes place or not is absolutely impossible: "It is possible that I was not called, me, and it is not ruled out that none, no One, no-one has ever called any One, any single one, no-one." *Judéités— Questions pour Jacques Derrida* (Paris: Galilée, 2003), p. 41. Precisely this is, in fact, possible. But the Abraham conceived by Kafka is not only *possibly* not called; he is not an Abraham who *doubts* his call, who could still cherish the hope to be called; he is, as Kafka writes, "an Abraham who comes uncalled"! And he comes "uncalled" because the suspension of the call can only then be seriously considered a suspension if it succeeds as the epoché of calledness without the *reservatio phaenomenologica* that it is on this account not yet the epoché of callability.

7. Walter Benjamin, *Selected Writings,* ed. Marcus Bullock and Michael Jennings (Cambridge, Mass.: Belknapp Press, 1996–2003), vol II, 806.

8. Kafka, *Description of a Struggle,* 209.

9. Immanuel Kant, *Critique of Pure Reason,* trans. Paul Guyer and Allen Wood (Cambridge, U.K.: Cambridge University Press, 1999), A, VII.

10. Martin Heidegger, *Being and Time,* trans. John Macquarrie and Edward Robinson (New York: Harper and Row, 1962), 322. "Der Ruf redet im unheimlichen Modus des Schweigens. . . . Das 'es ruft mich' ist eine ausgezeichnete Rede des Daseins. Der durch die Angst gestimmte Ruf ermöglicht dem Dasein allererst den Entwurf seiner selbst auf sein eigenstes Seinkönnen." Martin Heidegger, *Sein und Zeit* (Tübingen: Niemeyer Verlag, 1967), 57, 277.

11. Franz Kafka, *Wedding Preparations in the Country, and Other Posthumous Prose Writings,* notes by Max Brod, trans. Ernst Kaiser and Eithne Wilkins (London: Secker and Warburg, 1954), 296–97. "Es ist ein Mandat. Ich kann meiner Natur nach nur ein Mandat übernehmen, das niemand mir gegeben hat. In diesem Widerspruch, immer nur in einem Widerspruch kann ich leben. Aber wohl jeder, denn lebend stirbt man, sterbend lebt man." Nachgelassene Schriften und Fragmente, ed. Jost Schillemeit (Frankfurt am Main: S. Fischer, 1992), vol. II, 321.

12. Kafka, *Wedding Preparations in the Country,* 326. This note can be read as the condensed continuation of the text that begins with the words: "The great swimmer!" It is stated there: "Honored festival guests! I have, admittedly, a world record. . . . Actually, I can't even swim. I've always wanted to learn, but no opportunity has presented itself." Immediately afterward, the world record–holder and Olympic winner affirms—as the unoccupied servant does—that he does not understand a word spoken by those to whom he speaks: ". . . and despite great exertion I don't understand a single word of what is spoken here . . . it doesn't disturb me very much that I don't understand you, and it also appears not to disturb you very much that you don't understand me. From the speech of the honored previous speaker, I believe I know only that it was inconsolably sad, but this knowledge is not only enough for me; it is even too much for me."

Kafka, *Wedding Preparations in the Country,* 316. Deleuze and Guattari refer to the "great swimmer" in order to demonstrate that the foundational structure of Kafka's texts is that of life in a foreign language and to characterize their strategy as the displacement away from centers of power that determine what one can say and what one cannot—a displacement whose point of convergence is what they designate as "absolute deterritorialization." Gilles Deleuze and Felix Guattari, *Kafka: Toward a Minor Literature,* trans. Dana Polan (Minneapolis: University of Minnesota Press, 1986). They do not mention in this context that the world-champion in swimming cannot even swim and that therefore the deterritorialization is continued in a de-aquatization. Its absolute, however, is the de-potentialization asserted in the note cited here.

13. In his chapter "The Reading Box," in *Berlin Childhood around 1900,* Walter Benjamin pays homage to Kafka's deliberation by paraphrasing it in his concluding reflection—without naming Kafka, who admittedly does not only play an important role in this part of his memoirs. It is stated there, after a discussion of learning to read and write: "Thus I can dream of the way I once learned to walk. But that doesn't help me. Now I can walk; no longer learn to walk." Walter Benjamin, *Berlin Childhood around 1900,* trans. Howard Eiland (Cambridge, Mass.: Harvard University Press, 2006), 142. While the "But that doesn't help me" is taken over almost word-for-word from Kafka's note, the deliberation, to which it lends its particular accent, is astonishingly weakened in Benjamin's text: Benjamin "can . . . walk, no longer learn to walk," Kafka's swimmer, however, "can, however, not swim." He has forgotten nothing of the pre-world, forgotten nothing of the "forgetting" that it exists, and for him there can therefore be no world that would not be hampered in its most elementary performances. He cannot forget—that means that he can do nothing of that which he is able to do.

14. Franz Kafka, *The Blue Octavo Notebooks,* ed. Max Brod, trans. Ernst Kaiser and Eithne Wilkins (Cambridge, U.K.: Exact Change, 1991), 28, 90.

15. Kafka, *Wedding Preparations in the Country,* 119.

16. Walter Benjamin, *Selected Writings,* eds. Marcus Bullock and Michael Jennings (Cambridge, Mass.: Belknap Press, 1996–2003), vol. IV, 390.

17. Kafka, *The Blue Octavo Notebooks,* 28.

Elissa Marder
Avital Ronell's Body Politics

> There is no natural, originary body:
> technology has not simply added itself, from the outside,
> or after the fact, as a foreign body. Or at least this foreign
> and dangerous supplement is "originarily" at work and in
> the place of the supposed ideal interiority of the "body
> and soul." It is indeed at the heart of the heart.
>
> —JACQUES DERRIDA,
> "THE RHETORIC OF DRUGS"

In Your Ear

> "Your mission, should you choose
> to accept it, is to learn how to read
> with your ears."

In a certain sense, one might begin by saying "she told us so," but perhaps we did not hear her well enough. For a long time now, over many years and in her many important works ranging from the early *Dictations* to the most recent *Test Drive*, Avital Ronell has been trying to open our ears to the ramifications of the politics of the body. Recent events in world history and science are only confirming what she has been telling us all along. Before AIDS, terrorism, drugs, information technology, and viruses were on everyone's lips, she was tuning in to the ways in which the question of the body opens up onto politics, ethics, religion, and war. Throughout her remarkable corpus (which is, as I write, very much alive), she has continued to show that the body calls for thinking. But to say that the body calls for thinking does not mean that the body invoked here is thinkable in any simple sense; it is not an object of thought but rather a mode, frequency, and tonal field that can only be read to the extent that it is heard. Such thinking, Ronell tells us, begins in your ear.

And, indeed, in her inimitable voice, Ronell prefaces *The Telephone Book* with the following challenge and appeal to the reader: "Your mission, should you choose to accept it, is to learn how to read with your ears. In addition to listening for the telephone, you are being asked to tune your ears to noise frequencies, to anticoding, to the inflated reserves of random indeterminateness—in a word, you are expected to stay open to the static and interference that will occupy these lines."[1]

Ronell's direct address to the reader is an invitation and a warning, as "reading with the ears" is inherently risky: it is always both a promise and a threat. As she herself elucidates, such a reading actively "engages the destabilization of the addressee" by scrambling known pathways of sense and sound, cutting off common connections, suspending meaning. Likewise, in her reading and writing practice, Avital Ronell opens her ears to the challenge of receiving the unconscious determinations and overdeterminations of contemporary politics and culture. She engages in an analytic practice of listening for "that which resists presentation." Drawing upon literature, philosophy, psychoanalysis, Ronell attends to the white noise of popular and unpopular culture in order to forge new lines of communication. And her texts open up a new form of analytic reading that sets forth an ethics, a politics, and a practice of "performative intervention" for which one might be tempted to invent the neologism: "techno-analysis."

At stake is nothing less than the future. As she puts it in the opening pages of *Finitude's Score:* "If I am in the position of giving you anything—and this is not clear to me—I know that one cannot hope to give anything but the future."[2] The gift of the future depends upon the ability to hear the repressed strains within the history of thought. The effects of these repressions are embodied everywhere in the materiality of daily life in all its registers. The history of what has not been thought but that calls for thinking secretes its traces and produces symptoms, effects, pathologies, waste products, and technological appliances in its wake.

When, therefore, Avital Ronell picks up the telephone in *The Telephone Book,* she takes up the task of showing that the question concerning technology is inextricable from the challenge of opening up the body as a question. To open up the body as question entails acknowledging that the "body" is not the silent "other" of thought but rather its medium, its very condition of possibility. Although she had already put the concept of the body to work in *Dictations: Haunted Writing,* in *The Telephone Book* Ronell explicitly and systematically inaugurates her (ongoing) interrogation into the ways in which technological objects come into being as symptomatic responses to certain conceptions and repressions of the body. In its attempts to bypass the body, the history of Western thought, philosophy, and culture has repressed the body and failed to read its traces. But embedded within the history of these repressive gestures, the body continues to assert its demands differently, setting up alternative networks and pathways of meaning. Ronell borrows from psychoanalysis by burrowing into its textual complexities and its contradictions; its method, material, and madness.

And, as she also points out, Freud himself acknowledges the telephonic dimension of psychoanalytic interpretation by explicitly comparing the transference as a telephonic communication and the position of the analyst as a receptor of messages that arrive through unconscious telephonic networks:

> To put it in a formula: he [the doctor] must turn his own unconscious like a receptive organ towards the transmitting unconscious of the patient. He must adjust himself to the patient as a telephone receiver is adjusted to the transmitting microphone. Just as the receiver converts back into sound-waves the electric oscillations in the telephone line which were set up by sound waves, so the doctor's unconscious is able, from the derivatives of the unconscious which are communicated to him, to reconstruct that unconscious, which has determined the patient's free associations. (115–16)

The reader who dares to take up the challenge posed in and by *The Telephone Book* must in this sense "become" a telephone by adopting a stance of "free floating reception."[3] The reader is simultaneously placed on the line and cut off from it, as ear reading opens up an outside that folds back upon itself like the invaginated ear itself. Let us remember, as Jacques Lacan has pointed out, "in the field of the unconscious, the ears are the only orifice that cannot be closed."[4] (Lacan's gloss on the ears comes to us through *The Telephone Book,* transmitted by Ronell, who also cites Derrida citing Freud on this point). This opening and openness of the ears renders the self open to the outside, to its others (that is, to everything that is not itself and everything that it is not) as well as to others. As such, this openness (like all openings) is also a wound and a trace of incompletion, finitude, and absence. As opening, it carves out a space that can always be left empty, filled with absence. In this sense, the ear is endowed with cryptic powers and possibilities. The specter of the absent other and/or the absence of the self always lurks within its folds.

Throughout her work, Ronell insistently calls attention to the specifically uncanny and improper properties of the ear. In *The Telephone Book* and *Finitude's Score,* she explains the significance of the difference between the ear and other bodily orifices as follows: "Unlike the mouth, the ear needs a silent partner, a double and phantom of itself. The mouth doubles itself by metonymic displacement, getting on the shuttle to vaginal and anal sites" (*TB,* 193; *FS,* 241).

The ear is simultaneously strangely singular and duplicitously plural. As Ronell indicates in the preceding passage, the ambiguities of the ear(s) stem in part from the fact that although we may each be morphologically endowed with "two ears," our ears do not belong to us and we do not hear with our own ears alone. In its "communicative" function, the ear relies on being given to another and shared across other bodies. In this sense, my "other" ear belongs not to me, but to the other. It is the ear of the other.[5] Although only the ear of the other can respond to my call to be heard, the ear of the other cannot be "present" to me. It is, as Ronell describes it, "a silent partner, a double and phantom of itself." By comparing the ear to the mouth, Ronell implies that while both mouth and ear are the primary organs of communication, the ear communicates only with the other and with others, whereas the mouth has the capacity to retreat from the other and turn inward onto the self by establishing autoerotic lines of communication.

But because the ear is, in some sense, defenseless in its appeal to an absent (or potentially absent) other, it is the most receptive, fragile, and easily bruised human orifice. Its very constitution as an organ destines it to be dependent on and vulnerable to the response or nonresponse of the other. As Ronell insists, this means that the ear cannot live without an "other" ear, cannot function by itself, cut off from a world of others. But this also means, paradoxically, that the authentic experience of solitude begins in the ear. Only the ear knows what it means to be truly alone and bereft. The solitary ear is always in some relation to mourning, listening for lost others and its phantom twin. (If people who talk to themselves are deemed to be crazy, the madness lies not in the moment of speaking [an act that would resemble in all ways the act of speaking to another] but in the act of hearing one's own voice. For one cannot hear "one's own voice" as such: it is always the voice of the other as it comes through the ear.)

In *The Telephone Book,* Ronell listens for the special effects that the telephone produces on the way we answer (or fail to answer) the call of the other as it comes to us through the ear. "The telephone," she writes, is a "structure that is not equivalent to its technical history, the telephone . . . indicates more than a technical object. In our first listening, under the pressure of 'accepting a call,' the telephone in fact will emerge as a synecdoche of technology" (*TB*, 13). As "synecdoche of technology," the telephone comes into being as both a reaction and a response to the body function for which it serves as prosthesis and supplement. The telephone (like all technology) is not opposed to the body, but rather mimes, repeats, amplifies, and elaborates a certain (repressed) history of the body. Hence like the ear(s) upon which it is modeled, the telephone is radically double and duplicitous: it both incarnates and disavows the vulnerability and openness of the ear(s) to which it is addressed: "In sum, Alexander Graham Bell carried a dead ear to his mother's house that summer. It is the ear of the Other whose identity is manifold. The telephone, whose labor pains were felt in the ear, has already in this limited example of its birthmark so complex a matrix, that the question of its placement as a thing, object or machine, scientific, gynecological, or objet d'art still bears upon us" (*TB*, 193–94).

Furthermore, the technological body in question is both feminine and maternal. As we can begin to hear in this passage, the telephone is conceived as a fetishistic extension of the body of the mother.

The Prosthetic Maternal

> If one were to set an event, a date, or a time bomb in order to see the beginning of the modern concept of technology touch off, then this event gets stirred up by the invention of condensed milk. In fact, something like the history of positive technology is unthinkable without the extension of this maternal substance into its technological other: in other words, its precise mode of preservation and survival. (*TB*, 340)

Among the many startling and original premises of *The Telephone Book* is the notion that the birth of the telephone has a significant relation to anxieties concerning the maternal function in the technological age and that its emergence constitutes an important event in the history of mourning. Indeed, throughout the book, Ronell demonstrates the multiple ways in which the very investment in a certain repressive concept of the mother (as the grounding and stable incarnation of "nature," "origin," "connection," "meaning," "presence," "life") is one of the critical sources of the technological drive. Paradoxically, therefore, the technological drive emerges from an attempt to (re)produce a "mother" who would and could preserve the (philosophical, masculine) fantasy of "full presence," life, and unending connection. Technology is the result of a fantasy to make artificial life more lifelike than life by denying death, absence, disconnection, the improper, and sexual difference.

One way of reading *The Telephone Book*, then, is as an interpretation (in the sense one gives to the word in the phrase "interpretation of dreams") of the causal drives and the consequences of this fantasy on history, politics, and culture: a study of telephonic instincts and their vicissitudes. Because, as Ronell points out, the "technological drive" is most often linked to an attempt to repress the body's finitude, the technological urge aims to deny the reality of the body's vulnerability and mortality by replacing (or supplementing) it with a body that does not know death; a body of "pure life." Thus the driving fantasy of technology is the (re)production of an *Über-mutter* capable of procreating this "pure life." "Pure life," however (as Freud explores in *Beyond the Pleasure Principle*), often resembles death more than it does "life" as it privileges preservation, immobility, and absolute resistance to change or difference. Consequently, the technological *Über-mutter* is inherently both monstrous and repressive.

Ronell explores this structure and the effects of this dynamic throughout *The Telephone Book*. However, in the final section of the book, she performs a "techno-analysis" of the problem by providing us with a kind of case history of the birth of the telephone. Alexander Graham Bell's biography emerges as an important element in Ronell's "studies in technology." By reading this biography through the ears, she constructs a certain anamnesis of the psycho-historical investments inscribed in the telephone's conception. Ronell glosses Bell's (oto)biography thus:

> "The conception of the telephone," he adds in 1916, "took place during the summer visit to my father's residence in Brantford, in the summer of 1874, and the apparatus was just as it was subsequently made, a one-membrane telephone on either end" (M, 73). He had gone a step further there, inscribing himself in the paterno-maternalizing space of invention. In his father's house he conceived something like a child by a dead ear, conceived with or for his father, which means that he as his mother conceived his father's child—a brother collapsed into a one-membrane telephone "on either end," as he puts it, on the end of a beginning, a calendrical birthday or on the end of the end, as the other end, precisely, to which one reaches for some telespark that tells the end of the other. One membrane with two ends, giving birth to the gift of death, shouting vowels at the moment of conception, watching oneself be overcome with tracings made on smoked glass. (*TB*, 334)

> In case you think we have forgotten about the mother's vampiric energy, it has been put into storage, left coiled up in the telephone. For if Bell conceived a telephone with his father in order to bring back the two children, he was identifying the machine with "Ma-ma!" that is, he was caught up in taking her place, multiplying her, folding her invaginated ears into those of the pair of brothers left behind in Europe. (*TB*, 335)

As Ronell tells it, Bell gives birth to the telephone by twice replacing the mother. He himself takes the place of the mother by transforming a dead ear into a pseudo womb quickened by his voice. The telephonic offspring that he conceives is endowed with maternal properties. Furthermore, she calls attention to the fact that the telephone is conceived "in the father's house." As she hears it, the replacement replicant mother is addressed to the father either in response to his (paternal) desire or to a fantasy of paternal desire. In either case, Bell attempts to please the father by giving him a telephonic child—a gift of life that would surpass all life by being a life-giving gift. But, as Ronell points out, the gift of a life-giving gift is actually a gift of death as it annihilates the vital distance that separates us from the other. In this sense, it "tells the end of the other." She then goes on to elucidate that the repressed mother is encrypted in this father-son exchange and her "vampiric energy" remains "put in storage, left coiled in the telephone."

From its conception, then, the telephone usurps the maternal function.[6] But the energy bound and "coiled" in this repressed mother (who is neither living nor dead) lies encrypted in the telephone system and haunts the relations it makes possible. When mommy becomes mummified in the telephone lines, the techno-maternal figure assumes new functions in the historical/hysterical organization of the modern psyche. Roughly speaking, these new tasks concern: fetishistic forms of (failed) mourning and the amplification of a pathologically punishing, (maternal) superego. As maternal prosthesis, the telephone lends itself specifically to these two functions because it can simulate a sustained (re)connection to the other by constituting, as Ronell puts it, "the maternal cord reissued" (*TB*, 4). When it answers to a desire to remain permanently bound to the mother, the telephone becomes used as a fetish to ward off the experience of separation, absence, or death. And, because there can be no telephone without another telephone, the telephonic matrix binds all its units together through a techno-maternal network in which each individual number loses its singularity by becoming answerable to a symbolic collectivity. This collectivity, furthermore, reproduces itself by transmitting voices that dictate orders into the ear. The first such order of the telephone is the demand to answer its call. The call from the other that comes to us through the telephone retains something of the voice of the (undead) mother who returns, with a vengeance, to issue imperatives and regulate compliance. As Ronell puts it, "[t]here is always a remnant of the persecuting, accusatory mother in the telephone system, suggesting that the entire dimension of the monolithic parental unit can never as such be silenced" (*TB*, 144). When this toxic mixture of failed mourning and superego dysfunction manifest in the sphere of the political, they most often take the form of fascism, nationalism, totalitarianism, and other repressive systems of state (remote) control.

But perhaps we have moved too quickly. In order to understand how and why the telephone becomes associated with state control, we must first look more closely at how the question concerning technology is haunted by the body of the mother. In one of the densest and most difficult passages of *The Telephone Book*, Ronell establishes a connection between the advent of technology, the incommensurability of "catastrophe," and the (reactive) inability and failure to mourn the loss of the mother. She writes:

> Technology . . . is inseparable from catastrophe in a radically explicit way. Cutting lines and catastrophizing, the telephone has been associated with a maternalized force. Now, when mourning is broached by an idealization and interiorization of the mother's image, which implies her loss and the withdrawal of the maternal, the telephone maintains this line of discon- nection while dissimulating the loss, acting like a pacifier. But at the same time it acts as a monument to an irreducible disconnection and thus runs like incorporation, a kind of pathology inhibiting mourning, offering an alternative to the process of introjection. In this sense the telephone operates along lines whose structures promote phantasmic, unmediated, instantaneous, magical, sometimes hallucinatory flashes. What happens to the perished Other when mourning is inhibited? The refusal to mourn causes the lost "love object" to be preserved in a crypt like a mummy, maintained as the binding around what is not there. Somewhat like frozen-dried foods, the passageway is sealed off and marked (in the psyche) with the place and date in commemoration. (*TB*, 341)

If mourning (of any kind) is always defined by a refusal to let go of the departed other, the work of mourning entails gradually becoming able to accept the fact that the connection with the beloved other has been irrevocably severed. And because (as Freud famously observed) no one willingly gives up a connection to the beloved other, in its less pathological manifestations, the psyche in mourning seeks consolations and compen- sations for the loss of the beloved object in different ways: by becoming like the lost loved one through identification and by finding new others to love. In pathological mourning, however, as Ronell invokes it above, there is no renunciation possible; the loss is simultaneously radically disavowed and experienced as catastrophic, unendurable, and inexpressible.[7] As the incarnation of our primordial attachment to and separation from the other, the mother becomes the matrix for all future connections and disconnec- tions. In this sense, the mother prefigures the telephone and the telephone emerges in response to anxiety about separation from the mother. But as technological incarnation of the mother, the telephone mimics the maternal function perversely by annihilating distance with the ghost of presence. As a mechanical reproduction of a (catastrophic and unbearable) lost connec- tion to the mother, the telephone will take on the function of an auxiliary organ in the service of melancholic commemoration and cannibalistic incorporation and preservation.

In "Mourning and Melancholia," Freud explains that the pathological inability to let go of the lost object is expressed as a desire to eat the other: "The ego wants to incorporate this object into itself, and, in accordance with the oral or cannibalistic phase of libidinal development in which it is, it wants to do so by devouring it" ("MM," 249–50). But as Ronell suggests, the telephone radically amplifies this melancholic gesture by becoming a prosthetic body part in which the eaten but undigested mother is contained and preserved. Furthermore, when swallowed by the telephone, this undigested mater becomes simultaneously inaccessible and all powerful: on the one hand, her body is too deeply frozen within the psyche to be touched, while her ghostly, idealized image becomes projected outward and produces "instantaneous," "magical," "hallucinatory flashes."

But if, as we have suggested, the telephone serves as a technological substitute for a lost relation to the mother, its function as prosthesis is not merely to replace the lost object but also to repair the wounds caused by the trauma of its loss. For this reason, the telephone rewires the connections of the erogenous zones through which contact was made (and lost) with the archaic mother in order to make sure that she is now kept permanently available and on hold. The fragile orifices of ear, mouth, breast, and anus through which bodies first encounter others now become joined together through an internal network that is contained and preserved in the phone system. The telephone now regulates all access to the outside. As replacement for a source of love and nourishment, the telephone mediates relations with the other through an autoerotic body reorganization that dispenses freeze-dried food and the fantasy of an unbreakable connection. When the mother becomes telephonically ingested, however, her imperishable mechanical voice implants itself in the psyche. The implanted voice takes over the command control of the psyche by supplanting superego functions.

At this juncture it should come as no surprise to learn that there is a substantial literature devoted to telephone perversions and pathologies within clinical psychoanalysis.[8] For the purposes of this discussion, it is worth pointing out that within the psychoanalytic context, the telephone has most generally been understood as a fetish (used either for sexual gratification or to attenuate separation anxiety, or both) and as an external manifestation of a particular kind of punitive superego. For example, in his essay "The Symbol of Telephoning," Leonard Shengold suggests that when the telephone is used as a fetish, it is related to addiction and masturbation and its purpose is to regulate the connection to the other. He writes that:

"[t]he use of the telephone as a kind of addiction can, as masturbation, have a calming effect—not only in relation to castration anxiety, but as a measure against separation anxiety and even more primitive dangers. In patients who are psychotic or 'borderline,' the telephoning can maintain some object ties at a bearable distance, providing separation without loss and contact without fusion" ("ST," 466).

In the same essay, he also reminds us that the "telephone's association with sound evokes Freud's emphasis on the special relation of the superego to the auditory. The telephone can serve as a prosthetic extension or an externalization of the conscious in order to carry out such superego functions as control and censorship" (465). From its inception, then, psychoanalysis has always (if more or less implicitly) conceived of the superego in relation to the telephone.

More recently, however, Janine Chasseguet-Smirgel has explored how the inability to renounce the primal fusion of the mother can lead to "the development of an anal-sadistic superego where the longing to become one with the mother coincides with the necessity of obeying her orders. . . . It totally (or almost entirely) takes the place of the evolved superego and has a degree of autonomy in the psychic apparatus. The subject does not simply obey orders from outside, he has internalized the necessity of complying with orders. . . ."[9] This all-powerful anal superego comes into being as a traumatic response to an ancient and archaic failure to separate from the mother and subsequent inability to mourn the loss. Chasseguet-Smirgel goes on to argue that this anal-sadistic superego is linked to a pathological hatred of anything perceived as threatening to the primal "union" with the mother. And, because all "others" are foreign, anything that cannot be absorbed into the union is perceived as "filth" that must be eliminated and annihilated at all cost. For this reason, Chasseguet-Smirgel suggests that this anal-sadistic, pseudo-superego can express itself through genocidal fantasies as well as other excessive attempts at eliminating "dirt" in order to protect and purify itself from any and all outside "contamination."

In Chasseguet-Smirgel's description of the excessively punitive and uncompromising demands of this anal-sadistic superego, we hear strains of the commanding mechanical voice that Ronell discovers buried in the maternal prosthesis that is the telephone. Through its desperate and regressive attempts to simulate perfect fusion with the archaic lost object, the anal-sadistic superego takes the form of a repressive machine designed to maintain autoerotic law and order by eliminating all impurities in its system. By establishing this connection between the anal-sadistic (maternally derived) superego and the telephone, we can better understand why the telephone lends itself so easily to fascist aims. In the opening pages of *The Telephone Book,* Ronell provides an example of the ways in which the telephone can facilitate fascist ends by fabricating a synthetic form of organic unity: "The German telefilm *Heimat* (1987) organizes part of its narrative around the erection of a telephone system. The telephone connects where there has been little or no relation, it globalizes and unifies, suturing a country like a wound. The telephone participates in the myths of organic unity, where one discerns a shelter or defense against castration. A state casts a net of connectness around itself from which the deadly flower of unity can grow under the sun of constant surveillance" (*TB,* 8).

As this quotation suggests (and as we have seen in the preceding pages), the technological drive is haunted by a nostalgic, reactionary investment in perpetuating a fantasy about the unity and purity of a biological body that never was. In its regressive attempts to fabricate such a body, the telephone simulates maternal bio-functions and attempts to protect itself hygienically and sustain itself through homeostasis. However, as we shall see, the attempt to eliminate the other ends up producing new and potent forms of toxic waste.

The Toxic Maternal

> The *toxic maternal* means that while mother's milk is poison, it still supplies the crucial nourishment that the subject seeks. It suggests, moreover, that the maternal is too close, invading the orifices and skin with no screen protection, as it were, no intervening law to sever the ever-pumping umbilicus. (*CW,* 118–19)

As we have already seen, the commands emanating from the (undead and unmourned) mother trapped in the telephone wires are repressive and oppressive. In its tendency to control channels of communication by wiring subjects together, making them "answerable" to a collective system, the body politics generated by the telephone system can be linked to political fantasies of national purity. But the very bio-technological drive that produces the social structure of the telephone system also produces its own allergic response to that very system. One name for that allergic response is "drugs." In *Crack Wars,* Avital Ronell extends her exploration of body technologies to show how the declaration of a so-called "war on drugs" exposes an internal link that connects this attack on drugs to failed mourning, repressive politics, and contemporary forms of warfare.[10] In this sense, Ronell's claims about drugs, mourning, and the pathology that she calls the "toxic maternal" in *Crack Wars* can be read as an elaboration—perhaps even an effect—of the logic that produced the telephone as maternal prosthesis in *The Telephone Book*.

In *Crack Wars*, Ronell explores how drugs make it possible for the addict to commemorate lost and absent others by numbing the pain of the loss and making oneself absent. Drug addicts transform the self into a vessel for the absence of the other. Where the telephone reflects the desire to consume and absorb the (repressed and undead) mother, the drug user metabolizes nothing.[11] Instead of eating the undead mother, the person who is wasted on drugs is actually being eaten by an unconscious relation to the other as irrevocably lost. As she so strikingly puts it in her powerful reading of Flaubert's *Madame Bovary*, "something is eating at Madame Bovary. She has a 'depraved appetite,' which is to say, she accepts as comestible what by natural or normed evaluation ought to be refused. Intricate parasitism" (*CW*, 122). Ronell goes on to explain that Emma Bovary's perverse eating habits and inability to nurture her own daughter owe to the fact that she is otherwise occupied in feeding an unknown, unburied other:

> Something is growing in Emma of which the repelled child, Berthe, is a symptom. The other in its absence must somehow be kept alive and preserved; this requires certain metonymies of feeding. To retain the other, the subject, wanting to satisfy its depraved hunger, follows a foreign regime, filling an emptiness that somehow leaves the subject full. The body becomes the site for exercising the rights of a missing person. This person, or parasite, as interiorized other, is imperious. It demands immediate satisfaction of a felt lack. . . . There's no giving up the other. (*CW*, 125)

Taken in this context, drug addiction can be understood as a symptomatic response to the overwhelming and invasive demands of the telephonic immune system. Where the telephone user denies loss and overcomes distance by simulating presence, the drug addict disconnects and drops out from the collective body politic. Ronell writes that the "drug addict offers her body to the production of hallucination, vision or trance, a production assembled in the violence of non-address. This form of internal saturation of self, unhooked from a grander effective circuit, marks the constitutive adestination of the addict's address" (*CW*, 106).

Thus, unlike the telephone, which simulates presence in absence, drugs promote disassociation and de-socialization. In bio-political terms, however, this disassociation and de-socialization becomes expressed as a perversion of body functions regulating intake and output, production, consumption, and waste. Instead of producing waste that can be eliminated from the system as filth to be disposed of, the addict becomes an internal waste product within the economy of the social system. The self "wasted" on and by drugs produces toxic waste in place of a self. As wasted self, the addict inhabits the social order, is radically disconnected from it, but cannot be eliminated from it. In this sense, the addict is doubly parasitical: he or she "hosts" an alien other within and he or she becomes an alien other that threatens to destabilize the boundaries between inside and outside, self and other, ally or enemy. As an internal outsider who threatens the ability to draw clear boundaries, the drug addict's (self) destruction is received as a threat to the health of the collective. In an essay entitled "The Rhetoric of Drugs," Jacques Derrida describes how the parasitical status of drugs means that there is no such thing as "solitary" drug use: "So it cannot be said that the pleasure of drug use [*la jouissance toxicomanique*] is in itself forbidden. Rather we forbid a pleasure that is at once solitary, desocializing, and yet contagious for the socius. . . . Besides, you might even say that the act of drug use is structured like a language and so could not be purely private. Straightaway, drug use threatens the social bond."[12]

As Derrida suggests in this essay, as a parasite that infects and contaminates the social body, drugs are seen to be inherently contagious. Both Derrida and Ronell explore how drugs open up the question of the body as something that cannot be contained, purified, or protected from contagion. Put another way, drugs force us to acknowledge that there is no such thing as a "healthy" body. To the extent that bodies are alive, they are always already inhabited by alien others and are vulnerable to death by contagion at every touch. Attempts to quarantine or purge the foreign bodies that lurk within the self become expressed as violent acts of war. In *Crack Wars*, for example, Ronell explicitly relates drugs to both genocide and viral infection: " . . . indeed, it would be difficult to dissociate drugs from a history of modern warfare and genocide. One could begin perhaps in the contiguous neighborhood of the ethnocide of the American Indian by alcohol or strategic, viral infection, and then could never end. . . ." (*CW*, 52) Furthermore, as Ronell and Derrida both argue, thinking about politics and war must take into account how hygienic exercises to ward off foreign invasion or cleanse internal infection produce what they have called an autoimmune situation where the self turns against itself because it cannot maintain or sustain a pure boundary between itself and its others. Ronell's work, however, specifically emphasizes how autoimmune (political) responses can be linked to the technological drive and its accompanying repression of the feminine body. Throughout her writings, she examines how modern war technologies are consistently feminized as a hygienic attempt to ward off (masculine) fear about the actual power, vulnerability, and irreducible otherness of the feminine body. In other words, technology is the defensive, militarized reaction to the fact that, for male culture, the feminine body remains the first threatening foreign body.

Foreign Bodies and Toxic Shock

> No liberation without appliances, no war machine without a girl's name, no desire for survival without the feminine. No mode of connectivity, in short, without the Emergency Feminine. ("The Worst Neighborhoods of the Real," *FS*, 221)

If, as we have suggested, modern technology can (at least in part) be understood as a militant defense against the threat of the female body, we can begin to appreciate why war technology and technological warfare take the form of a particularly reactive repression and denial of the feminine. One of the *leitmotiFS* that runs through the essays assembled in *Finitude's Score* is that the specific brutality of war in the technological age is accompanied by a symptomatic radical disavowal and denial of feminine difference. The annihilation of the enemy other is related to a simultaneous negation of the feminine and a repudiation of the body as such. War waged by technobodies, who embody the fantasy of triumph over life, results in a form of violence in which the death of the other is rendered totally unreal. Because the body's finitude is repressed in technological war, it produces the illusion not only that the enemy other is nobody but also that he (or she) has no body. Writing about nuclear war in an essay entitled "Starting from Scratch: Mastermix," Ronell argues that if we read with our ears, we can hear how the body that is repressed in technological war returns in the form of a symptomatic rhetorical trope:

> As everyone knows, total nuclear war cannot as such begin, it can only end—the moment it takes place, nuclear war will be over. Its taking place, therefore, constitutes an original end of sorts, the final fall of the fall, the spectacular fallout. Displacement of the body: arms have become arms that race, erasing the bodies' members, heads turned into war heads, and so on. By several rhetorical maneuvers, then, the body has already been evacuated from the site of battle, a battleground no longer being grounded as a circumscribable place where a class of warriors might engage one another in a limited, classical way. Nuclear war is conducted by no bodies: a symbolic mutation in the very concept of war that has created, I think, a condition through which every body is carrying war upon itself, now. ("SSM," *FS*, 210–11)

Ronell suggests that when the body is removed from the battlefield, it itself becomes a war zone. Technological attempts to cleanse the body of its frailties and impurities end up producing endless antibodies that make war everywhere. A living body is only alive to the extent that it remains open to the outside for sustenance and hence also open to the absolute inevitability of its own death. However, when the body's openings to the outside are shut down and sealed up in an attempt to protect itself from death and alien others, these internal anxieties about the body's limits become projected outward and are externalized as "disembodied" war zones. Ronell suggests that the pathologies of modern war can be traced back to disturbances in and of the body:

> Where does war take place? . . . Not in an imaginary outside, no longer in a firmly circumscribed space of the battlefield, but in two ways—war's atomization marks the civilian body and the language that envelopes it. I wanted to scan incorporations of war, scouring the national unconscious. The war zone extends to the intestinal tract, or begins there. If we could throw it up, we would reverse the dialectic of assimilation. It is crucial to place the battlefield, especially when it is no longer localizable as such but still relegated to a hallucinated exteriority. ("SSM," FS, 207)

If, as she provocatively claims, "the war zone extends to the intestinal tract, or begins there," this is so because the intestinal tract is the body site where all material decisions about that which is other to the self (incorporation, assimilation, rejection, constipation) actually take place. And if, as she suggests, we need to "throw it up," it is in order that we be able to give up the foreign matter that has been taken in without needing to contain, preserve, or conserve it. Indeed, given our earlier discussion of how the unmourned mother is encrypted in the belly of the telephone, we might imagine that Ronell is suggesting that foreign matter that we need to vomit might also be a figure for the mother as genuinely other—that is, as another living being who cannot be merely assimilated into the self or preserved there indefinitely.

Throughout *Finitude's Score,* Ronell tracks how the body's repression impacts on the war zone. Several of the essays were written during and/or in response to the war that is now referred to as the "First" Gulf War, waged under the first President George Bush as opposed to its bloody sequel, the ongoing Iraq war brought to us by Bush II. As Ronell pointed out at the time, the driving fantasy of the U.S. military during the First Gulf War was that modern technology would enable "us" ("us" being the "U.S.") to fight and win a "bloodless war." In the essay "Activist Supplement," she relates this fantasy to a fear of feminine finitude:

> I am not an essentialist feminist, but . . . it is urgent to recognize that the
> body of a woman has a fundamental relationship to death and despair, to
> finitude—and life. While the woman's body produces the eternal return
> of the "bloody mess of organic matter," the cyborg soldier, located in com-
> mand and control systems, exercises on the fields of denial. Intentional
> Reality eliminates the body as an organic, finite, damageable, eviscerable,
> castratable, rushable entity, thus closing off orifices and stemming leakage
> and excrement. ("AS," *FS,* 300)

Ronell is certainly not "an essentialist feminist." But if she experiences
the need to make that point explicitly, it may be because there is a certain
politics of reading in which the mere mention of the "feminine" or of the
"body" suffices to produce familiar and predictable patterns of misrecogni-
tion. Throughout her work, however, Ronell brings us back to a thinking
of the body by showing how strangely and powerfully the effects produced
by the body's repression think for us and think in our place.

In the corpus discussed in these pages, we have seen how technology can
be viewed as a material manifestation of particular political, philosophical,
psycho-sexual failure to open the ears to the (feminine) body. Latent political investments, affects, and concepts become localized in and around the
orifices of the body politic and are eliminated technologically. Throughout
her work, Ronell performs readings of the body that challenge our pre-
conceptions and produce shocks of (non) recognition. Through her (non
essentialist) feminine writing, we discover that the body does not conform
to our imaginary or technological fantasies about it; rather it has powerful non-anthropomorphic resources in its absolute strangeness. Ronell's
texts invite us to open our ears to the unsettling strangeness of the body.
She shows that every body is always already a foreign body and asks us to
grapple with the political and ethical consequences of that fact. Contrary
to the ways in which it has been most often domesticated, colonized, and
appropriated by philosophy, religion, and culture, no body can be reduced
to the property of a self. Bodies are rent with orifices, apertures, drives, and
vital functions that open up the living self to all forms of otherness. And,
as she points out throughout her work, the body is not only the site of this
alterity, but also the battleground for a defensive response to it. Attempts
to make the body invulnerable and impermeable, to regulate its intake and
output, to police its erotic zones and deny its inevitable exposure to its own
finitude, are played out materially and expressed as forms of technology,
politics, and mourning. The body politic secretes its toxins as war.

NOTES

1. Avital Ronell, *The Telephone Book: Technology—Schizophrenia—Electric Speech* (Lincoln: University of Nebraska Press, 1989). Subsequent references to this work will be indicated in the body of the text by the abbreviation *TB* followed by the page number.

2. Avital Ronell, *Finitude's Score: Essays for the End of the Millennium*, 8 (Lincoln: University of Nebraska Press, 1994). Subsequent references to this work will be indicated in the body of the text by the abbreviation *FS* followed by the page number.

3. Ronell herself glosses this important passage in Freud in several different ways in *The Telephone Book*. In particular, however, she performs a complex and extraordinary reading of unconscious transmission and its relationship to "organ function" within psychoanalysis in pages 99–106. She writes, for example:

    > To tie up some of these loosened wires, it is useful to note that the question of sight-retreat and of unconscious transmissions is articulated in psychoanalysis in terms of citing a telephonics, that is in terms of putting through calls from the unconscious, always subject to being cut off. (99) . . .
    >
    > Freud claims that vision can be disrupted by something like an internally punishing voice. The voice gets the upper hand, shutting down visual apprehension, when the eye is felt to be abusing its "organ of sight for evil, sensual pleasures."(100) . . .
    >
    > The extent to which the telephone feeds into the psychogenic disturbance of which Freud writes, or in fact simulates it, needs to be seriously considered. Understanding the organ *as such*, in its singular unity, still needs to be determined. But the kind of organ which the telephone duplicates, replaces or protects may itself be subject to multiple displacements (psychoanalysis has argued convincingly for the symbolic exchangeability of anus and ear, for instance). If by this logic, the telephone begins to behave like "an actual genital," we may be opening the shutters on the scandal which accompanied its conception. (104–5)

    I have unfortunately been compelled to simplify this discussion in the interests of expository clarity. I urge the reader to consult her texts in order to appreciate how profoundly the richness of her thought is embedded in the poetic density of her writing.

4. For this discussion concerning the openness of the ear, see: Jacques Lacan, *The Four Fundamental Concepts of Psycho-Analysis* (London: Hogarth Press, 1977).

5. The expression comes, of course, from Jacques Derrida. See: Jacques Derrida and Christie McDonald, *The Ear of the Other: Otobiography, Transference, Translation: Texts and Discussions with Jacques Derrida* (New York: Schocken Books, 1985).

6. For a related discussion of technology and the maternal function, please see my essays on photography and the mother. Elissa Marder, "Blade Runner's Moving Still," *Camera Obscura: A Journal of Feminism, Culture, and Media Studies* 27 (1991), Elissa Marder, "Nothing to Say: Fragments on the Mother in the Age of Mechanical Reproduction," *Esprit Créateur* 40.1 (2000).

7. For an important study on technology and failed mourning, see Laurence A. Rickels, *Aberrations of Mourning: Writing on German Crypts* (Detroit: Wayne State University Press, 1988).

8. See, for example: Janine Chasseguet-Smirgel, *Creativity and Perversion*, 1st American ed. (New York: W.W. Norton, 1984), Janine Chasseguet-Smirgel, "Altglas, Altpapier: (Empty Bottles, Waste Paper): Reflections on Certain Disorders of the Superego in Relation to Houseproud Mothers," *Psychoanalytic Inquiry* 11 (1991), Arlene Kramer Richards, "A Romance with Pain: A Telephone Perversion in a Woman?" *International Journal of Psychoanalysis* 70 (1989), Leonard Shengold, "The Symbol of Telephoning," *Journal of the American Psychoanalytical Association* 30 (1982).

9. Chasseguet-Smirgel, "Altglas, Altpapier: (Empty Bottles, Waste Paper), 554.

10. Avital Ronell, *Crack Wars: Literature Addiction Mania,* (Lincoln: University of Nebraska Press, 1992). All future references to this book referring to this edition will be indicated by the abbreviation *CW* followed by page numbers in the body of the text.

11. For a more detailed engagement with Ronell's reading of *Madame Bovary* in relation to questions of time and addiction, see: Elissa Marder, *Dead Time: Temporal Disorders in the Wake of Modernity (Baudelaire and Flaubert)* (Stanford, Calif.: Stanford University Press, 2001).

12. Jacques Derrida, "The Rhetoric of Drugs," trans. Michael Israel, in *Points . . . : Interviews, 1974–1994,* ed. Elisabeth Weber (Stanford, Calif.: Stanford University Press, 1995). 250.

WORKS CITED

Chasseguet-Smirgel, Janine. "Altglas, Altpapier: (Empty Bottles, Waste Paper): Reflections on Certain Disorders of the Superego in Relation to Houseproud Mothers." *Psychoanalytic Inquiry* 11 (1991): 537–58.
———. *Creativity and Perversion*. 1st American ed. New York: W.W. Norton, 1984.
Derrida, Jacques. "The Rhetoric of Drugs." Trans. Michael Israel. In *Points . . . : Interviews, 1974–1994*. Ed. Elisabeth Weber. Stanford, Calif.: Stanford University Press, 1995. 228–54.
Derrida, Jacques, and Christie McDonald. *The Ear of the Other: Otobiography, Transference, Translation: Texts and Discussions with Jacques Derrida*. New York: Schocken Books, 1985.
Lacan, Jacques. *The Four Fundamental Concepts of Psycho-Analysis*. London: Hogarth Press, 1977.

Marder, Elissa. "Blade Runner's Moving Still." *Camera Obscura: A Journal of Feminism, Culture, and Media Studies* 27 (1991): 77–87.

———. *Dead Time: Temporal Disorders in the Wake of Modernity (Baudelaire and Flaubert)*. Stanford, Calif.: Stanford University Press, 2001.

———. "Nothing to Say: Fragments on the Mother in the Age of Mechanical Reproduction." *Esprit Créateur* 40.1 (2000): 25–35.

Richards, Arlene Kramer. "A Romance with Pain: A Telephone Perversion in a Woman?" *International Journal of Psychoanalysis* 70 (1989): 153–64.

Rickels, Laurence A. *Aberrations of Mourning: Writing on German Crypts*. Detroit: Wayne State University Press, 1988.

Ronell, Avital. *Crack Wars: Literature Addiction Mania*. Lincoln: University of Nebraska Press, 1992.

———. *Finitude's Score: Essays for the End of the Millennium*. Lincoln: University of Nebraska Press, 1994.

———. *The Telephone Book: Technology—Schizophrenia—Electric Speech*. Lincoln: University of Nebraska Press, 1989.

Shengold, Leonard. "The Symbol of Telephoning." *Journal of the American Psychoanalytical Association* 30 (1982): 461–70.

Pierre Alferi
Serial

Une pièce brisée	A broken coin
une boîte noire	a black box
une balle de cuivre	a brass bullet
sept perles:	seven pearls:
qu'est-il arrivé à marie?	what happened to mary?
avec qui se marie marie?	who will marry mary?
Un express perdu	A lost express
un pays caché	a hidden land
une ville fantôme	a ghost city
une maison sans clé;	a house without a key;
l'aventurière que j'aimais	my beloved adventurer
attachée bâillonnée.	bound and gagged.
L'homme qui a disparu—	The man who disappeared—
masque pourpre, bas de cuir	purple mask and leatherstocking
gant rouge, main déformée	red glove and clutching hand
doigts de velours, griffe d'airain	velvet fingers and iron claw
tache cramoisie	crimson stain
x noir.	black x.

Un disque ardent
un fantôme gris
une ombre protectrice
—l'ombre crie:
haut les mains!
brûlez leurs granges!

Une voix sur la ligne
une voix du ciel:
joue le jeu!
dix cicatrices font un homme
—combattre le destin
s'en tirer
agir ou périr
se battre pour la gloire
chasser le tigre en inde
l'or des pirates
le mystère de la double croix
les miracles de la jungle.

Le cercle rouge?
signe fatal
le rayon invisible?
fortune fantôme
le troisième œil?
mauvais œil.

Ensevelis dans la neige:
les maraudeurs du rail
les dessalés
les hommes radars de la lune
les tireurs du nord-ouest
les vautours de la mer.

Pris au piège:
june la fugitive avec homonculus
scotty des scouts avec une fille de
    l'oncle sam
l'épouse négligée avec le roi de la
    radio

A flaming disk
a grey ghost
a shielding shadow
the shadow screaming:
hands up!
burn 'em up barnes!

A voice on the wire
a voice from the sky:
play ball!
ten scars make a man:
fighting fate
breaking through
do or die
fighting for fame
hunting tigers in India
the pirate gold
the mystery of the double cross
the miracles of the jungle.

The red circle?
fatal warning
the invisible ray?
phantom fortune
the third eye?
evil eye.

Snowed in:
railroad raiders
sea raiders
radar men from the moon
gunfighters of the northwest
vultures of the sea.

Trapped:
runaway june with homonculus
scotty of the scouts with a
    daughter of uncle sam
the neglected wife with the
    radio king

le mystérieux docteur satan avec
   la fille de la jungle
la tigresse avec jimmie dale alias
   le phoque gris
hutch l'ouragan avec lucille love
   la fille mystère
brenda starr avec le capitaine
   video
l'archet vert avec la fille de
   don q
la femme panthère du congo
   avec l'homme de minuit
le chevalier blanc avec la veuve
   noire.

Insaisissables :
le monstre et le singe
les loups de la culture et les
   araignées
le renard bleu, l'étalon
   d'or
les fauves du paradis
l'œil du taureau, de l'aigle
son ombre
la marque de la grenouille
le trajet d'un homme
la trace évanescente
de la pieuvre et de l'épervier
les empreintes digitales.

the mysterious doctor satan with
   the jungle girl
the tiger women with jimmie dale
   alias the grey seal
hurricane hutch with lucille love,
   girl of mystery
brenda starr with captain
   video
the green archer with the
   daughter of don q
the panther girl of the kongo
   with the midnight man
the white horseman with the
   black widow.

Elusive:
the monster and the ape
the wolves of culture and the
   spiders
the blue fox and the golden
   stallion
the beasts of paradise
the bull's eye and the eagle's eye
their shadows
the mark of the frog
the way of a man
the vanishing trail
of the octopus and the hawk
the finger prints.

Gil Anidjar
War Bodies

SHE WAR

WAR for AR is primary. This should not come as a surprise. AR knows
WAR. Which does not mean that she brings or bears some prophetic utterance, the moving image of a road warrior to come, nor that she asks us
to reflect on war's future, on how bad it might become or how horrible it
will get. Instead, she engages and confronts a near and constant danger, the
vulnerabilities and inflicted wounds of old (and young) in the militarized
zones of knowledge. That is why it may be possible to date, with a fair
degree of precision, when war occurs, when it is declared, in her writings.
Historical and geopolitical conditions confirm, moreover, that an onset of
a war of the world, a war of the new world and, more precisely, the *new war
order*, inscribed itself upon her work, as it did upon few, all too few, and
more urgently, more overwhelmingly so.[1] Reading Ronell, one is made to
acknowledge that everything is as if polemology, increasingly constitutive
of the political, had been given yet another turn of its imperial screw. I am
referring to the Gulf War for now, the first war ever declared not so much on
war itself—by 1991, the war to end all wars had been a common place since,
well, since forever, really—but one declared and unleashed on a specific war,
namely, the Vietnam War.[2] Much more lethal, and almost literally so, considering the exponential increase in the amount of bombs dropped during
these wars, is the fact that this "war as test" (*TD*, 347n23&24) constituted
the endless beginning of a war that is still going, and going, and going.[3] And

with it, so are hundreds of thousands among the inhabitants of Iraq—of the world, really. This is said while suspending, for the moment, the question of whether war (and even *a* war) could ever be treated as a circumscribable, recognizable, or identifiable theme in the world, much less as the object of a *felicitous* declaration or description, the referent of a *constant;* whether war could ever be treated or comprehensively covered. An essential moment in the permanent production and reproduction of inequality and oppression, war has long exceeded the kind of binary logic that would manifest or maintain anything like two "sides." This is what Ronell, in the tradition of the oppressed, teaches us. Always one-sided, and increasingly so, war lacks integrity. War dis-integrates—others first, but then also those who claim to "conduct" it. War is being in the world, Emmanuel Lévinas warned, and it must be granted a measure of thematic explicitness for the purpose of poised reflection on its scandalous banality, and for righteous indignation. "Noise-machine, schizo leash, war-zone shots in the dark, lover's discourse or phantomic conference call" (*TB*, 265), the expanding field of war's brutal traces into everything—here the telephone; for Léon Daudet, the car, as Benjamin reminds us; now everywhere—can be perceptibly followed in Ronell's unwavering and fearless attention to the "nearly military strategic deployment of language" (*TD*, 34), and in what she calls "the *militerary* regime" that organizes her texts (*FS*, 120 and 221) and, all things being unequal, the rest of the fabric of our lives.[4]

But Ronell's "earliest" war is also the latest, the last and final, war. It is therefore not identical to these old, though ever-present wars, nor is it really the Gulf War. I am hesitant to name it because one war can always hide another, and besides, it is not clear that this was, or that there is, *one* war. It is as if rather than war being the pursuit of politics by other means, as Clausewitz famously has it, politics (and culture, economics, religion, and everything really) had undergone a radical mutation and transformed into nothing but war.[5] War thus became the pursuit of everything by any means necessary. And "note that there is War and there are also wars" (211), especially when you start counting limited or invisible wars, not to mention forgotten wars.[6] Who, after all, remembers "the Telephone Wars of the Egyptians and the Hebrews" (*TB*, 296)? Who recalls that "the polemics surrounding drugs historically became a War only when crack emerged"? That it was crack that first "brought war unto the law" (*CW*, 19)? Do you even know "how the Gulf War became a technological test site in which our national body scored HIV-negative" (*FS*, xi)? There are, to begin addressing these questions, methods of transmission "whose origins are in the Civil War, but which extend toward all wars and pestilence, designating in the first place an alternate telegraph system or secret coding. A *civil* war, as it were, conducted through language ducts" (93). There is evidence, at any rate, that such is the case for Avital Ronell. Yet, to remain philologically and rhetorically disciplined (war for AR is nothing if not "War Words" [*TB*, 14]), one will have to say that war is primarily, even originally, war only and insofar as it is essentially *new*. This is why war became manifest in the first text she explicitly dedicated to the one war that announced itself as the latest news: the latest ever. Whether "nuclear war constitutes itself in and by rumor" or whether it sets off journalistic reporting as the "desire for instantaneity that projects a sensational nuclear blast" (*FS*, 209), it is a war that announces itself with the radical novelty of the just-about-to-happen, a novel and spectacular fallout bringing down the end of all things. Certainly, there has always been war, but what nuclear war revealed—or historically coincided with—is that war is new(s). More precisely, beyond the apparent senselessness of war, "the absolute scandal of death," and from the beginning, this absolute and total, infinite war, this war without bounds, has ultimately inscribed itself everywhere only to the extent that it has become ineluctably tied to the body.

So much for a smashing insight, you might say. She would and has, in fact, explicitly said, among other relevant things, that "the war zone extends to the intestinal tract, or begins there" (*FS*, 207). But whose body is this here talked about? Considering that Ronell rarely engages in navel-gazing, it may be important to point out that her recurring concern with this and other body parts comes up in the following announcement, namely, that she "had been working on rumorological paranoïa and the telephone, trying to trace the umbilical logic that attaches certain utterances to the paternal belly of the state" (*FS*, 207). It is in the context of another navel, then, another's navel and another narcissism, if not an allonarcissism, a narcissism of the other state, that Ronell at once refuses to abstract or universalize war while engaging the relation between war and the state, the (political) body of every body ("every body: this includes the body politic and its internal organs, i.e., the security organs of the state" [*TB*, 109]). She does so most strikingly by examining her/our own place in this body, her place within and between the university and "the war machine that keeps it well lubricated" (*FS*, 207). Indeed, for the ivory-tower terrorist, "universities have all too often been the locus of collaboration and intellectual complicity with war" (210). Along with the question "where does war take place?" then, which gets asked here for the first time (the answer, by the way, is: everywhere and nowhere, but some places more than others), we are swiftly introduced to

118

the multiple bodies of war.[7] And everything is already in place, that is to say, everything is already out of place.

> I wanted to address this and also the state's inscription of the body, the way it registers, imprints, and invents a coded body. Where does war take place? Or the radicality of absolute war? Not in an imaginary outside, no longer in a firmly circumscribed space of the battlefield, but in two ways—war's atomization marks the civilian body and the language that envelops it. I wanted to scan incorporations of war . . . (*FS*, 207)

Later, Ronell will revisit this scene of autoimmune deficiency—the state inscribes war on itself, on its "own" body rather than on an imaginary outside—and narrate the onset of war along with that of illness, exploring everything that links "the sadism of doctors," the "drama of chronic fatigue," and "those wretched soldiers felled by 'Gulf War Syndrome'" (*TD*, 59). The body and language are themselves "marked" by war, incorporated by war. War is thereby revealed as akin to stupidity—what am I saying? War *is* stupidity—that "gratuitous if inerasable inscription that tags our bodies and is scratched on memorializing monuments" (*S*, 12). Stupidity is "a condition of war" (15). In the passage quoted above, war duplicates the scene of writing constituted by the state, a scene that is always already a multiple, and oddly productive, even (self)creative one ("it registers, imprints, and invents a coded body"). War is another *autre scène,* means with too many ends and targets in sight.[8] Inescapably, and endlessly, so. "In the war zone, where one cannot escape situating the texts under discussion, a variety of speech act continues to wage battle" (*FS*, 93). War is itself the reproductive multiplication of such texts and speech acts, scenes of writing that make the state a work of war, a war of the works, as it were. War "itself" is that other scene which cannot (fail to) take place (Ronell formulates what appears to be an exception, the exception constituted by a specific kind of war, but this exception will soon become the rule: "insofar as nuclear war cannot as such take place—when it does, it's over—then its proper domain is rhetoric and the field of the Other" [*FS*, 208]). There are already "implicit contracts that draw up bodies" and it is war that writes them (*S*, 244). War writes the body of the civilian as well as the body of language. In and upon these two bodies, these two *war buddies,* what Ronell calls "incorporations of war" are not simply brought about and introduced to the creative scene of world devastation, although they are that, too. Nor are these bodies a new and improved instantiation of the Hobbesian "war of all against all." In ways we will still have to read, Ronell tells us that they are not so much war machines as incorporations of war. *War, Inc.*—the new world order—is war generalized, internationalized, and globalized; war as the pursuit of itself by any means (hence the operations of the autoimmune), and, in ways we still have to take the measure of, the transformation of bodies—corporate or corpo(sur)real, although it must be said that corporations have an easier time at it; they make an easier transition—into war bodies.

> Displacements of the body: arms have become arms that race, erasing the bodies' members, heads turned into war heads, and so on. By several rhetorical maneuvers, then, the body has already been evacuated from the site of battle, a battleground no longer being grounded as a circum-scribable place where a class of warriors might engage one another in a limited classical way.
> Nuclear war is conducted by no bodies: a symbolic mutation in the very concept of war that has created, I think, a condition through which every body is carrying war upon itself, now. (*FS,* 211)

The substitution of war bodies for the body—a singular entity, if it is ever one, which will have to be interrogated and followed retrospectively, as it were, and from the perspective we are now forced to adopt—involves multiple displacements and transformations, substitutions and mutations, effacements, erasure and "rhetorical maneuvers," the evacuation of the body, the disappearance of place and of the classical battle fight. There are, at once, war bodies and "no bodies." These nobodies—war is generalized—are every body. "Every body is carrying war upon itself, now." But with this advent of war bodies, the allegedly precise dating proposed earlier for the explicit occurrence of war in the writings of Avital Ronell has now entirely lost ground.

This should have been obvious from the beginning. And in a way, it is always about the beginning. For if the body is at war (with "itself" as well as with others) prior to the facts that we have begun to explore, namely that war is a writing (and an erasing) of bodies, if war has become constitutive of bodies ("one need only consider the way wars are waged on material sites and objects, and the way the state uses drugs in order to take possession of the body" *TD,* 19), then Ronell's writing was always and from the beginning a writing of war. It was always "itself" a body of war, the embodied occurrence of war bodies.

War Buddies

Invoking a certain literality—occurrences of the word "body" and its in-flections—I will attempt to both affirm and break bibliographic protocols. What after all could constitute the limits of a bibliography on the body? Or a count of its material occurrences? I turn to Ronell's books, then, intending to read them, still training to do so, in order to substantiate an admittedly simple and simplifying claim on bodies of war and on bodies at war. More precisely, perhaps, I aim to do the necessary grind work toward a kind of body part, an index that would concern itself with the numerous bodies that figure and, equally intransitively, dis-figure, appearing only to vanish, in Avital Ronell's writings. I insist on literality because I do not intend to open or even follow too widely the semantic ranges of the term "body" in her work, and because the body always projects a particular body, itself linked to a certain kind of literality. It is *this body* before it is my or anyone else's body (within the Western tradition, on the margins of which she works, such literality articulates itself at the limit previously known as "carnal," as in "carnal Israel," the pound of flesh and so forth).[9] "A literality that is no longer legible, this body at once withholds itself and produces resistant signs of itself" (*S*, 186). I insist on literality as a kind of horizon, then, in order to prepare the kind of a-thetic reading (I do not say athletic reading, although that would hardly be less pertinent in Ronell's case), a reading she practices and advocates at times, and one that seems particularly urgent, if not necessarily possible here: "a reading of non-essence which is at the base of the valuation wars raging in the textual body" (*CW*, 100). Under the conditions now prevailing (and perhaps this was always the case), "the body presents itself as an entity that does not exist, or barely exists, except perhaps in failure or exaggeration, in beauty or mortification" (192). Ultimately, however, I underscore literality for no other purpose than to contain the otherwise impossible task of counting, or even approaching, all the bodies—"there are often up to ten bodies to count," explains Ronell, "to honor, to nurture, including the subtle, back and energetic bodies" (*TD*, 118). Nor am I necessarily interested in joining, as this particular instance would have it, "Madame Bovary's body count" (*CW*, 124). At stake, then, is a rigorously insistent, forceful yet gentle thinking of the body, indeed, a constant concern for the body that demands exigent discipline and even *askesis*, the management of energies, proper eating (as in "Learning to Like Spinach," *D*, 25) and sleeping habits, and a responsibility toward health. Ronell is meticulously and joyfully serious about this. She means health—as one is said to "mean business"—and she affirms it as a Nietzschean value. She means health while directing us toward "the possibility of an altogether other health," having to do with "the properly *improper* character of the body" (*CW*, 64). "It would be entirely possible, therefore, to conceive somatological reordering, we could say, as the body achieves a new interpretation of exteriority toward which it seeks attunement" (*TB*,

116). One—everyone—"became the artisan of one's own body, fiddling around, experimenting, creating new parts or treating the psyche like an organ, a sick organ. One became a maniacal *bricoleur* of one's own body" (*CW*, 75). This is why experimentation wins the day, why "it seems as though everything—nature, body, investment, belief—has needed to be tested" (*TD*, 5). Minimally, one could say of Ronell what she herself says about Paul de Man's oeuvre (de Man himself commenting on Rousseau), namely, that "the body at least will haunt and return with convulsive lurches throughout the oeuvre, inscribing the stammering reserved for machinic disorder" (*S*, 98). Body trouble. In sickness and in health. Or at least "a kind of mechanized vision of the body" (*TB*, 118). Sometimes, the body constitutes "a massive disruption of inherited meaning," which is why it must (yet cannot) be read, attended to in its essential relation to time and place. "The body is in the world and pins down the vague locality of world, but when brought into view, it threatens the solidity of the world" (*S*, 180). But "how has the body been drawn into the disposal systems of our technological age?" (*CW*, 63). This is hardly a personal question ("*Her own body*'—what a joke!" [*CW*, 78]). At any rate, it is not only personal but one is made to feel, on one's flesh, as it were, that it could in fact get there, very up close and personal. "I'm not all that discreet about body's writhing habits," she writes (*S*, 26). Which is perhaps one of the reasons "why one has the uncanny sense of riding the wave of a personal pathology when finding oneself engaged in 'war' " (*FS*, x). And you should read the interviews.[10]

Every body, then, means that Ronell's texts—those she reads and those she writes, if the difference can be made to hold—are "like body parts of a missing corpus" ("Misery," 24), sheltering their own embodiments, splitting themselves off "into the poesy of body parts" (*FS*, 254). But "we can't just go around thinking that these bodies are easily reclaimable or anchored in reference" (*S*, 186). The texts are not so much enacting "the migration of the body into discursive practice (to speak in the dialect of the new historicism)" (*TD*, 94) as much as they are suffused with bodies. The Goethean body dominates, perhaps, but there are others: domestic and foreign bodies (in multiple injections), wasted, abandoned, forbidden, and trash-bodies, glorious, pure or borrowed bodies, hijacked bodies, minoritized bodies, and bodies arrested, tortured and condemned and throughout, indeed, always "bodies menaced by pulverization" (*TD*, 117); sublime and textual bodies, coded and natural bodies, phallic and phantom bodies and dead bodies, and more often than not, women's bodies too, sick, transfixed, and spilling, like the mother body—"the first body is symbolically rooted in what we might call the *toxic maternal*" (*CW*, 118). There is also the body of mania and the body of a cow (and those of horses, beginning with Nietzsche's body); the body of telephony and "the connection between a broken, stammering body and the telephone" (*TB*, 312). There is even, in addition (in addiction) to other institutional bodies, a philosophical body, the body of the worker engaged in class warfare, and that, repeatedly inscribed, of the young student body. Sometimes, "the procedure, simple yet incalculable, implodes the concentrated student body." Sometimes, "language falters, the student body cracks" (*TD*, 127). There is "the *suppléance* of an addict's knowing-body" and "the body-broken, the racially hallucinated other" (*CW*, 77). And there is, of course, "the political body—and what a body it was!—plugging orifices, building muscle" (ibid.). Among all these, one body, at least, "had to be tossed into the bargain, invaded and scarred" (*TD*, 88). Everything occurs "as if to emphasize the impossible separation of domains, notably, where the body ends" (*S*, 183). Ronell's texts concern themselves with contamination, fragmentation, and "the possibility of mutilation" (*D*, 32). "The ways of bodies, what drew them toward health or condemned them to stasis" are there to be read, and sometimes it is as if the body "belonged, finally, to another order of being" (*S*, 45). "Bodies are being exchanged, appropriated, and sacrificed" (*D*, 178). And this is, once again, only the beginning.

In the beginning, there was Goethe, who, first at everything, "pioneered the moment when the body became the test site and a secondary prop for a transcendentalizing consciousness" (*TD*, 160). That is to say that Goethe's body (and the body in and after Goethe) was on the line from the very beginning. "Thus Goethe made his contribution to science, a science that cuts as deeply into the Freudian body as one dare imagine" (*D*, 40). Incarnate and disincarnate, this body and its ghost proceeded to move on, "Goethe's ghost moves on . . . dictaphoning the rest of his corpus to the one who has known to exchange bodies" (139). Like every body, perhaps ("At first lost, the child's ghost would find a telephone connection in the body that housed the spirit of a petrified subject. The spirit inhabits the body, its many voices demanding a reply" [*TB*, 179]), yet in its own, highly singular fashion, this corpus carries a parasite; it constitutes a case of "literary parasitism" (*D*, 65). This is why it becomes necessary to follow Eckermann and "the course of an alien body (*Fremdkörper*) into the Goethean corpus" (ibid.). This body does not give up, it rather takes up, the ghost. "Everything that follows will have been naturalized (for the most part) as Eckermann's drive and will bear the mark of his body's desire to embody" (81). No wonder that when Eckermann writes, "he calls representations of Goethe's body to mind . . . the body does claim a place here" (87). "In fact," Ronell explains in a section of *Dictations* entitled "Body Building," it is Goethe who "gives his body to Eckermann so that he can constitute it as a body. Eckermann's task, as Goethe defines it, will be to transform the fragments and remains . . . into the body of Goethe's works" (107). And so, "once again, Eckermann carries two bodies as he walks toward Weimar" (186). This is the beginning of the body as buddy system and, along with other operations, it may justifiably lead, therefore, to "a reading of genius as something 'lodged in the body'—a resident phantom or alien body, a *Fremdkörper*. . . . And Goethe cannot resist talking to Eckermann about the physical constitution ('körperliche Konstitution') of a writer" (113). This un-democratic constitution involves all the activities of the body, its processes and its processing of that which enters the body, and comes out of it. "This brings us back to the large question, which is never held at a distance from what Eckermann writes or Goethe says, of the relationship between property and (self)possession (*Eigentum*) and the extraneous or foreign (*das Fremde*) that pertains to *excrementum*" (138). This "large question" is still relevant today, becoming exponentially larger and all-encompassing, and although there is no simple answer to it, we do know that any answer would bridge the insistently reinscribed gaps between inside and outside, between the natural and the artificial, moving from one to the other, policing the border, as quickly as one can set up a new and always improving department of homeland security. "As that which can swallow and throw up—naturally or artificially—the body rigorously engages the dynamics of becoming, surpassing itself without reducing itself to a passageway" (*CW,* 64).

There are movements and functions, then, official functions and body functions, where every body is invited, the living, the dead, the angels, and even God and his "double body" (*S,* 196). This is in and from the beginning, again. And again. God's beginning. For true to Himself and to His numerous modalities of non-presence, God is, well, divine, that is, ubiquitous, if not omnipresent and far from omnipotent, in Ronell's work, minimally signaling a constant pondering, perhaps even a impious attempt at "re-creating the very essence of religiosity" (*TB,* 283), at least "a map of God's tactical assault on woman," which is akin to his "organized defense against science" (*TD,* 243–44). From the living sacred to the bumbling idiot as "quasi-sacred being" and to the sacred alien—"there would be no God without the foreigner" (*S,* 206)—it may be increasingly difficult to deny that "our politics and theories prove still to be under God's thumb" (*CW,* 61), attending to and responding to the loving and not so loving demands of "religious phantasmagoria" and other "internal religious wars" (*CW,* 131), not to mention "religious mania" and its "global rebound today" (*S,* 45). On a number of occasions, at any rate, in which Ronell comes perhaps closest to deploying a figure of "God's juggler," it is not only the thumb, but the body, indeed, the bodies of God that are on the line ("This put God on the line," *TB*, 323), a line that Ronell holds or treads by investing the text with "decidedly theological inflection." There is a "hypertheology of the telephone" (*FS*, 250). Not, of course, that either technology or "religion [were] deemed capable of offering a clean bill of health" (*S*, 45). Indeed, beginning with her attention to "Freud's reading of the body in godlike annexation, whose phantasmatic order deduces durable electric organs for the body's future" (*TB*, 89) and going back to "monotheism's suppression and abolition of divine party lines" (*TB*, 296); well before Mel Gibson's latest contribution to the cultural sedimentations of Christianity, Ronell had underscored "the invention of the tormented body . . . the disquieting exhibition of Holbein's dead Christ—the scandal of the bruised and bloody body of Christ . . . his reduction to a body that succumbs to its own destruction" (*S*, 176–77). Clearly, it has been a while since "the circuit was installed with the discovery of God's insufficiency . . . Shit was happening. God's fundamental breakdown, His out-of-serviceness and withdrawal from the scene" led to some major rewrites (*CW*, 75). There are divine bodies—they are all over *Stupidity*—and (assuming there is a difference, which is precisely what is at issue) there are technological ones, electric and technological bodies and body parts. There is, in other words, the matter of a "necessary articulation" brought up, which is "insinuated between a communication media and body extensions, . . corporeal citation marks: crutches holding up a body the way citations are propped up" (*TB*, 127).

If bodies are going to be read—forgive the lame repetition—it is because we have been subjugated by language. And although "we may go on living, surviving the recognition that our bodies, traversed by language, have been optioned out to death . . . with bodies overwritten, we are weighed down by language, which lives through us" (*S*, 241). Ultimately, if to no other end in sight, "language is body; it enters the body, forming and deforming it, putting up a force field to which organs respond" (*S*, 266). It is also because there are "languages of the body" (*TB*, 118), "the poesy of body parts" (339), moments of linguistic and technological irruption, ingestion and excretion, modalities of violent insertion into or by a means, a tool of electric speech, "the body reterritorialized, broken into, entered by the telephone cord. Somewhere someone has said that the enema was the first telephone line to the body. She connects the spinal to the telephone cord" (129). This is what it might mean to be "attached to the body of telephony" (313). And there is hope, or a chance of hope or of a call. At least, there is a chance of change. For every body.

When the body seems destined to experimentation, things are no longer introjected but trashed: dejected. The body proper regains its corruptible, organic status. Exposed to this mutability, the body cannot preserve its identity, but has a chance of seeing this fall, or ejection, sublimated or revalorized. Nautilus vs. the addict. When some bodies introduce drugs as a response to the call of addiction, every body is on the line: tampering and engineering, rebuilding and demolition, self-medication and vitamins become the occupations of every singularity. Sometimes the state has a hand in it. (*CW,* 7)

One should be careful not to reduce addiction to illness, much less illness to war, but some of the lines between them have been drawn and even put in motion by the militarization of medicine and by the war on drugs, among others. Moreover, within the confines of illness, which "visits you at will and does what it wants to your body," there is hallucination, a "store of toxicity" that spills (*S,* 182), and there is cleansing, even ethnic cleansing (in the Middle Ages, "doctors and theologians were one, and the plague, for example, was seen to originate in those carriers that were recognized, after much research, as Jews" [*FS,* 42]. What remains unchanged, at any rate, is "the tradition by which epidemics come to be associated with minorities including, nowadays, the greater part of the so-called Third World" [ibid.] and "the conspiracy of medicine and religion collapses" [*CW,* 144]). At any rate, "it's a fight." Illness is a fight, which "can be a losing battle or a healing without cure, one big healing crisis. It's war" (*S,* 182). And this war, like all other wars, occurs in your body. "Your body—your body is *fighting for you*" (ibid.).

What War? (The Story of US)

"And so we go to war" (*S,* 15). In fact, among a number of "other conflictual pairs" that introduce us to the war buddy system, one would have to single out once again the original warrior bodies of Goethe and Eckermann. "Armed for battle on the field of science, Goethe is the warrior whom Eckermann challenges" (*D,* 145). Then again, one should consider the "thematic of intense double-crossing" that surround the figure of Goethe, and then "which of the two Goethes?" "There are at least two sparring in each piece of writing" (*FS,* 131). No wonder, then, that Goethe's position—sometimes "the stance of a reactive warrior who is not afraid to cut to the quick" (*FS,* 180)—was always "already linked to devastation" (*D,* 22) and to a "mode of fragmentation that contains within it, like a potential explosive, the possibility of mutilation" (32). We have seen that Goethe pioneered the body as test site (among many other things) but have yet to consider that, essentially linked to Goethe, testing itself ("testing itself" constituting an impossible phrase after *The Test Drive*, but anyway) "counts as warfare today" (*TD*, 167). "We have seen that testing counts as warfare, and elsewhere I have tried to demonstrate how war is conducted on the imago of the maternal body" (241). Later—if temporal markers make any sense here—there would be other "polemical turf wars" (15), there would be Turing, who, at war with himself, "cracked the code and turned the tide, determining the outcome of the war" (51). There would be Schönberg and Freud, who "form a war-machine couple that attacks the visual fantasy, the realm of idols and Apollonian drawing power" (*FS*, 31); there would be Batman and Robin, America and the world, and then, there will be Nietzsche's war on Wagner. All around, there will be a battle of names, exemplified by Goethe or God—but at bottom, rock bottom, the name is always war. "War: when was war not waged in His name?" (*TD*, 244). *Dichtung und* WAR, poesy and truth, "dish*war*" (*FS*, 212).

> But we have been taught early on, by Homer and by Hölderlin himself, that going to the poet often involves going to war. Whether reading polemological maps, devising strategies of attack or retreat, surveilling a hostile territory, practicing poses of surrender, or getting iced by a particular turn of phrase or wind, the poetic and war efforts appear often to overlap. (*S*, 5)

Carried by the winds of war that traverse Ronell's writing, I have attempted to pursue the modalities and transformation of the poetic (and Lacanian) insight regarding the relations between language and war and the body of war. "The signifier turns the body into the Other's territory, medium, or colony. The body contorts and collapses into a language site" (*S*, 241). We had seen that "language is body," but we needed to attend to the way in which bodies are war. This is what *Crack Wars* is most explicitly about, of course, but it should be obvious by now that the significance of this fact reaches into a wider field, "from the consistency of polemics to daily mutations in what we call war (on the streets, at work, out of work, or in your body)" (*FS*, x). Clearly, "we do not know how to think war as something we should wage, which is why we think we can conduct warfare as if it were extraneous, momentary, simulated, and not engaging the very core of our being" (297). This is the story of US, the story of America. Hence, in order to think war, Ronell demands critique ("the extent to which war is waged in the name of certain readings, whether perverted or not, indicates that it is susceptible to a critique. You cannot criticize nature; you cannot offer a critique of the earthquake as such, but you can and must criticize, that is, *read* Desert Storm" [294]). She demands more vocal inquiry into the transformations of a war—here, again, the Gulf War, but all of "America's wars," really, as part of the "transgenerational chain of experimentation," which does not exclude war among its links but channels warlike aggression" (*TD*, 217)—from phantasm to intervention and into "the symptom par excellence for the uncontrolled translation of the [AIDS] syndrome into other bodies" (*FS*, 43 and 301). Finally, she demands that accounts be given for the "good intentions" that contributed "to the destruction of the reactional coherency of indigenous communities, serving only to weaken their resolve to defend themselves within and outside their political bodies" (45). And then, of course, there is still the question of "why does a body—institutional, political, biological—not know that it is, under certain conditions, attacking itself, misconstruing a self as nonself?" (51)

NOTES

1. Close to Ronell, see Jean-Luc Nancy's 1991 analysis of what he calls the "return of war" in "War, Right, Sovereignty—*Techne*" in Nancy, *Being Singular Plural*, trans. Robert D. Richardson and Anne E. O'Byrne (Stanford, Calif.: Stanford University Press, 2000), 101–43.

2. As Ronell went on to show, and as became more and more apparent since, thanks in part to the effort of Steven Spielberg, behind the Vietnam War was always World War II (Ronell, "Support Our Tropes" in *FS*). For a poignant reading of Ronell's work that follows the consequences of this other dating of war, see Eduardo Cadava, "Toward an Ethics of Decision" in *diacritics* 24:4 (Winter 1994): 4–29.

3. Most recently in *The Test Drive*, Ronell writes of "the unending Gulf War" as constituting "a privileged instance" for her reflections on testing (*TD*, 18, and see, e.g., 347n23&24). For more on the history of bombing technology prior to September 11, 2001 (more "progress" having been made since), see Sven Lindqvist, *A History of Bombing*, trans. Linda H. Rugg (New York: New Press, 2001).

4. Commenting on "the extraordinary expansion of the field of the testable [*die Erweiterung des Feldes des Testierbaren*] brought about for the individual through economic conditions," Walter Benjamin had primarily located this "metamorphosis" in the body of the film actor (constantly "subjected to a series of optical tests"), that of the director ("the camera director in the studio occupies a place identical with that of the examiner during aptitude tests"), and of the audience ("the audience takes the position of the camera; its approach is that of testing"). Ultimately, for Benjamin, this is a process "from which the star and the director emerge victorious," and it is a process that culminates in war as the paradoxical failure and success of the body, of an incorporation of

technology. "The destructiveness of war furnishes proof that society has not been mature enough to incorporate technology as its organ" (Walter Benjamin, "The Work of Art in the Age of Mechanical Reproduction," trans. Harry Zohn in Benjamin, *Illuminations: Essays and Reflections,* Hannah Arendt, ed. [New York: Schocken, 1969], 217–51).True to Benjamin's insight on the history of the victors, Ronell dedicates her attention to other bodies.

5. Michel Foucault describes some of the mutations of the discourse on and of war in *"Il faut défendre la société." Cours au Collège de France. 1976* (Paris: Gallimard/Seuil, 1997). Most pertinently, Foucault argues that if Clausewitz could claim that war is the pursuit of politics by other means, it is because earlier, "politics had become the pursuit of war by other means" (147). Recall that Clausewitz defined war as "an act of force to compel our enemy to do our will," to transform the enemy into a means to our ends (Carl von Clausewitz, *On War,* edited and translated by Michael Howard and Peter Paret [Princeton, N.J.: Princeton University Press, 1989], 75). In other words, war is about the colonization of the enemy's *body* and its transformation into an instrument of our desires. What I am attempting to describe in Ronell's work is the way she charts the extension of that colonization of the body to every body.

6. For a succinct discussion, see Eqbal Ahmad, *Confronting Empire: Interviews with David Barsamian* (Cambridge, Mass.: South End Press, 2000).

7. Reflecting on Freud and on the academy—the latter a consistent site of meditation and interrogation on research and pedagogy all the way to *The Test Drive* (e.g., *FS,* 7, 108, 207; *TD,* 202), the former too, but this time everywhere— Ronell early on evokes "mobilization" and the university as providing a kind of immunized zone, a place for undaunted fossilization, free from the crush of exogenous attack" (*D,* 24). The truce between the university and the state of war will be short lived, however. For a history of this transformation over the period Ronell attends to, see *Les sciences pour la guerre. 1940–1960,* Amy Dahan and Dominique Pestre, eds. (Paris: Éditions de l'École des Hautes Études en Sciences Sociales, 2004).

8. Ronell will soon invoke Walter Benjamin's 1925 essay on war, "Die Waffen von Morgen (Tomorrow's Arms)" in *Gesammelte Schriften,* Hrgb. Tillman Rexroth, Bd. IV: 1 (Frankfurt am Main: Suhrkamp, 1972), 473–76. There, she explains, "Benjamin writes of the possibility of an invisible war, anticipating scenes (or rather nonscenes) of chemical and biological warfare that would take place in our cities—in a space, therefore, that is no longer remote from the *polis,* and about which we would have no absolute certitude" (*FS,* 211).

9. Daniel Boyarin, *Carnal Israel: Reading Sex in Talmudic Culture* (Berkeley: University of California Press, 1993). Proximate as well, and deserving of a more extensive study that would also have to engage Avital Ronell's laughter, are the correspondences with what Mikhail Bakhtin calls "the grotesque body." This is a body that is "not separated from the world. It is not a closed, completed unit; it is unfinished, outgrows itself, transgresses its own limits. The stress is

laid on those parts of the body that are open to the outside world, that is, the parts through which the world enters the body or emerges from it, or through which the body itself goes out to meet the world" (Mikhail Bakhtin, *Rabelais and His World,* trans. Helene Iswolsky [Cambridge, Mass.: M.I.T. Press, 1968], 26; Bakhtin relates the culture of laughter to Goethe and to the German romantics who occupy Ronell throughout her work).

10. See, e.g., "Avital Ronell" in *RE/Search* (1991), special issue on "Angry Women," 127–53 (interview conducted by Andrea Juno) and D. Diane Davis, "Confessions of an Anacoluthon: Avital Ronell on Writing, Technology, Pedagogy, Politics" in *JAC* 20: 2 (Spring 2000): 243–81.

Samuel Weber
The Indefinite Article
or the Love of a Phrase

What leads one to love a phrase
and where can such a love lead?
Can it lead to friendship?
Can it keep faith?

—JACQUES DERRIDA,
"THE REASON OF THE STRONGEST"

The love in question, we should recall, addresses not just language as such, or words in isolation, but phrases like "une fois pour toutes," which I have been translating, all too approximately, as "once and for all." The question is all the more pertinent, because Derrida's writing is a constant love affair with phrases. Phrases that come and go, but that leave their mark, always singular and yet always related to one another. A family of phrases. One such, in what would seem to be an entirely different register, is "la démocratie à venir"— "democracy to come." It is a phrase, as Derrida admits in the midst of his last major essay, "La raison du plus fort" ("The Reason of the Strongest"), that has made him pay dearly for the affection he has shown it:

> A second preliminary question tortures me. It resembles a kind of remorse at having used and abused the expression "democracy to come." And above all, in the process, in using and abusing, to have repeated, while feigning to innovate, a (mere) truism. As though I had merely wanted to say: "You know, the perfect democracy, full and vital, does not exist; not only has it never existed, not only does it not exist at present, but, indefinitely deferred, it will always remain to come, it will never be present in the present, will never present itself, will never come, will remain always to come, like the impossible itself." If I had only said or wanted to say that, wouldn't I have reproduced, indeed plagiarized the classical discourses of political philosophy? (French, 107 / English, 73)

If the fascinating power of phrases is everywhere in evidence throughout Derrida's writing, nowhere does it play a more decisive role than in this essay, which responds to the phrase that "tortures" Derrida to the point of remorse: "la démocratie à venir." Indeed, the entire text can be read as an effort not just to unpack the phrase and free its author of a certain remorse, but also to suggest some of the political implications of phrases with respect to what is called "democracy." In what follows, I want to look at one particular phrase that occupies Derrida in the final concluding section of his text, which indeed takes its point of departure from it. It is an all too familiar phrase, with momentous implications, although not ones that are easily placed in relation to questions of democracy. For its author is Martin Heidegger, who, in the famous or infamous *Der Spiegel* interview from which the phrase is taken, acknowledges—and Derrida by no means clearly demurs—that he is "not convinced that democracy" is the political form best capable of responding to or confronting the challenges "of modern technology" (157–58 / 111–12).

The phrase that Derrida will cite and recite, turn and return, is Heidegger's famous pronouncement usually translated in English as "Only a God can save us." In German: "Nur noch ein Gott kann uns retten." The French translation differs slightly but significantly from this English version; it reads: "Seulement un dieu peut encore nous sauver." The English version, the most compact of the three, simply effaces the German word "noch," which in French is translated as "encore." But this translation, although it reproduces French equivalents of all the words in Heidegger's phrase, ignores what Walter Benjamin, in his essay "Task of the Translator," argues should be the defining principle of all translation: what he calls "literalness of syntax" (*Wörtlichkeit der Syntax*). Benjamin acknowledges, however, that the application of such a principle can easily produce monstrous results. And in this respect, English would be no exception. For Heidegger's formulation is ambiguous through its placement of the word "noch." He could have easily avoided the ambiguity, could have declared "Nur ein Gott kann uns retten." But he insisted, and surely not fortuitously, on inserting the word "noch," and that changes everything. For it opens the possibility of two very different, although not necessarily contradictory, readings, and hence situates itself in the hiatus between these two possibilities. Everything depends on the placing of the accent, which in turn scans the phrase. For Heidegger's declaration can be read as consisting of two different microphrases: "Nur noch ..." or " ... noch ein": in English, "Only still (or yet) ..." and "one more." The French translation opts for the more plausible of these two possibilities, when it translates "Seulement un dieu peut encore nous sauver"—"Only a god can still save us." Placing the accent on the "Nur noch . . ." it reads this phrase adverbially, as modifying "save" (*retten*) and thus feels justified in transposing the French equivalent of "noch" and placing it directly before the verb, *sauver*. However, if that was all Heidegger had wanted to say, he could easily have written as much in German: "Nur ein Gott kann uns noch retten." His text would then have said precisely what the French translation says it says. In this case, he would indeed have produced the "sententious phrase" which, in an even more truncated and sententious form has come home to us in its English version: "Only a God can save us."

But the fact that Heidegger writes "Nur noch ein Gott kann uns retten" and not "Nur ein Gott kann uns noch retten" leaves open the second possibility to which I have already briefly referred. Not simply that we can, at this point, only be saved by a God, but also that the God in question will be "Nur noch ein Gott"—which is to say, "Only yet or still another God." To allow for this possibility in English would result in the monstrosity to which Benjamin referred, and which he exemplified through reference to Friedrich Hölderlin's translations of Sophocles. It would read something like: "Only yet another God can still save us." Small wonder, therefore, that the English translators preferred to avoid the problem entirely by simply dropping the "noch" as keeping what they doubtless took to be the nominal essence, or meat of the phrase: "If we are to be saved, only a God can do it."

It should be noted that this simpler, meat-and-potatoes version of Heidegger's pronouncement is by no means excluded by the more literal but also monstrous translation I have provided, but it certainly is complicated by an element of uncertainty. The uncertainty it introduces could well be compared to what Derrida, in this concluding section of the essay, discerns in the "figure of the half-turn," which he in turn relates to what he calls "the dimension of the half-measure," a phrase that formalizes one of the decisive oscillations emerging out of his discussion of "democracy to come," namely, that "between the commensurable and the incommensurable." The unresolvable question of their common measure produces a movement of oscillation[1] that can also be found in the ambiguity of Heidegger's declaration, that "Nur noch ein Gott kann uns retten."

To be sure, as Derrida demonstrates, even ignoring the ambiguity of "Nur noch"—"Only yet" or "only still"—Heidegger's pronouncement is far more complex than commonly understood, through its use of "ein" as indefinite article, "ein," to determine and undetermine the "God" that is the only hope left of "Rettung." Through his use of "ein" as an indefinite article—as "an" rather than "one"—the God Heidegger invokes, so Derrida, can no longer be identified with the one and only God of certain monotheisms, as a "God" that is "one" in the sense of being identical with himself: sovereign, self-same, "ipsocentric" and "ipsocratic" (38 / 17). But Derrida goes on to distinguish a God that is identifiable only through the indefinite article from the "last God" defined by Heidegger in his *Beiträge zur Philosophie* as a God whose "lastness" is defined as being "not the end, but rather the other beginning of immeasurable possibilities of our history."[2] By stressing that the "ein" in Heidegger's phrase is used as an *indefinite article,* Derrida emphasizes the irreducible indeterminacy and alterity of that "God" who alone can "still save us." Such a God can neither be determined as one and the same nor as the End that inaugurates a new Beginning. It is "a God," not "one God."

In this respect, however, Heidegger's formulation, if it is read as gesturing toward "a God that *alone* can *still* save us," *still* saves as its ultimate horizon the notion of "saving" itself, which is to say, "saving" as the salvation and perpetuation of the sovereign self, of the self as sovereign, which is to say, of the self as ultimately immortal. Derrida will therefore go on to invoke other texts of Heidegger, notably his lectures on Hölderlin, in order to show how the notion of *Retten* is complicated and enriched by Heidegger himself so as to include not just personal *salvation* or healing but also *salutation* as the *welcoming address of the other, Grüßen* as well as *Heilen.*(160 / 114).[3]

And yet, the split possibility of reading Heidegger's phrase as either "Nur noch . . ." or " . . . noch ein Gott"—as "Only still" or "one more"—and above all, the possibility of reading both, already destabilizes any attempt to determine the notion of "Retten" in a univocal manner. Everything would depend on how the phrase is scanned. If the accent falls on "Nur noch," what emerges is the exclusive aspect of the God invoked. But if the accent falls on " . . . noch ein" the God invoked is inscribed in a sequence, and its supplementary, iterative dimension is stressed. There is no measure, no criterion that can exclude such a reading or decide for the one or for the other. In this case, which corresponds to the seventh type of Empsonian ambiguity,[4] the indefinite article "ein"—"a"—defines an alterity that is determined through its position in an iterative series; what is invoked or addressed in this phrase is something that is both familiar and yet impossible to define or delimit. This something has to do with the trajectory traced by the figure of the ellipse, already mentioned, and which provides a kind of emblem for this entire essay.

In suggesting at the outset that the dual meaning of the word "ellipse" has something essential to do with "democracy," Derrida invokes another of his favored phrases: "The ellipse does not simply name a lack. It is also the curved figure with more than one center. We are already between the

134

'minus one' and the 'more than one' (*plus d'un*). Between the 'minus one' and the 'more than one' (*plus d'un*), democracy bears perhaps a certain essential affinity with this turn or this trope . . ." (19 / 1).

The couple of phrases, "*moins un—plus d'un*" traces the ambivalent trajectory of a "democracy" that is both less and more than itself, that turns around the notion of self—ipseity—while exposing if not destroying it in the name of self-protection (autoimmunity). But this vicious circle, which both reveals and dissimulates the exposure of the self to the other, also entails the possibility of an alternative to such self-destruction, but only when this "possibility" is thought together with that which it usually excludes—its impossibility. This "impossibility," Derrida argues, must not be thought as being merely "privative": it entails everything that cannot be planned, projected, and calculated in advance, an openness to that which is to come. And yet, such openness cannot be directed as a future that would exclude the present or be its virtual form. It must be experienced in the form of urgency, as that which "seizes me *here and now,* in a manner that is non virtualizable, in actuality and not in potentiality" (123 / 84). It is this that stamps the phrase "démocratie à venir" as being neither simply "constative" nor simply "performative," but as involving an alternative to their opposition: "The 'to' of 'to come' hesitates between the imperative injunction (appeal to a performative) and the patient *perhaps (peut-être, can be*) of messianicity (non-performative exposure to what comes, to what can always not come or have already come)" (132 / 91).

It is this "non-performative exposure to what comes" but also "to what can always not come or have already come" that leads Derrida to inflect Heidegger's notion of *Retten* in the direction of *Grüßen* as "only another God who alone can still save us." And yet, even when stretched to include salutation and away from salvation, Heidegger's phrase still declares that the greeting must come from "a God" to us. Just how this greeting can be experienced is something that the phrase itself leaves entirely open.

In developing a discourse on "democracy to come" that hesitates between promise and expectation, between injunction and description, Derrida reserves the right, and indeed the necessity, to "withdraw into the secret of an irony, of irony in general or of that figure of rhetoric called irony." But, he adds: "But here is one more turn and it is political: is not democracy also that which gives irony the right to occupy public space? Yes, it opens public space, the publicity of public space, by granting the right to a change of tone (*Wechsel der Töne*), to irony as to fiction, to the simulacrum, to the secret, to literature, etc. And thus, to a certain non-public public within the public . . ." (133 / 92).

The right to a certain irony, which also means to a certain non-public within the public, was demonstrated by the reception of Derrida's text by a portion of his audience, when he first presented it at Cérisy-la-Salle in the summer of 2002. The fact that he organized his concluding remarks around the phrase of Heidegger's we have been discussing, and in particular around three German words—*Retten, Heilen, Grüßen*—shocked many in his audience and provoked an extremely agitated response from certain members of it (those of you here today who were present then will, no doubt, remember the heated discussion that followed this talk). For anyone familiar with Germany, and with the German language as used in the years between 1933 and 1945, the word "Grüß" could hardly be disassociated from what Avital Ronell has aptly labeled its "evil twin"[5]—its use to designate the "Hitlergrüß," the gesture with which his followers greeted Hitler and which wished him well. And, of course, this gesture in turn was inseparable from the word *Heil.* What the shocked protesters in the audience at Cérisy did not realize—did not want to, perhaps, or could not—was that Derrida's entire discourse that day, as well as his writings elsewhere, was an effort to "separate as irreconcilable the notion of *salut* as greeting or salutation—as 'hailing'—of the other from every *salut* as salvation (in the sense of the safe, the immune, health, and security)" (160 / 114)—but also to acknowledge their *irreducible proximity.* It is this proximity, of course, that makes the effort to separate greeting from salvation, *Grüß* from *Heil,* both necessary and extremely difficult. For it cannot simply oppose itself to its other as a new form of salvation. The result is an extremely precarious undertaking— "precarious and questioning," as Ronell puts it (ibid.), the direction of which Derrida spells out thus: "If one holds the greeting or salutation of the other, of what is to come, to be irreducible and heterogeneous to any search of *salut* as salvation, you can guess toward the edges of what sort of abyss we are drawn" (160 / 114).

The effort to insist on the heterogeneity of *salutation* and of *salvation* does not "save" one from the abyss. Rather, it acknowledges the irresistible power that "draws" one toward it. And the English word, "draws," here is something of a euphemism for the French word used by Derrida: *aspirés,* literally: *aspire,* "sucked," but with every breath, as it were. The pull toward the abyss results from the breath of life, from life as "aspiration" that leads us inescapably toward the edge—*vers les parages*—of an abyss that remains nameless.

It is the very namelessness of this abyss—a "*khôra* that *receives* rather than gives" (14 / xiv)—that perhaps generates the attraction, and with it the love of and fascination with certain phrases, and in particular with their ironic dimension that turns halfway against themselves, against what they want to say or seem to want to say. It is this ironic half-turn that we have been retracing in the phrase of Heidegger. It is not necessarily deliberate, and in any case is certainly not explicit. But in its oscillation between two possible *Lesarten*, two possible ways of being read—between that which privileges the "Nur noch . . ." and that which stresses the "noch ein . . ." the phrase of Heidegger suspends its own sententiousness, its own ability to form a coherent sentence with a consistent meaning, and instead begins to oscillate. For it is one thing to announce that salvation can *still* come only from "a God" and quite something else to link it to the recurrence of "still *another* God." And yet, once this alternative appears, and the announcement begins to oscillate between the indefinite uniqueness of only "a God" on the one hand, and the excessive iteration of "yet another God" on the other, the very notion of *Retten* loses its consoling stability and begins to waver—and perhaps also to dance. In any case, to sway in the wind—in that "northeast wind" that is the poet's favorite "because it promises fiery spirit and good voyage to sailors."[6] Even and especially if it is a voyage going nowhere. Like the phrase, "Tout autre est toute autre"—yet another of those that mark Derrida's later texts, which in repeating itself changes its stripes while going nowhere. Or like "a God" that travels between singularity and superfluity, between uniqueness and repetition, and in so doing never stays the same nor becomes entirely different. What is left, perhaps, is the serial ambiguity of a recurrent event that is "plus d'un"—more than one and no longer one—that however calls others to account.

Or, as Derrida puts it as he prepares to present this long essay at the fourth, and last, Cérisy "décade" dedicated to his work, "une fois encore": "Une fois encore, certes, mais pour moi, une fois encore c'est toujours à nouveau, de façon chaque fois toute neuve, une fois encore une première fois. Non pas une seule fois pour toutes mais une fois pour toutes la première fois." [One more time, to be sure, but for me, one more time that is ever anew, in a way that each time is entirely new, once again a first time. Not a single time once and for all, but once and for all, the first time] (19 / 1—my translation—SW).

A phrase is never simply "once and for all," in the sense of being entirely unique. It comes to be recognizable *as a phrase* only through its recurrence. Which is to say, through a certain iterability. And, as Derrida reminds us, referring to Austin, "a word never has meaning: only a phrase has meaning" (105 / 71). The meaning of a phrase thus has to do with the manner in which it has been iterated, but also with the manners in which it can be iterated. There is no time left (today for me) to lay out the various ways in which

Derrida iterates: that is, cites and transforms the meanings attached to the phrases that have marked the word "democracy"—not to indicate the way that these iterations help open that word to what is to come. There is only time, perhaps, to recall a brief remark made shortly after placing his talk at Cérisy-la-Salle under sign of the ellipse. This remark comes after responding to a question of fidelity: "Fidélité à venir, à l'avenir. Est-ce possible?" (Fidelity to come, to the future. Is it possible?) To this question Derrida responds with what he describes as "a sort of oath in the form of an obscure aphorism—still illegible because once again (*une fois de plus*) untranslatable, *in the silent displacement of its syntax and accents*. The oath would say: yes, there is friendship to (be) thought (*oui, il y a de l'amitié à penser)"* (23 / 4).

The enunciation of this phrase, oath, or aphorism, is then turned and rephrased by Derrida, through a "regular displacement of accents on the body in movement, on the animate or animal body of this phrase," in ways that I will have to leave you to read or reread, but which, in the end, through "the displacements of accents" also "displaces the meaning" of the phrase "like the coils or rings (anneaux) of a snake." Having thus transformed his oath into a "snake," Derrida ventures the following remark: "This oath is in danger of resembling a snake. At once, threat and promise, they are a threat and chance not to be missed; for it is not certain that the serpent is simply, as a certain reading of Genesis would have us believe, a figure of the devil, 'along the axis of evil.' *Only a certain poetics can dislodge and deflect* (détourner: turn askance) *a dominant interpretation*—whether of the Bible or of any other canonical text" (23 / 5).

In this sense, no text is more "poetical" than this text of Derrida. Its poetics, however, is one of uncertainty, or rather, one of *indefinite singularity*, which seeks to keep faith with phrases by allowing them to salute the impossible that is not just to come but is coming, here and now.

Afterword: "Go on Now and Greet"—"daselbst"

The remarks above were first presented at a conference on Derrida's "Democracy to Come," held at Cornell University. Avital Ronell was one of the participants. At the conference she gave me an offprint of her recently published PMLA article, "On the Misery of Theory without Poetry: Heidegger's Reading of Hölderlin's 'Andenken.'" In that essay she links the problem of "greeting" (*Grüßen*) with the dubious trend in literary studies over the past decades to ignore the specificity of poetry. That greeting is a problem, indeed a growing problem, has been driven home to me over the past years by a certain tendency to regard it as a superfluous form, an obstacle in the way of getting down to business. The problem becomes immediately conspicuous when one has the possibility of comparing the way in which people make contact in the United States and in Europe—or at least in that part of "old Europe" with which I am fairly familiar (mainly France and Germany). In the latter two countries it is still—and I have to add this qualifier: *noch*—considered an important part of civility to greet people when making contact with them. This is particularly evident with telephone calls, but also to some extent with Internet contact as well: one begins a conversation by wishing the other well, which means to an extent acknowledging the other as someone different from oneself, but also as something other than a strict means to an end (of whatever aim one has in mind). From a strictly utilitarian point of view, this may seem superfluous: you can buy a newspaper or speak to someone on the phone more rapidly, more efficiently, without stopping to greet them. But this is immediately experienced by the other—the old European other, at least—as impolite, not to say as uncivil.

What could this culturally specific but also growing tendency to dispense with salutation, with greetings, have to do with the neglect or devalorization of poetry in literary studies—and not just there? In the words of Colin Powell, responding to critiques of his United Nations presentation justifying the decision to go to war against Iraq, the emphasis today is on "moving forward" and not spending time to "look back." The United States is still—*noch*—(but for how long?) the only country and culture, to my admittedly limited knowledge, in which the phrase "that's history" means it is over and done with, and not worth while remembering or even forgetting.

Poetry does not move forward toward a clear-cut and discernible goal, one that could be separated from the movement in its direction and thus serve as a new and absolutely self-contained starting point. And this, perhaps, is one of the major reasons why a certain valorization of "meaning" associated with "theory"—but by no means limited to it—could have encouraged the trend away from the study of, and above all engagement with, poetry and toward the privileging of certain forms of narrative, which know where they are going and how best to get there.

As Avital Ronell has shown, with, against, and beyond Heidegger's lectures and writings on the subject, Hölderlin's "Andenken" is just such a poem, and indeed a reflection on poetry: "Bound to the impossible task of commemorative retrieval, 'Andenken' persistently reorients the discussion concerning a decisive locality and the placing of the political, blowing apart the premises on which one could build a substantial work or project

139

of asserted nonalienation and secured returns—a political work or project mirroring the narcissistic totality of a state" (31).

Poetry is "bound to the impossible task of commemorative retrieval" precisely insofar as its sequencing is not informed by the grammatical-semantical-teleological logic of narrative progression, of a movement toward a goal that would be self-contained and impervious to time—and to singularity. Poetry—and exemplarily the poems of Hölderlin—call upon themselves to "go and greet"—not necessarily persons, and certainly not "individuals," but things like rivers and gardens, "the beautiful Garonne/ And the gardens of Bourdeaux"—which, however, are anything but merely "natural." Such addressees are as unique and as indefinite as that "God" that Heidegger, read by Derrida, invokes. They are not the stuff of citizenry but of those that the City has rejected and sought to eliminate—"refugees," to use the opposition Ronell borrows from Arendt.

But above all, the Greeting that is Poetry, but that still exists outside and beyond it, however threatened, is as Ronell writes, one that "reorients the discussion concerning a decisive locality and the placing of the political," resituating what has been called the political in respect to localities that have become *indecisive* or undecidable—localized, as Hölderlin localizes the "rivers and gardens" that define the direction of his greeting, and yet undeterminable, if by determination we mean the description of a place that could be identified once and for all. De Man once quoted Goethe criticizing Hölderlin's poetry as not "anschaulich" enough—not sufficiently visualizable, and yet the determination of place is never simply abandoned to abstraction in his verse. The greeting is always destined to go toward a unique place, even if that place remains ultimately *unvorstellbar*, unimaginable, unrepresentable:

Geh aber nun und grüße	[Go on now and greet
Die schöne Garonne,	The beautiful Garonne,
Und die Gärten von Bourdeaux	And the gardens of Bourdeaux
Dort, wo am scharfen Ufer	There, where down the sharp bank
Hingehet der Steg und in den Strom	The path leads on and into the stream
Tief fällt der Bach, darüber aber	Falls deeply the brook, yet over which
Hinschauet ein edel Paar	Surveys a noble pair
Von Eichen und Silberpappeln;	Of oaks and silver poplars;
Noch denkt das mir wohl . . .	Still such thoughts come to me . . .]
("Andenken," v. 5–13)	

It is difficult in a translation to do justice to the use of spatial connotations in Hölderlin's use of words like "Dort," "Hingehet," "darüber," "Hinschauet"—

except to suggest that, as Heidegger emphasizes in *Being and Time,* in German "dort" (there) is not the same as "da," which is also translated as "there," but which can also mean "then" or perhaps: "there . . . and then?" It is precisely in the tension between "dort" and "da" that the trajectory of the poetic greeting emerges: "There" (dort) "where the sharp bank" descends to the river, the visibility and definability of the scene is withdrawn precisely through its description: it is "surveyed" not by human spectators but by a "noble pair" of trees, which do not merely look "over" it but look away past it, "Hinschauet." Wherever the "da" emerges, it is in the sense of that dislocation in which Ronell discerns the challenge to traditional politics, but also to the whole system of values that are associated with its emphasis on the territorially delimitable state—including the values that inform a certain criticism, and indeed, a certain notion of knowledge and of truth.

And indeed, as Ronell has demonstrated, it is the introduction of a uniquely unexpected—at least by a thinker such as Heidegger—figure: "The brown-skinned women" that irrevocably disrupts the effort to assimilate poetry to a certain mode of thinking. For those women remain both uniquely located and uniquely indeterminable, and this feature is condensed in the German word "daselbst":

An Feiertage gehn	[On holidays come and go
Die braunen Frauen daselbst	Brown women there-self
Auf seidnen Boden,	On silken ground
Zur Märzenzeit,	At the time of March,
Wenn gleich ist Nacht und Tag . . .	When night and day are alike . . .]
("Andenken," v. 17–21)	

As Ronell notes, the use of "daselbst" was already in Hölderlin's time considered archaic, and Heidegger also emphasizes its "prosaicness." But it is also worth remarking that the mention of the "brown-skinned women" is through the use of this word both emphatically located—the word usually means "in this very place"—and no less emphatically dislocated. For the "self-same place," the "self" of the "da" is impossible to determine univocally.[7] Neither with respect to the "dark-skinned women" (*braune Frauen*) nor with respect to the place in which they "come and go." The time of year can be precisely described (March-time, when day and night are of equal length, equidistant between the two solstices), but the bottom, the ground—the *Boden*—remains "silken" and therefore perhaps also slippery.

What the greeting recalls, then, is a past that is all the more present for its not being ultimately locatable: a past that was once, and as once, remains . . . for all, and forever open to an uncertain future.

Is it because of the uncertainty of this future, which seems increasingly difficult to bear, that the decline of greeting seems coupled with the ubiquitous, "Have a good day!"
But can the day to come be good without a greeting?

NOTES

1. Perhaps not without a certain affinity to what Heidegger, in his 1942 seminar on Hölderlin's poem, "The Ister," describes as the *Gegenwendigkeit*—the "counterturning"—of the "spirit of the river." It should be noted that "gegen" in German can mean not just "against" but also "toward," and thus describes a complex movement that is irreducible to any unidirectionality.
2. Martin Heidegger, *Beiträge zur Philosophie (Vom Ereignis)* (Frankfurt am Main: V. Klostermann, 1989), GA 65, pp. 411, 416; cited in Jacques Derrida, *La raison du plus fort*, p. 156. English version: p. 111.
3. Avital Ronell has illuminated the motif of Greeting—*Grüßen*—with respect to Heidegger's reading of Hölderlin's poem, "Andenken," in a remarkably suggestive essay: "On the Misery of Theory without Poetry: Heidegger's Reading of Hölderlin's 'Andenken'" (PMLA 2005, 16–32). I will return to some of those suggestions at the end of this paper.
4. William Empson, *Seven Types of Ambiguity* (New York: Vintage Books, 1975).
5. Ronell, "On the Misery . . . ," p. 31.
6. Hölderlin, "Andenken."
7. This holds for the women as well, and if their appearance—"dark-skinned"—raises the question of "gender and race," as Ronell observes, it raises it as a question, not as an answer. For the adjective "braun" in German can apply to sunburned skin as well as to racial characteristics, and this makes it as difficult to appropriate the "dark-skinned women" for a racial problematic as it is to precisely situate them. All of this contributes to the unique indefiniteness that is underscored in the use of the word "daselbst": the "self" of the "da" is singular and finite, but therefore never definitively identifiable.

Shireen R. K. Patell

Learning Impossibility:
Pedagogy, Aporia, Ethics

> Le maître n'est donc pas destiné à aplanir le champ
> des relations, mais à les bouleverser; non pas à faciliter
> les chemins de savoir, mais d'abord à les rendre non
> seulement plus difficiles, mais proprement infrayables.
>
> —MAURICE BLANCHOT, ENTRETIEN INFINI

> It is better to fail in teaching what should not be taught
> than to succeed in teaching what is not true.
>
> —PAUL DE MAN, "THE RESISTANCE TO THEORY"

> How can one thank the beloved teacher?
> (I mean, without bringing a dead mouse
> to the door, as if one were a cat.)
>
> —AVITAL RONELL, THE TEST DRIVE

Can I Read You?

Even if inaudible, this question perhaps attends every textual encounter. Before *May I read you?* or *Do I read you?*, before even *before*, this: Can I read you? For even if I do read you, it is not certain that "I *can* read you"—each term in that locution is pressured, shaken, fissured by the very passage of reading.

And if you were the one who vitally gave me reading, reading as a strange, depropriative task, the question is even more pressing: can I read you? How?

I shall here be direct about the acute scene of writing in which I find myself: How can I read my teacher, my mentor, my friend, Avital Ronell? Marking the particular exquisite difficulty of this writing occasion is just one fine trace of her teaching. To express the impact of her thought, her writing, and her teaching, not just on me but on us, I cannot help but respond to this reading/writing call by submitting to the cognitive limit, reading elsewhere, guided by the pull of that other scene, reading in and as a displacement. She always returns to the pedagogical scene—or maybe "returns" is the wrong word because we have never left it. We are in and of it. Only in a displaced way might "I" read my teacher. And yet, displaced, who are we, I and teacher? Submitting to the impossible as the very response to the granting of responsibility—the articulation of responsibility itself—this is also the mark of being in the pedagogical scene, a strange place, staged over an abyss that terrifies and thrills. Teaching is always addressed, somehow, to the enigma of our survival despite the breakup of ground.

I will try and approach this abyss by attending to Ronell's pedagogical theory and the *other* other economy that subtends it—the ineluctability of a rupture non-Oedipal that accompanies every itinerary of learning, Oedipal or other. This writing will be an entry into the atopical field of "abysstemology" with which Ronell concludes her reading of the Rat Man in "The Sujet Suppositaire." In that essay, devoted to an elaboration of what she calls "Oedipedagogy," Ronell reads the "pedagogical deposit" into the student body: "The 'truth' of such a transmission is measured by the test of alterity which the student body, an excretory installation, produces, or, more properly speaking, in relation to the receptacle through which the teaching subject (who does not know what it knows) attempts to find articulation in the Other."[1] In the Oedipedagogical scene, the aporetic structure of transmission is intensified, and the drama is one of both conveying and covering over gaps in being. Even in the midst of this articulation of Oedipedagogy, however, Ronell implies that the Oedipal economies do not exhaust or saturate the pedagogical field when she specifies a certain *type* of pedagogical scene, "particularly one structured by Oedipal constraints" (*FS*, 109) and thus suggests that not every teaching scene is determined only by Oedipal pathways. She concludes her reading of Rat Man at an abyss of radical doubt "where one simply cannot decide for one semantic field over the other" (*FS*, 126). This undecidability motors the tropological compulsion and "[Rat Man and Freud] produce a desire that is reconstituted as source and origin, surveyed by the control tower that monitors indecision in the face of *some terror.*" It is to this indeterminate terror as the displaced and displacing core of the pedagogical scene to which I will submit this, my reading practice.

I will tend to swerve between teaching and reading, or render them around a slash, marked or not, always to invoke them as a kind of unshakeable couple. Ronell teaches reading, and teaches reading by reading, as if reading and teaching were always being cowritten. Reading the teaching-scene as a revival mise-en-scène of the *Urszene,* Ronell is constantly attentive to the pedagogical encounter as the staging ground of fantasy. Site of transmission, it cannot help but be a transferential switchboard, as she makes clear in *The Telephone Book*.

Reading Ronell, AR, teacher, my teacher, on the scene of teaching, I find myself multiply inscribed in and by this scene. It is not a matter of positioning myself there in a reading/writing abyss—I am there. And being there, I am displaced. The passage through this impossibility is the uptake of a teaching that comes from *elsewhere*. Yet Ronell's readings of the pedagogical scene as a metonym for the *Urszene* trace another type of primary repressed that is absolutely exterior to the libidinal economy, even as an *aneconomic* eruption; the death instinct remains, despite Freud's exquisite rhetorical and theoretical moves, ineluctably bound to the pleasure principle as its transgression and thus ratification.

Ronell gestures to another abyss that yawns "beneath" the fantasy screen that cannot be covered over or contained by any fantasy, but that rends fantasy as such, leaving a scar that marks the spot of an impossible teaching, one that succeeds only if it fails. Reading Ronell reading allows us to begin to understand desire itself as the performative effect of fantasy, and especially the fantasy that the libidinal economy is the upsurge of all figuration; that is, desire, even construed as an object-cause or *objet petit a* might itself be a fantasy of projecting the possibility of there being any kind of object at all, with all of its positioning power. Instead, there may be nothing but sheer objectlessness, which is to say sheer subjectlessness, abyss without predication, displacement without desire. But we are not yet there. Or we are always already there, without place. Without.

I cannot do justice to all of the dangerous, intricate economies involved in trying to read and thus thank the ones who gifted you with the impossibility of reading—the knotted double and triple binds that Jacques Derrida and Avital Ronell trace without untying. But, rehearse them or not, I am haunted by the risks of reading, and I cannot—

She always tells me to just begin. To submit to the odd pull of writing, a pull that comes from somewhere on that *other* scene. To begin, to just begin or justly begin, is always to respond to a certain commandment to "Begin *again*"—to begin with a hat tip to the failure that shadows every task, to the non-origin of writing. There is no proper entry to reading, to reading reading, and so I will plunge into an abyss of reading: the reading of reading and its resistance that heads up *Finitude's Score*, as its introduction, and that perhaps exposes one version of what Ronell elsewhere calls the "pedagogical ordeal."[2]

It is a piano lesson, a scene from Marguerite Duras's *Moderato Cantabile*. The teacher has asked the student the meaning of *moderato cantabile*, the

145

musical notation that heads up his score. "I don't know," responds the student to the rising wrath of the piano teacher. Put on the spot in the abyss of reading, on the receiving end of a demand for meaning, the student is petrified, frozen in resistance. The tension of the piano lesson stages what Ronell calls a "topography of the *meta* [that] dominates the text, pointing constantly to an inscription that would supercede what is presented as readable" (*FS*, 8). This meta effect means that the scene is internally cleaved—both the promise and fatality of meaning dehiscing and deferring in the endless demand that meaning, finally, appear. Calling for the closure of meaning, the demand of the piano teacher plunges the student into the gap that on one register propels the disseminative movement that Derrida refers to as "tropic supplementarity," where reading never meets itself without a resistant excess.[3] Here the student is frozen at the threshold of that dizzying tropological adventure, the clash of sense and reference, caught in the "whirligig" of undecidability, as Paul de Man describes it.[4] The boy is pitched into the hiatus at the far side of the semantic range. Reading Ronell reading a scene of reading, we are doubly mise en abyme, interpellated into reading a scene of reading resistance that is also reading us reading, and thus resisting us. Resistance is not opposed to reading, does not only paralyze it, but propels its interminable paths, always displaced elsewhere. The piano teacher embodying the denial of these abyssal trajectories in and of learning asks the student for the meaning once and for all, and Ronell, aware of the impossibility of this demand, and teaching us about it, cannot help but be both teacher and student in the scene.

Indeed, Ronell emphasizes that in this *Urszene* of reading (resistance), as opposed to the "seated figures [teacher, student, mother who watches the piano lesson], you . . . are mobile; you identify-with each of the three characters in this tensed scene of reading" (*FS*, 7). You, who? Reader? Ronell? Ronell, reproducing through the essential reversals of the shifters, the depropriative effects of writing and reading, of writing about reading? The mobility of the *you* indexes the transit of the signifier, the circulation that produces effects of sense. The circulating identification recalls Jean Laplanche's and Jean-Bertrand Pontalis's specification that the subject of the primal fantasy is actually desubjectivated in the *Urphantasie* and thus not only circulates throughout the scene without fixity but is anamorphed into the very "syntax of the sequence in question."[5] In this way, both the pedagogical scene and the reading encounter as sites of transferential fantasy do not consolidate ego, but instead expose it to expropriation, depropriation, dissemination, and other intensities of undoing. And yet this expropriative effect of reading is in tension with any pedagogical demand for the transmission of mastery, which is the horizon of any teaching.

You are being put through the paces; you must demonstrate mastery; you must master the material, cover it, command it. It is to this tension between the pedagogical demand for transmissibility and the uncertain epistemological object of that pedagogy that Paul de Man points when thinking about the resistance to theory:

> Scholarship has, in principle, to be eminently teachable. . . . As a controlled reflection on the formation of method, theory rightly proves to be entirely compatible with teaching. . . . A question arises only if a tension develops between methods of understanding and the knowledge which those methods allow one to reach. If there is indeed something about literature, as such, which allows for a discrepancy between truth and method, between *Wahrheit* and *Methode,* then scholarship and theory are no longer necessarily compatible; as a first casualty of this complication, the notion of "literature as such" as well as the clear distinction between history and interpretation can no longer be taken for granted.[6]

De Man identifies an epistemological abyss that yawns open when one carefully analyzes the linguistic patterning of any text, a cleavage that makes truth and method diverge. The non-coincidence of grammar and rhetoric both propels the sublating force of theory and pierces the promise (or fantasy) of totalization that it drives. It is precisely this internal fatality that de Man names "the resistance to theory," a resistance concurrently salutary and defeating, and thus the resistance of undecidability itself: "Nothing can overcome the resistance to theory since theory *is* itself this resistance . . . it cannot help but flourish, and the more it is resisted the more it flourishes, since the language it speaks is the language of self-resistance. What remains impossible to decide is whether this flourishing is a triumph, or a fall" (*RT,* 4). In this way, the success of theory is predicated on its inexorable failure, and indeed de Man's text is an artifact of "failure," a failed assignment to write an essay on literary theory for a pedagogical volume entitled *Introduction to Scholarship in Modern Language and Literature.* De Man immediately discovered that the main interest of literary theory was the impossibility of its definition, and his text was declined when it was decided by the committee that this impossibility was at odds with "the pedagogical objectives of the volume."

This failed assignment of de Man's begs the question of the contingency of impossibility when it comes to the pedagogical goal—is this impossibility that de Man locates when it comes to formalizing the claims of literary theory, a contingent feature unworthy of attention, or is it enfolded into the scene of every literary teaching as its very chance and risk? Though de Man and Ronell seem to be neighbors at the edge of an epistemological abyss, a transferential gulf separates their reading practices and styles. Whereas Ronell continually marks the transferential staging that marks the teaching scene, de Man dismisses all such transferential circuits with not a small trace of disdain: "Overfacile opinion notwithstanding, teaching is not primarily an intersubjective relationship between people but a cognitive process in which self and other are only tangentially and contiguously involved. The only teaching worthy of the name is scholarly, not personal; analogies between teaching and various aspects of show business or guidance counseling are more often than not excuses for having abdicated the task" (*RT,* 4). To be sure, this passage may also be read against the grain as confirming the psychoanalytic understanding of the tropological construction of the subject and object of knowledge. In this estimation of the object of teaching, however, de Man curiously reinstalls the objectivity or autonomy of the pedagogical referent by means of marginalizing all bodies and contingencies at the very moment that he is also going to espy the aporetic wedge between *Wahrheit* and *Methode* when it comes to teaching theory. Indeed the embodied beings stand in the place of contingency itself—("self and other are only tangentially and contiguously involved"), both of these adverbs themselves signifiers of touching, the very touching of bodies that is rendered secondary if not inessential to the pedagogical task, as if the signifier itself and the upheavals of its strange ontology were not body too, entering in our bodies and producing effects. Focusing on the "cognitive processes," de Man eliminates transference and performative force (teaching is *not* a performance, some kind of "show business") from the scene of teaching. Yet this divestiture of body and return to "cognitive processes" may itself be an effect of the phallus that de Man deflates. The bracketing of bodies, transference, and performance may actually be in the service of erecting the kind of disembodied truth that marks the allure of the *sujet supposé savoir.* Waving off transference, de Man invites it and, denying the transferential allure of the pedagogical scene, de Man perhaps articulates a fantasy of non-transference, a fantasy of non-fantasy, thus engaging the transferential circuitry by denying it. At the very moment where truth and method diverge, his reaffirmation of the impersonal character of scholarship marks a fantasy of non-fantasy and thus engages the transferential circuitry it denies. We are at the tropological edge of the libidinal economy.

It is the teaching of literary theory that reveals the aporetic encounter of truth and method and introduces the success of failure, the noncontemporaneous articulation of truth and pedagogical success, a glitch in the transmission system; literary theory instantiates an interruption of pedagogy as pedagogy. De Man produces a near aphorism at this disjuncture: "It is better to fail in teaching what should not be taught than to succeed in teaching what is not true." The professor of literary theory, or what de Man would simply call *reading*, cannot help but fail and thus succeed. Yet, for de Man, the abyss at the heart of teaching is a linguistic effect that does not redound to the tropological economies of the unconscious but to the divergence of syntax and semantics, of grammar and rhetoric. Despite this epistemological upheaval, however, in de Man's quasi-aphorism, what is true—however negative—still wins the day and literally has the last word.

When it comes to teaching reading and all of the aporetic tensions that attend it, it is precisely the rigorous impossibility of a smooth transmission that Ronell reads for us, what she calls "the non-purity of the reading scene," the fact that it is always interrupted, subject to static, intrusion, and other interference (*FS*, 14). For Ronell, the teaching reading scene and its interrupted transmission is the mise-en-scène of both a transferential network *and* the exquisite linguistic effects of rhetoric's and grammar's divergence, both of which provoke a groundless responsibility that is the tracing of an ethical impulse catalyzed by the confrontation with alterity. As Ronell writes of the boy in the piano lesson, asked to read his *Spaltung*, he is assigned an impossible task: "Read your part, your share, that part of you which can be 'yours' only in the vertiginous movement of depropriation to which you submit by what we call reading. . . . In the familiar unfamiliarity of this place where you will find yourself, read your part, *do* your share" (*FS*, 9). The boy, still reading only literally, can experience this demand to take on his share only as a standstill. Later, we will see how the maternal margins take up the child's traumatizing charge. For now, we are in the hiatus of an impossible demand to read.

While the scene can only frustrate the piano teacher, the interrupted conveyance signaled by this aporia as a positive impossibility is, in fact, the very matter of teaching reading. I might have said "theory" in the place of "teaching reading," for, in many ways, Ronell's text and thought demonstrate that "doing theory" is literary reading without apology or epistemological security (clearance). Ronell, always operating a switchboard, works at the edges of the cognitive limit, circuiting the transferential flows and setting the stage for the impossible passage that is teaching. Not retreating from the abysses in and of teaching reading, Ronell's thought allows the convocation of different thinkers around these aporetic interruptions of finitude's score and allows their differences to be thought together. For Ronell, the pedagogical scene activates the transferential network and excites a vigilance that, following Emmanuel Lévinas, is "not a hypertrophy of consciousness," but a submission to the desubjectivation provoked by the demand for meaning.[7] For psychoanalysis this desubjectivation dialectically prepares the libidinal economy, whereas for Lévinas it hails the ethical responsibility of the one-to-come, that is you, me. De Man, for his part, might read these names—fantasy, ethics—as articulations of the power of representation or (dis)figuration to cover over the very gap between rhetoric and grammar that skews every representation. Ronell's work suggests that the putative gaps between different lines of thought are an effect of "finitude's score" and that the *palimpsest* of traces approaching the abysses that catachrestically subtend our language and being is precisely what articulates the ethical responsibility of the one depropriated, desubjectivated, exposed by the uncanny experience of reading.

Ronell explicitly calls attention to our multiple embeddedness in the scene of teaching reading and plays on the deforming anamorphosis of desubjectivation when she recalls you to the *Urszene*, the primal scene of reading, "you who have been both the victim and the transmitter of this exhortation to produce a meaningful title" (*FS*, 7). When Ronell hails "you," she thus summons not the specificity of a one—the particularity of a "reader"—but the multitude that inscribes *you* as the impossibility of being-just-one. And this you is also she, for through the *you* transits what Derrida calls the *destinerrance* of address. The shifters' reversals are not scripted only by the syntax spanning and constituting the difference between *I* and *you*, a difference that Derrida would understand as the tracing of the same and the passage of *différance*; the anarchic architecture of alterity is already within each position as a more radical difference than the thematic alternation of the *I* and *you* as grammatical shifters could ever bear.

In Ronell's text, the *you* undergoes the trial of reading to which the piano student is submitted intradiegetically, a trial that reveals that "reading is never done alone or for oneself alone; even if the father is absent from the scene, or displaced to the phallic teacher, he seems to make his way back." Here, Ronell suggests that there is no space beyond the *nom-du-père*. Shadowing the scene of every reading, every teaching, throbbing even through the resistance, is the law of the father that compels and paralyzes the subject. Can the rupture inscribed in the scene of learning ever be other than a parricidal fantasy, even if on one economic track that rupture inevitability submits to the conciliatory violence of the castration narrative? Is there another beyond the pedagogical-pleasure-principle that articulates not only the "non-erotic aggressivity"[8] of the death instinct but also the upsurge of ethical responsibility from the outside that Lévinas names true teaching? In that aporetic encounter, teaching takes place as the granting of an unbearable responsibility for the singularity of the other and the unsubstitutability of the other's death.

It is to this kind of non-maieutic pedagogical practice that Ronell points in the preface to her book on Goethe and Eckermann, *Dictations: On Haunted Writing.* Thinking about conversation as teaching and teaching as conversation, she explores the splitting, multiplication, and incalculable reversals of the shifters, the disruption of the *you* and *I* in conversation:

> The fundamental dissymmetry governing Conversation, the distance at the origin and the rule of non-requital—these are so many markers of the condition of separation that keeps it going. . . . Conversation is not that which fuses you to me; but the experience of Conversation induces, once again, the vertigo of expropriation. It is not only the case that I am not identical to myself when I begin to converse with you, but more severely, perhaps: you are no longer the one that I have interiorized or memorized. Breaking the secret contract that sealed you within me, you, in Conversation, are no longer you, or the you at least of whom I have preserved the image. No longer the selfsame, you only correspond to yourself when I respond to you. Something else occurs between us, and I cannot say it is altogether you, it's not you and me but something else still.[9]

Conversation does not gather together in a shared space of relation two who remain two; instead the conversation spans without bridging the interval that is the disjunction not only between me and you, but *in* me and you. The radical asymmetry of conversation, an unsurpassable non-contemporaneousness, is perhaps rendered even more acute in the pedagogical scene, where a representational hierarchy is also thematically and overtly present and determinative of various transferential and other material economies.

Lévinas deliberately overlaps teaching and conversation, and Ronell's text welcomes and takes in a passage from his *Totality and Infinity:*

> To approach the Other in conversation is . . . therefore to *receive* from the Other beyond the capacity of the I, which means exactly to have an idea of infinity. But this also means: to be taught. The relation with the Other, or Conversation [*entretien*], is a non-allergic relation, an ethical relation; but inasmuch as it is welcomed this conversation is a teaching [*enseignement*]. Teaching is not reducible to maieutics; it comes from the exterior and brings me more that I can contain. In its nonviolent transitivity the very epiphany of the face is produced. (Lévinas quoted in *D*, xiii)

Retracing Descartes' "Third Meditation" and the proof of God that hinges on the idea of infinity, Lévinas imagines conversation as the staging of a nonmediating pedagogy, as an interruption that imparts a lesson from elsewhere—the introduction from the exteriority of an unknown and unknowable proximity to the other as infinity. Anti-Platonic in its understanding of the teaching scene as one not staked on the incremental birthing of an internal if forgotten knowledge, Lévinas imagines this cleave in the subject of knowledge as the very upsurge of ethical responsibility for the other. Expropriated by the proximity of the other's infinite alterity, the I is both exploded and oriented by this impossible demand. Yet, in *Totality and Infinity,* the interruptive force of this teaching is still imagined as the possibility of bypassing violence, as a pacific alternative to the violence of representational language; the face captures that nonviolent possibility. By the time that Lévinas elaborates an "otherwise than being," the ethical experience is characterized by persecution, trauma, psychosis, Derridean "non-synonymous substitutions" for what Lévinas calls "une bonne violence"—a good violence (*OB*, 43). In *Totality and Infinity,* the non-phenomenological status of the face renders it the site of interruption in the differential system of signs, provoking signification, but resisting it. It is this threshold position of the face at the edge of language that grants it the possibility of a non-violence. On the edge of language the face is produced in teaching as teaching, the articulation of a "non-violent transitivity." For Lévinas, "the notion of act invokes a violence essentially: the violence of transitivity, lacking in the transcendence of thought."[10] The relationship with the absolutely other as teaching produces a non-violent transitivity that flashes the epiphany of the face without the stabilization of thematic content, and indicates the responsibility called forth in the vocative dimension of language. For Lévinas, the face does not always coincide with itself in language, but marks a place of rupture in language, of language as rupture, and it is this rupturing of language as the very condition of responsibility that Ronell tracks with unflagging rigor.

Does the piano lesson play a kind of Lévinasian encounter with the face? Piano teacher keeps time for the scene of representation and the law, but the demand to read triggers a freeze frame of resistance as the little boy is confronted by an absolute alterity in the form of an unreadable text; Ronell zooms in: "There is the immobility of the child faced with the score." This allegorical face-to-face propels an emergency scene for semantic consolidation, forces the one called upon to read into a crisis of reference. This crisis upends the very possibility of literary criticism or reading, which proceeds by a kind of similitude or transitivity, even if practiced as a compare and contrast. Reading unravels methodology into disposition, both as an inclination and a transference of power to the text being read in its alterity, as an alterity. Reading, far from taking us to any unified understanding, wanders, errs perpetually; reading unravels—is always accompanied by an unreading, a *délire,* its own undoing, in the sense of a perpetual dismantling. As Ronell writes: "Reading produces an interruption of relation to self, partitioning the one who reads, breaking the specular reflection of any reading" (*FS,* 14). *Délire* is not just an unreading, but a madness. And this moment of unreading madness is built into the scene of teaching reading as its very condition of (im)possibility.

The metronome in the piano lesson still tocks incessantly in the background, cutting time into reliable units that are to meter sense. Let us return to that lesson, and watch for the madness of reading. The student has been tensed in resistance, unable to respond to the teacher's demand for meaning. Clocking time and waiting, teacher and metronome span open the time of measure and meaning, hold open the promise of the semantic register, the representational grid. We will see how that *other* scene interrupts in the form of a piercing scream from the street, from the outside, just as the reading one—the student—encounters its split, its morcelating mobility and perverse multiplication, its precarious location in any present scene.

The multiple destabilizations and deformalizations of the reading one reveal both the chance and the violence of reading (resistance). The disseminative "structure" of the one who reads reveals an openness to inscription as the very possibility of learning, but also to inscription as the mark of ultimate unreadability with the traumatic effects of this epistemological blow. Beyond whatever effects of signification are conveyed, the impossible lesson of teaching reading is the ineluctable encounter with interruption, impasse, aporia, non-recuperation, the interruption of sense, and non-closural finitude as the very condition of any transmission. As Ronell writes, casting a backward and forward glance on her pedagogical inscriptions: "Teaching (how to read) remains elusive and blinding as it remains the promise of future illumination. But it is a future that will never have completed its task in the present" (*FS,* 6–7). Without this exposure to the impossibility of having taught reading or of having learned it "properly," there would be no teaching or learning at all, for rote memorization, or hewing to a prior narrative, regurgitating the internalized dictates of law, does not strengthen and reinforce the law but reveals a fatality in the law (of reading) itself. If the law can only force automatic repetition and slavish semantic reproduction, then its truth is reduced to habit, a mere norm inculcated, revealing the abyssal construction of the law's authority itself. For the law of reading to have been internalized properly, there has to be the possibility of a misreading, or a resistant reading, and yet this aleatory quality inscribed in the uptake of law's lesson also means that the lesson, even when successful, perhaps especially when successful, can backfire on the law.

For Ronell, the abyssal aspect of law comes through as a law (of reading) that dictates nothing, but commands nonetheless. Its very emptiness grants it a kind of a power, because it is the projection site for transference and fantasy. It pulses an exigency without content or form, signaling its demand without any authority save for the obedience of the response it commands and the perpetual repetition of its own form, that is, emptiness. Law's relentlessness produces effects of authority precisely by covering over this internal emptiness, for "as law, it emits nothing more than a signal; it shows the way in which the score *should* be read. The interpretation of the score would be left to the reader" (*FS*, 7). This strange hetero-autonomy of the reader signals the law's aporetic sovereignty, one that is both veiled and revealed by the resistance of reading itself. This resistance is, perhaps, an index of the perceived inscrutable sovereignty of the demand to read, as if the law could indeed compel the correct reading, the ultimate one, the right answer; at the same time, we cannot be assured that resistance is external to the law's field, and not already of it. It is undecidable whether the resistance of reading confirms or contests the force of law's authority.

Even resisting the law of reading, the piano student seems to curve to its appeal nonetheless, articulating its ungrounded force of authority in the very petrification of the traumatic instant. Whether reading or resisting reading, you are under the implacable sway of the empty law of reading that demands sense, even as it exposes its failure. The aporetic structure of reading's demand—read what you cannot read—is a repetition of the aporetic structure in the law itself. What is staged in the scene of reading the score is the impossible confrontation with the one-who-read's *Spaltung*. This abyssal staging, however, also threatens the representative of the law—the piano teacher. Teacher stifles a cry of exasperation, which, Ronell emphasizes, is a non-semantic indication of "the hidden experience of impotence. . . . The teacher recognized in the performance of pedagogy her end of the line too" (*FS*, 10). Because the pedagogical scene is also the mimetic staging ground of the teacher's, and thereby the law's authority, a crisis in reference threatens to spark the powering down of law.

The piano teacher's weakness erupts eventually as a rage. Ronell reads the violence precipitated by her palpable weakness, this concomitance of violence and vulnerability in the law. At first, Ronell notes, the piano teacher's phallic rectitude maintains composure: "the teacher, possibly a writer, occupies in this scene the provocative place of the paternal metaphor, teaching law by disciplining the child, threatening him, punctuating the little boy's reply with the metonymy of beating time" (*FS*, 10). The law's violence, however, sublimated into all the forms of discipline, suggests that, between the boy and teacher, it may be the boy who is the stronger reader, the one who has internalized the "truth" of the law, the emptiness of the law's demand for meaning: "The demonstration of the imperative to read shows the strongest figure, backed by institution and tradition, to be the more impressionistic and thematic reader, weak though capable of flexing the muscle of received meaning" (*FS*, 10). The representational teacher fails the test of rigorous reading, a failure that the sedimentation of meaning attempts to hide through the flexing of officially sanctioned violence—discipline.

The boy's withholding, his non-response in the hiatus, demonstrates the impossible lesson of reading as the impossibility of absolute semantic security. The resistant boy as disarticulating limit to the infinite extension of the semantic field does not figure a new mastery—mastery of the unmasterable—but arises as a response to the excessive nature of the law itself and its demand. The law attempts to smother the madness and perversity within it by continually clamping down on such *elsewhere,* as if its obsession with the "perverse" and its madness for sense were not a sign of its own perversion and madness.

The little boy is frozen by this secret knowledge of the law's perversity, nonplussed by the promiscuity of the law's demand: "His malaise is traced not so much to the conviction that what he is doing has no meaning as to the immoderateness of her demand for meaning" (*FS*, 10). Although measuring the beats and clocking the response time, the law itself is without measure. The non-response of the boy constitutes a kind of civic disobedience and sends the law into a frenzy: "The child decided not to answer. The lady looked again at the object before her, her rage mounting. . . . 'You're going to say it this minute,' the lady shouted. The child showed no surprise. He still didn't reply. Then the lady struck the keyboard a third time, so hard that the pencil broke." Ronell analyzes the narcissistic crisis for the law that is precipitated by the young boy's refusal to respond; the non-response mirrors the law's weakness, signaling "the impotence of the phallic function to teach meaning or stimulate memory." Revealing the impotence of the phallic function, however, the non-response mirrors the law's weakness only by shattering the very possibility of mimetic reflection. Indeed the shattering of the mimetic possibility of meaning is what is implicated in the traumatic demand to read your score, a demand that breaks the specular circuitry of self-gathering, or reveals the gathering of self-consciousness to be but a mirror screen laid over the *Spaltung* that divides the illusory *res cogitans* from the *res cogitatum,* and cleaves the smooth constitution of both.

The resistant reader, deer in the headlights of the law's demand, is articulating the demands from that other scene, is somehow sounding out the claims of finitude's score precisely by remaining mute on the meaning of the phrase *moderato cantabile.* As if staking a claim for the right to privacy, the boy refuses to speak, but in so doing, he is silently responding to "the question which will resonate from the field of another scene, an exteriority beyond appropriation, [which] concerns the story of human finitude" (*FS,* 10). And this story, precisely, touches upon the immoderateness of finitude itself, the fact of its "*excessive* nature, not only because of the inappropriability of its meaning (human finitude: *factum est*) but, as the experience of sheer exposition, because of the way it refuses to disclose itself fully" (*FS,* 5–6). The excessive nature of finitude, its resistance to semantic appropriation, is at the heart of the pedagogical scene, but must be kept at a distance by the long arm of the law of reading. When confronted with the lesson of finitude's score sealed in the boy's refusal to speak, the law breaks down and devolves to the violence that always ultimately subtends it. Ronell's analysis of the law of reading, however, suggests that the empty law that dictates without particular content also catalyzes the musculature of what we might call the law of representational or mimetic reading. The law as representation, however, with its semantic promises is itself a fantasy stretched over an abyss that structures and destructures law.

It is not clear, however, that the piano teacher is the only teacher in the scene, for there emerges another one in the margins of the law's failure, who imparts the lesson that cannot simply be imparted, the very lesson of finitude's score: Anne Desbaresdes, the mother of our stricken piano student. And indeed, if the pedagogical *Urszene* is one of desubjectivation and expropriation, then it is not surprising that the teaching function should itself be split, mobile, multiple. The mother, Anne Desbaresdes, taps into an other scene of pedagogy that she holds open, displacing the mimetic circuitry of mastery demanded by teacher; Ronell reads the mother's complicity with the boy's refusal to respond, emphasizing that "it is her task to telepathize with her son, transmitting secrets of another more remote and less literal reading" (*FS,* 11). Anne Desbaresdes picks up the circuit of her son's traumatic encounter with his score. In this *Urszene,* where father is displaced by a demanding piano teacher and mother is already identifying with son rather than the phallic substitute, we find ourselves in a surprisingly non-Oedipal staging of the confrontation with the threat of castration, a threat that fails to discipline and instead backfires on the law. Cabled to son in the abyss of non-knowledge, "Anne Desbaresdes, unable to teach anything but bound by the desire to know, fixes a limit of pedagogy which will prove to have opened another type of research facility." Here, at the limit of the pedagogical scene, revealing the law's inability to totalize itself, we can see Ronell too, always at the frame and never fully embedded in the reassuring fantasies of simple transmissibility.

The son has been charged, imparted with the task of reading his part, doing his part. Frozen in the shattered mirror stage, among the shards of mimetic security, the son's traumatic learning instant returns as a piercing scream from outside, a sonic intrusion that spins the wheel of shifting identifications, and puts Anne Desbaresdes in her son's position, in your position, in my position, but always differently. She cannot decline the call from elsewhere that charges her with a reading responsibility, to read for a meaning that she already knows cannot arrive as such: "There was the traumatic call from elsewhere that did and did not target you. In any case, you were always charged with figuring out the meaning" (*FS*, 12). The murder on the street below arrives into the piano lesson as a scream that signals an event, the ultimate content and meaning of which will never be known. It sweeps up Anne Desbaresdes in the transferential and disseminative drifts that pass through the pedagogical scene as its staging ground and it pitches her into a confrontation with the death of the other, with the absolute alterity that according to Lévinas pulls us into the ethical tension of a hyperbolic responsibility.

The piercing scream slashes open the space of the piano lesson with a "story that erupts, as a primal scene, into the room to create a tear in the fabric of a primal, if primitive scene of reading. Anne knows only the death of the other with whom she comes nonetheless to identify—the death of the other to whom I am exposed" (*FS*, 12). Thus the primal scene itself splits open, dehiscing, recursively, regressively, revealing no origin, but always a displacement elsewhere. You will have noticed already that in Ronell's syntax, at the moment of the identification, there is an em-dash that thwarts the identification by keeping it mobile, repeating the phrase as an anacoluthon and shifting to the shifter, the *I* that cannot constitute itself as such, the I as a dash and a crash into the hall of mirrors of any would-be mimesis.

Reading the *Urszene* of reading as the staging of the law's power and its displaced and displacing need for mimetic responses, Ronell is vigilant about specifying that tensed in any pedagogy—whether the representational practice demanding stable meaning in the piano lesson, or the exquisite trajectories of non-knowledge traced in the koan—is a violence ineluctable. Attempting to erase it or ignore it only ensures that it will gather force and magnitude and appear elsewhere. The koan will expose the violence that attends the uptake of a lesson from elsewhere that does not consolidate subjectivity but swerves from it: "The Zen pupil looks inwardly, but this is not the same as a subjectivity: the pupil is led to an inner experience without interiority, to understanding without cognition, without a history" (*TD*, 114). This nonsubjective inwardness is the *différance* of the shored-up self-consciousness of a metaphysical subject, that forerunner of the student going through the paces in the university. The painful contemplation of the koan "exceeds the experience of reading—if such an untroped domain can be understood to take hold. The body that has submitted itself to the task of answering gets hit" (*TD*, 121). The epistemological blow of the koan is accompanied by a corporal blow. The violence of the koan teaching pitches the Zen pupil into a zone of non-cognition, beyond reading. Is this the same syncope or rift in being in which our piano student will find himself caught, thrown beyond reading in the midst of its impossible demands? Like the piano student, the student of the koan finds herself lurched into a nonrepresentational zone where "there will be no movement of the reflective gaze that can put together or ensure the *composure* of the one who is made to read the score. No ideology of gathering or self-recollection where reading would mean looking past language" (*FS*, 10). This aporetic experience of learning to read means that whatever the transits of pedagogy, they do not happen without a certain measure of violence, a violence that cannot be erased from the scene but can only be anamorphed into various positions in its staging.

Not shying from the S/M frame and traumatic structure of the pedagogical scene, Ronell explains: "The scene of the piano lesson, moored in the customary regulations that have required the pupil to leave home, amasses the sadomasochistic edges of learning, exposing the piano student to a moment of ontological syncope, a between-time nowhere, opening another way of transposing 'finitude's score'" (*FS*, 8). The scene of the piano lesson, staked on the piano teacher's unquestioning assumption of the transmissibility and reproduction of knowledge and meaning, reveals the pedagogical violence all the more violent because unacknowledged and desperately attempting to mute "finitude's score." For Ronell, the figure of the child itself marks "the anguish of the *différend* . . . where speech falters and language chokes in the throat of a political body, where the questions of fair representation is peremptorily dismissed or not addressed at all."[11] She emphasizes that this condition—what Lévinas characterizes as ethical "persecution . . . the precise moment when one . . . is touched without the mediation of logos"—is not confined to chronological childhood.[12] The child, unable to consent, finds himself in a "pedagogical torture scene" that goes so far as to undo the mutually representational structure of sadomasochism as contract (at least graduate students have submitted themselves willingly to the structures of pedagogical authority, and think they know to what it is they are submitting).

Importantly, for Ronell, the rupture in the piano lesson, although it may be a reaction to the law's perversity, is not strictly an Oedipal rupture but an "ontological syncope" or hiatus that terrifies. For the Zen pupil, the uptake of mastery does not trace parricidal path: "The experience of enlightenment has little (nothing) to do with self, with triumphal narratives of self-gathering or with the bloated accomplishments of successive sieges of alien territory" (*FS* 121). This non-triumphal mastery, unlike the victories of those whom Ronell elsewhere calls metaphysical action heroes, succeeds "without *stealing* that place for himself according to the precepts of a familiar parricidal approval." We might think of the ontological syncope that allows for non-triumphal mastery as a rift in being from the "point of view" of the desubjectivated locus of learning. Put on the spot, the student is shuttled to the horror of being without representation, without recourse to sense, without the ground of knowledge; but this abyssal encounter may well be the attunement to finitude's score.

The temporal breach of the hiatus, however, also indicates what Lévinas calls the *il y a,* sheer existence without extension that precedes the hypostasis of any beings; it is the irremissibility of being itself. The traumatic reminder of the *il y a* is not of a psychoanalytic nature, according to Lévinas, for the *il y a* is an "impersonality that is completely the contrary of the unconscious. This impersonality concerns the absence of a master, it concerns being without a being."[13] On Lévinas's reading, even the unbounded and unknowable unconscious participates in the establishment of the mastery of ego. Ronell's complex treatment of the pedagogical scene, however, allows us to understand how the unconscious and the *il y a* might somehow, even if aporetically or abyssally, encounter one another.

Against the backdrop of the *il y a*'s sheer horror, Lévinas will eventually analyze the synchronicity or synchronous temporality (both comforting and threatening) of the "totality"—the realm of representation and thematizing consciousness in which we most often daily live. The yawning *il y a* is thus covered over by the synchronous time of representation. Frozen in the *Urszene* of reading, the little boy in the piano lesson perhaps glimpses the temporal hiatus of the *il y a* and is exposed to the ontological violence that preconditions every figure, representation, discourse, and fantasy as the unknowable core of existence—or is this syncope the very upsurge of ethical responsibility, the asignificatory sign of having learned an intransmissable, non-maieutic lesson?

In the syncope to which the nonresponding little boy is consigned by the breakdown of law, do we glimpse the *il y a;* the diachrony of another responsibility that supercedes the law's demand; or both? The traumatic syncope seems to be the opening of both the relentlessness of being's impersonality—the abyssal *il y a*—and the diachronic, interruptive ethical upsurge that is the exception to this neutral and neutralizing totality. This contemporaneousness of two disjunctive registers may well have something to do with the pedagogical scene as the staging ground of fantasy. As Laplanche and Pontalis remind us concerning fantasy: "Freud even considers fantasy as the privileged point where one may catch in the raw the process of transition from one system to another, repression, or the return of the repressed material."[14] In this way, the pedagogical scene, with all of its transferential circuitry, is another mise-en-scène of desire, where we may catch a glimpse of the conversion from one system to another, even if these grids be in a differential, aporetic, or disjunctive relation—the impossible conversion of the *il y a* into both representation and ethical interruption, for example.

What psychoanalysis discerns as the staging ground of fantasy, a screen stretched over an abyss as a site of translation, de Man essentially understands as the targeted confusion of ideology. The rift in being might be an exploitable effect of language or the failure of reference. Where Freud might locate the economics of the pleasure principle, de Man reads the ideological confusion of two distinct orders, and he comes to this definition of ideology precisely when trying to stabilize the difference between two materialities, that of the signifier and that of the phenomenon, "the materiality of the signifier" versus "the materiality of what it signifies" (*RT,* 11). De Man argues that this distinction is easy enough to maintain the closer one is to phenomenal materiality, but that the distinction soon blurs as one moves up the metaphysical food chain toward the ideal: "No one will try to grow grapes by the luminosity of the word 'day,' but it is very difficult not to conceive the pattern of one's past and one's future existence as in accordance with temporal and spatial schemes that belong to fictional narratives. This does not mean that fictional narratives are not part of the world and reality; their impact may well be all too strong for comfort. What we call ideology is precisely the confusion of linguistic with natural reality, of reference with phenomenalism" (*RT,* 11). De Man's insistence on the gap between reference and phenomenalism underscores the pedagogical import of the impossible teaching of the "linguistics of literariness" for it becomes "a powerful and indispensable tool in the un-masking of aberrations, as well as the determining factor in accounting for their occurrence." Deformalist reading practices partially resist ideological recuperations by revealing the rhetorical effects by which ideology persists. There is no true mastery, however, when it comes to the linguistics of literariness, and the internalization of rhetoric's epistemological upsets does not ensure that readers can except themselves from the confusion of ideology, because the very rhetorical dynamics that would clear up the confusion also cause it.

The piano student and his mother, Anne Desbaresdes, perhaps anarcho–de Manians, register this double bind, the recursive figuration of meaning and its underlying insubstantiality, otherwise. Always cabling the other scene, Ronell's analysis of the ectopian eruption of a traumatic knowledge—the murder on the street and the piercing scream that breaks (it) into the frozen space of the piano lesson—exposes the meaninglessness that haunts every lesson as an embedded violence that resists and invites symbolization at once; the "ectopian drama . . . signal[s] the meaning of violence which, precisely, is to have no meaning, to exceed our grasp, or to mark the absolute scandal of death, though it can be followed in certain cases by the symbolicity that grants it a veil of meaning and the stability of ritual" (*FS*, 14). This non-dialectical alternation of abyss and symbolicity is also traced in Lévinas's understanding of how the ethical subject is uprooted from the *il y a*, an uprooting that begins as a syntactic operation (what he calls hypostasis or the becoming substantive) that is more than linguistic or metaphorical—it brings the subject into being: "The hypostasis, the appearance of the substantive is not only the appearance of a new grammatical category, it signifies the suspension of the *il y a* anonyme, the appearance of a private domain, a name, a noun . . ." (*EE*, 141). This hypostasis emerges as the appearance of a mastery over being (an appearance de Man might read as sheer rhetorical or ideological effect, a linguistic operation disguised as an ontological movement): "The existent, that which is, is the subject of the verb to be and thereby exercises a mastery over the fatality of being now become the subject's attribute." And yet, just behind or below these representational possibilities "yawn[s] the chaos . . . the abyss, the absence of place, the *il y a*" (*EE*, 121). Thus the abyss simultaneously stimulates representation and haunts it as its own impossibility. Literature both takes us to the edge of this abyss and reeconomizes it or reintegrates it as a principle of negativity that allows for regathering. Harassed by the *il y a*, the literary text courts it, even yearns for it, and keeps it at bay. Throughout her work, Ronell is attuned to the caesuric rhythms that choreograph literature, reading, and finally the impossibility of literature or reading simply disclosing what they know.

Ronell's pedagogical theory traced in the atopical field of "abysstemology" operates a palimpsest around the impossibility that animates Lévinasian ethics, the psychoanalytic understanding of fantasy, and the de Manian reading of the linguistics of literariness, a palimpsest that brings together all of these reading possibilities without harmonizing them, brings them together and keeps them apart. Working the interruptions, gaps, traumatic intrusions, aporia, and other syncopes, Ronell's text takes calls from the unconscious, the undecidable, and the otherwise-than-being without according any of them absolute priority or right of first refusal, and this disposition provides the alternative energy for the illocutionary and ethical force of her "abysstemology."

Ronell's work situates her there where Derrida finds the "university's unconditional principle of resistance"—where unconditional theorization "itself will always suppose a performative profession of faith, a belief, a decision, a public engagement, an ethico-political responsibility."[15] The abyssal resistance that Derrida locates in the *université sans condition,* the one to-come, is toggled to the illocutionary aetiology of a postfoundational responsibility. It is this abyssal resistance to which Ronell scrupulously attends in her writing, in her teaching, in her work. Or, I might say, she is always already in the *"université sans condition,"* the one à *venir;* her teaching scores the representational time that fantasmatically makes the university a uni, a one, just as it does the "subject." There, in the *"université sans condition"* the lesson of finitude's score leaves the subject undone, transmitting a knowledge unsharable and always propelling a reading elsewhere—today, tomorrow and tomorrow, and to-come.

Reading terminable, interminable: thus do I think and thank my teacher, my mentor, my friend, Avital.

NOTES

1.   Avital Ronell, *Finitude's Score* (Lincoln: University of Nebraska Press, 1998), 106. Henceforth *FS,* with page references in the text.
2.   Avital Ronell, *The Test Drive* (Champaign: University of Illinois Press, 2007), 279. Henceforth *TD,* with page references in the text.
3.   Jacques Derrida, "White Mythology," in *Margins of Philosophy,* trans. Alan Bass (Chicago: University of Chicago Press, 1982), 210.
4.   Paul de Man, "Autobiography as De-Facement," in *The Rhetoric of Romanticism* (New York: Columbia University Press, 1984), 70.
5.   Jean Laplanche and Jean-Bertrand Pontalis, "Fantasy and the Origins of Sexu-

ality," in *Formations of Fantasy,* ed. Victor Burgin, James Donald, and Cora Kaplan (New York: Routledge, 1987), 26.

6. Paul de Man, *The Resistance to Theory* (Minneapolis: University of Minnesota Press, 1986), 4. Henceforth *RT,* with page references in the text.

7. Emmanuel Lévinas, *Otherwise than Being,* trans. Alfonso Lingis (Pittsburgh: Duquesne University Press, 1998), 101.

8. Sigmund Freud, *Civilization and its Discontents,* trans. James Strachey (New York: W.W. Norton, 1989), 79.

9. Avital Ronell, *Dictations* (Champaign: University of Illinois Press, 2006), xiii.

10. Emmanuel Lévinas, *Totality and Infinity,* trans. Alfonso Lingis (Pittsburgh: Duquesne University Press, 1969), 27.

11. Avital Ronell, "On the Unrelenting Creepiness of Childhood," in *The Überreader,* ed. Diane Davis (Champaign: University of Illinois Press, 2008), 102.

12. Lévinas, *Otherwise than Being,* [translation modified], 121.

13. Emmanuel Lévinas, *De l'existence à l'existant* (Paris: Editions de Vrin, 1998) [my translations], 112. Henceforth *EE,* with page references in the text.

14. Laplanche and Pontalis, "Fantasy and the Origins of Sexuality," 20.

15. Jacques Derrida, *L'université sans condition* (Paris: Galilée, 2001) [my translations], 43.

Hent de Vries

Testing Existence, Exacting Thought:
Reading Ronell with Deleuze

Test everything; hold fast what is good.

—PAUL, I THESSALONIANS 5:21–22

Let each one test his own work, and then his reason
to boast will be in him alone and not in his neighbor.

—PAUL, GALATIANS 6:4

In *Spinoza: Practical Philosophy,* Gilles Deleuze writes that "existence is a test." He immediately adds: "But it is a physical or chemical test, an experimentation, the contrary of Judgment. . . . The physical-chemical test of states constitutes Ethics as opposed to moral judgment."[1] The motif of testing, as opposed to judging in its propositional definition, which is both Kantian and legal, not to mention moral, also appears earlier in Deleuze's writing, as does a repudiated "dogmatic" image of the test, which, in the words of *Difference and Repetition,* manifests a naïve commonsensical and epistemic "representation" of what constitutes genuine "problems" (or true "problematics") in science and the arts, in practical philosophy, including politics and law, and in life and existence as such. Here is what Deleuze, in the pivotal chapter devoted to "the image of thought," says about "tests":

> We are led to believe that problems are given ready-made, and that they disappear in the responses to the solution. Already, under this double aspect, they can be no more than phantoms. We are led to believe that the activity of thinking, along with truth and falsehood in relation to that activity, begins only with the search for solutions, that both of these concern only solutions. This belief probably has the same origin as the other postulates of the dogmatic image [of thought]: puerile examples taken out of context and arbitrarily erected into models. According to this infantile prejudice, the master sets a problem, our task is to solve it,

164

and the result is accredited true or false by a powerful authority. It is also a social prejudice with the visible interest of maintaining us in an infantile state, which calls upon us to solve problems that come from elsewhere, consoling or distracting us by telling us that we have won simply by being able to respond: the problem as obstacle and the respondent as Hercules. Such is the origin of the grotesque image of culture that we find in tests [*les tests*] and government referenda as well as in newspaper competitions (where everyone is called upon to choose according to his or her taste, on condition that this taste coincides with that of everyone else). Be yourselves—it being understood that this self must be that of others. As if we would not remain slaves as long as we do not possess a right to the problems, to a participation in and management of the problems. The dogmatic image of thought supports itself with psychologically puerile and socially reactionary examples (cases of recognition, error, simple propositions and solutions or responses) in order to prejudge what should be the most valued in regard to thought—namely, the genesis of the act of thinking and the *sense* of truth and falsehood.[2]

A little later, Deleuze identifies this tendency to reduce problems and the problematic to potential and possible solutions, couched in propositions or theoremes alone, with the "technical" character and novel form of an age-old "illusion," an at once "natural" and "philosophical" diversion or, as he likes to say, "denaturation" of the original task that "dialectics" has set itself since Aristotle.[3]

Deleuze and his discussion of the test—this time, in the context of his *Nietzsche and Philosophy*, "the test of the eternal return," a motif that also informs the argument of *Difference and Repetition*—makes a decisive appearance in Avital Ronell's *The Test Drive*.[4] As in her earlier work *Stupidity*, where she refers to Deleuze's discussion of *bêtise* (an equally important theme in *Difference and Repetition*), the striking resonance between Deleuze's discussion and her concern with the "test" and its "drive" provides a significant clue for receiving and analyzing her thinking. If I am not mistaken, Deleuze's conception of "existence as a test"—together with his concern with "experimentation," in constant discussion with the meaning of this term and its distortion in the propositions of science (including mathematics and the life sciences), as well as in judgments presupposed by dogmatic images of thought—provides an excellent foil that will help us situate and appreciate Ronell's if not most experimental, then at least most testing (in the sense of most exacting) work.

Conversely, I would claim, Ronell's latest work, in a reflection that radicalizes a perspective already opened in *The Telephone Book*—with its unsurpassed taste for exemplars and a radically post- (or, better, "aggravated")

Heideggerian engagement with the question of technology and a science that, *pace* the later Heidegger, continues to "think"—gives further depth and profile to some of Deleuze's overarching philosophical and material claims, many of which are formulated at an abstract conceptual level, at least in the writings from which we have taken our lead here.

Compare the quotes from Deleuze, with which we began with a programmatic opening statement from *The Test Drive:*

> A kind of questioning, a structure of incessant research—perhaps even a modality of being—testing scans the walls of experience, measuring, probing, determining the "what is" of the lived world. At the same time, but more fundamental still, the very structure of testing tends to overtake the certainty that it establishes when obeying the call of open finitude. An unpresumed fold in metaphysics, testing—that is, the types and systems of relatedness that fall under this term—asserts another logic of truth, one that subjects itself to incessant questioning while reserving a frame, a trace, a disclosive moment to which it refers.[5]

This passage echoes Deleuze's ambivalent appreciation of the motif and motivation of "testing." The test and its drive—unless it is the "test" and its underlying "drive" that should be distinguished and contrasted here—reveal a profound ambiguity in that they stand for a deep probing and an upsurging experimentation, on the one hand, and a (subsequent?) regimentation and petrification, on the other. Yet each of these moments guards a reference to—keeps a "frame," a "trace" of—the other. In other words, each of them betrays (that is, announces and recalls or interrupts) the other. The "genesis" of thought, of its "act" or "sense," on the one hand, and its relative stabilization, stasis, or categorization, on the other, mutually reveal and conceal each other. For good and for ill. Nothing could be said to exist— be thought—with the imbrication of these two conflicting perspectives on one and the same phenomenon, of these two aspects of one and the same reality, that is to say, of these two sides of the coin, tossed up in the air of experience, its trials and experiments.

* * *

Ronell's source of inspiration is more the thought and legacy of Jacques Derrida than that of Gilles Deleuze, and reference to the "trace" or "frame" reminds us of that intellectual filiation and fidelity. Although in all three authors an original reading of Nietzsche is central, it is above all Derrida who allows Ronell to move beyond the epistemic curtailment of the "experimental event," so prevalent in the history and philosophy of science and technology, and to inscribe into the very concept and experience of the event of existence and its testing—its trial and temptation—so-called "nonevents," elements and traces that border on the margins of the "experimental disposition."[6] Following Derrida, she reminds us at the outset that "the event falls under the heading of nonevent, an aggravation of the Heideggerian *Ereignis,* designating that which cannot be grasped or seen in its appropriation."[7]

Yet there is a sense in which this noneventual and nonappropriable character of the experiment of testing touches upon a motif that Deleuze, in a different register from Derrida but likewise in critical dialogue with Heidegger, sought to articulate throughout his career, and nowhere more forcefully than in *Difference and Repetition,* the first book in which, beyond his previous historical studies, he "tried to 'do' philosophy"[8] and the theoretical matrix that lays down the conceptual and ideational underpinnings of his philosophical and material as well as occasional writings. In that work, Deleuze takes Heidegger's notion of the *Nichts,* or Nothing, to signal a non-negative—and hence nondialectical—problematic whose shadow is cast over every assertion, every claim.

Like Deleuze, Ronell aspires to nothing less than a reorientation of thought, experience, and existence in the light of a "transcendent exercise," to cite Deleuze's surprising formulation, whose connotations and philosophical implications have ethico-religious as well as technologico-material dimensions. Like him—and like Derrida, although the latter takes a different point of departure and works with different conceptual tools toward different intellectual aims—Ronell seeks to undermine the simple distinction (the dualism, opposition, or binarism) between the conceptualization of the experiment of testing as a machinal, techno-scientific notion, on the one hand, and, on the other, its understanding in light of a more elusive idea of (noneventual or noneventual, that is to say, neither ontologico-hermeneutic nor possibilistic) otherness or othering.

As he states explicitly in the opening pages of *Difference and Repetition,* Deleuze thinks of "pure difference" or "complicated repetition" in terms of an "idea" of "becoming" and an "eternal return," all of them notions that not only reveal seemingly opposite sources of inspiration (Plato and Spinoza, Nietzsche and Kierkegaard, Bergson and Heidegger, to name only a few) but attempt to articulate a "dual aspect theory" of existence and experience, nature and the cosmos. The expression "dual aspect theory" is not his, but Stuart Hampshire's. Hampshire uses it to great effect in his powerful reading of Spinoza to understand the relationship between relentless determinism and freedom, causal mechanicism or automatism and *scientia intuitiva*—a relationship that recalls the duck-rabbit distinction and aspect seeing in Wittgenstein's *Philosophical Investigations* but has a wider relevance.[9]

For one thing, "pure difference" and "complex repetition" do not reveal themselves only—or even primarily—in modernity or in modern art. Although Deleuze invokes the force of poetry as well as the examples of *Wozzek*, Pop Art, Warhol, the new novel, and Butor, as well as, of course, new cinema,[10] these merely exemplify the structure and becoming of the actual as such, just as they also pertain to the domain of the artificial and the technological, the machinal and the digital.

Indeed, *Difference and Repetition* constitutes the theoretical matrix of all of Deleuze's philosophical, critical, and clinical work, that is to say, the axiomatics, foundation, and conceptual or ideational underpinnings of his more historical, material, thematic, and occasional writings (including, by his own account, his studies of literature, notably Proust, Kafka, and the great modern American novelists, the experimental studies composed with Felix Guattari, and so forth). We are thus not dealing merely with a systematic and philosophical Deleuze, to be distinguished from the later "anarcho-desirer," as some have characterized him, whether lovingly or critically. With its conception of "pure difference" and "complex repetition," *Difference and Repetition* gives us the essential ontological parameters, the transcendental deduction, indeed the "transcendent exercise" of the intellectual ambition that runs throughout all of Deleuze's books and interventions.

Alain Badiou, in *The Clamor of Being*, is right, perhaps, to characterize Deleuze's philosophical ambition as defending further steps on the way to a perennial philosophy, rather than as announcing philosophy's end.[11] Metaphysics, in its ancient and modern ontological articulation, is, in *Difference and Repetition* and its companion writings, not so much overcome as worked through, rearranged in its elements, and reassembled with the help of new concepts, ideas, and constellations, in view of novel aspirations, many of which have implications whose range and depth we have not yet fathomed. This is not to suggest that *Difference and Repetition* is a meta-theoretical study that offers us a merely formal framework or conceptual scheme of work to come or to be desired; indeed, everything in Deleuze's conception of the concept, the idea, the affect, or the percept works against such a classical understanding of the transcendental as having to do with given *a priori* conditions of possibility of all possible experience, whether abstract or empirical. Rather, the ambition of the book is to spell out a "logic of sense" (the title of another major study published at roughly the same time), to exemplify a "transcendent exercise" that seeks to "encounter"

168

the empirical as the actual (and hence not merely the possible), that is to say, as the ontological positivity whose singularity and universality escapes the traditional logic of analogy and resemblance, identity and equivalence, and thereby eludes the dialectic of the particular and the general, whose mediation is more presupposed and imposed than demonstrated by Hegelian logic. Yet Deleuze's insistence on a certain positivity—and hence on a certain empiricism—does not exclude invocation of the "virtual," indeed, of a certain ideality or objectivity. But the latter are part and parcel of the real as it presents itself to us, not a mere abstraction or potentiality.[12] This is a difficult thought, deeply indebted to the writings of Henri Bergson, of which one cannot easily find a parallel in either Derrida or Ronell, but may nonetheless offer an essential element for comprehending the different ways in which these authors engage the respective "archives"—both metaphysical and theological, psychoanalytic and technological—whose enduring ontological weight and increasing dissemination we have barely begun to assess.

Deleuze takes up a difficult position between the historical and conceptual alternatives of empiricism and rationalist dogmatism, naturalism and idealism, transcendentalism and historicism, universalism and relativism or culturalism, the philosophy of the infinite and the philosophy of finitude— but also, I would claim, while agreeing that this could be more readily contested—between the thought of immanence and that of transcendence.

Indeed, *Difference and Repetition* contains a critique of identity in view, or in the name, of an otherness, difference—indeed, of *l'Autre* or, as we read in the final pages of the book, with an almost Lévinasian twist, of *Autrui*. It launches an extensive assault on the derailment of the idea and practice of "dialectics," which pits Plato and Kant against Hegel (not unlike Adorno's *Negative Dialectics*, which substitutes for a dialectics of the Infinite a dialectics becoming infinite in its movement[13]); it incessantly rethinks the relationship between the concept and the non- or pre- and extra-conceptual in view of the critique of the paradigm of "representation" that emerged with Plato only to culminate in Descartes, but which Deleuze rethinks in light of a genealogical critique that reminds one of Foucault's *The Order of Things* (*Les mots et les choses*), as Deleuze himself explicitly notes.

And these are just a few of the main components of a thought that addresses the "test" of existence and the "thought" it exacts in the most novel and demanding of ways. Without exception, I would claim, they contribute concepts and analyses whose relevance to contemporary philosophical and, more broadly, critical concerns—not least those of Avital Ronell's most rewarding projects—is more than evident.

169

* * *

Yet in Ronell's work, motifs out of *Deleuze* cum Nietzsche are taken in divergent directions and developed in no less systematic yet highly original, suggestive, and rhetorical styles. This is not just because Ronell exposes Derridean intuitions (those of the "trace," the "frame," and the "noneventual"), which might seem largely implicit in Deleuze's (and, for that matter, Nietzsche's) writings, to a broader phenomenological panorama of forms of testing and being tested than the epistemic—dogmatic-representationalist—regime to which our opening quote from *Difference and Repetition* refers. The added value of Ronell's work lies also in its analytical, psychoanalytic, and, one might venture to say, wider therapeutic nature, in a Wittgensteinian no less rather than Freudian sense.

As we have already seen, Ronell insists that "the experimental turn" should not be seen as merely expressing "the oriented homogeneity of becoming," for the very reason that, by "its very nature, it interrupts itself, discontinues itself,"[14] and hence does not coincide with itself. The very process and trial of immanence would thus—non-dialectically, but quasi-automatically— yield its innermost other. Yet although this may appear to be the crucial point of contention between "philosophies of immanence," including those of Deleuze, Nietzsche, and Bergson, on the one hand, and the perspective Ronell herself espouses (again, in solidarity with Derrida), on the other, insight into the rhythm or punctuation of becomings, as opposed to some hypostasized eternal flux, is not absent from *Difference and Repetition* either. Read against the grain as much as read consistently, Deleuze's *magnum opus* points beyond the very position that it at times seems to articulate as well as argue against: the thesis, if not representation, of immanentism.

Ronell, for her part, exemplifies and dramatizes this insight into interruption in a host of disjunct instances, none of them easily reducible to a larger ontological perspective premised on the general doctrine of the univocity of Being (as distilled from, say, Duns Scotus, Spinoza, and Nietzsche) or its corollary and radicalized emphasis on singularities and pre-, para-, or post-personal individualities (as Deleuze advocates). Moreover, the disjunction of the most testing instances seems, in Ronell's account, both greater and more naturally oriented toward an experiential horizon, if not of resolution then at least of healing, of convalescence (indeed, of *Verwindung,* as the later Heidegger of *Gelassenheit* and *Die Technik und die Kehre* would have said). But how and in what perspective is this undertaken? To begin to answer that question, let me recall the central tenets and the variety of themes and topics that structure and inform Ronell's most recent book.

The Test Drive is conceptually and analytically astute just as it is wildly imaginative and, at moments, moving and witty. Its line of argumentation, which weaves together motifs from a wide range of disciplines, is masterly composed, yet gives the reader ample opportunity to pause, wonder, and object. So does the rhetorical organization of the text, which is interspersed with sections that are not so much excurses but modal variations on related themes, in which a different tone is adopted—now playful, disarmingly personal, or self-ironic, then again also touching.

A case in point is the little interior monologue put into the mouth of Edmund Husserl and inspired by his saddening correspondence with his most brilliant pupil, Martin Heidegger. In Ronell's rendering, Husserl muses about the fate of his legacy as well as about his encounter with a young visitor from Lithuania and Strasbourg, the Jewish thinker Emmanuel Lévinas. The latter would become one of the most radical innovators of the phenomenological method in France and beyond, first by publishing introductory scholarly essays and a lucid monograph on the master (*The Theory of Intuition in Husserl's Phenomenology*), in which he sides with the star-student Heidegger against the master, in an expository book that would inspire Sartre to leave for Germany to study phenomenology firsthand, then also by co-translating Husserl's *Cartesian Meditations,* and, finally, by using the phenomenological method to critique phenomenological ontology—and eventually also its method—tout court. Yet the amusing digression just as easily switches back into a serious and profound exposition of Husserl's deepest intentions, thereby reaffirming *The Test Drive*'s ultimate argumentative—and, I would argue, overall philosophical—thrust.

* * *

The Test Drive is a wonderfully written, cogently argued, exceptionally erudite, and stunningly original work of contemporary theorizing and philosophizing in its own right. It concerns historical, philosophical, literary, scientific, medical, as well as mediatic tropes of testing and experimentation that exceed the parameters and criteriological terms set for them by traditional, conventional, and more narrowly defined epistemic regimes, whether in the sciences or in the sociocultural domain, whether in love among persons or in the deepest of solitudes. Along the way, it addresses religious and theologico-political pitfalls and dilemmas as well.

Central to the conceptual, figural, rhetorical, and even visual investigation of all the registers of testing is the hypothesis of what Nietzsche called our "age of experimentation," an epoch caught up in terrible and increasing ambiguity. Such testing and experimentation should be understood in all

the ambivalent connotations of German *Versuch,* which combines the semantic connotations of testing with the associations of *Versuchung,* tempt-
ing or temptation, as well as those of trial and attempt (the "conjecture" or
"bold idea" in search of "falsification" of which Karl Popper makes so much
in his classic *Conjectures and Refutations,* single-handedly overcoming
logical empiricism's principle of inductive verification and epistemological
"phenomenalism"). As things now stand, so the argument goes, nothing
happens without checking, and the ever-expanded sites, sights, and plights
of experimental and experiential testing, Ronell suggestively observes, far
from clearing the ground and lifting our spirits only seem to "make the
wasteland grow."[15]

At the furthest extreme of this tendency—as Nietzsche foresaw in his
most perspicuous moments and as Hannah Arendt, well before Giorgio Agamben's musings about the "states of exception," concluded in her groundbreaking studies on totalitarianism—stands "the concentration camp as the
most unrestricted experimental laboratory in modern history, a part of the
will to scientific knowledge."[16] Arendt, significantly, spoke of "the experiment of total domination"[17] and demonstrated that its intellectual roots
reach all the way back into the depths of Western history and its intellectual
traditions, even though its most brutal twentieth-century manifestation
may have resulted from a no less fatal "banalization of evil" as well.

Yet, as Ronell reminds us, in Arendt this totalitarian risk—a standing
possibility rather than a logical consequence of the drive toward testing and
letting be tested in modernity—is far from justifying an all-out critique of
technological reason (as it would seem to do in Agamben). Arendt, and in
her footsteps Ronell, steers clear of the late (or latest) Heideggerian incrimi-
nations of technology as the recent and, perhaps, most fateful coinage of
the metaphysical forgetting of Being as such, of its sending (*Geschick*) and
event (*Ereignis*), of its ontologico-theological framing (*Gestell*) to which
our response could only be one of letting go (*Gelassenheit*), hibernation or
resignation, and not one of, precisely, experimentation.

What modern political history revealed, Ronell stresses, is not a tragic
fatality but a terrible, indeed horrifying, ambiguity, because, for all its un-
deniable capacity to produce and perpetuate the worst, the experiment is,
in a different—Nietzschean and, we might add, Deleuzian—reading, above
all "a freedom from the constraints of referential truth," just as it in no less
certain terms announces a possible liberation from history's all too massive Truths, or even from the non-propositional and non-representational
"Truth" reconceived in terms of unconcealment of which Heidegger spoke,
in *Sein und Zeit* and after.

No simple critique, then, let alone a naïve celebration of testing and the experimental mode—or, for that matter, our troubled modus vivendi with it—is to be found in *The Test Drive* or anywhere else in Ronell's preceding and accompanying writings. On the contrary, the entire book, including its written preparations and satellite studies, revolves around the intrinsic paradoxes and aporias of the test, of the experiment and the proof, and their potentially no less deadly than life-giving "drive." The many scientific and sociocultural articulations that Ronell surveys testify to nothing else.

* * *

The motif of the test, whose rhetoric Ronell had begun to discuss in the third chapter of her earlier *Stupidity* (though it could easily be argued that her other works are a long preparation for this theme and method of analysis), perhaps stands above all for "permanent innovation." It allows one to perceive and reintroduce a novel relationship—at once scientific, philosophical, and literary, though not reducible to any of these tested disciplinary domains—between the ancient and modern understandings of the notions of *technē* and *epistēmē*. The test is embedded in a larger historical, social, and cultural "experimental turn" and, indeed, "experimental disposition," whose metaphysical proportions it took a Nietzsche to fathom and whose extreme consequences—usually horrifying but sometimes also promising—it took the whole twentieth century to realize. Existence has been tested indeed, and the perils and chances it manifests are, perhaps, more exacting than we can bear to admit.

It is the larger intellectual history and ontological event of "the experimental turn," Ronell writes, that "houses the test and gives shape to its particular contours, transgresses, in breaking down and disassembling the ground of a tradition, the limits of knowledge and technicity or method." Yet, as the now strained, then merely hypothetical relationship to all things, words, gestures, and powers, in short, minds and moods, the experimental turn—and especially its central expression and vehicle, namely, the test and its proof, the trying out or trial—is neither inserted into a unilinear, homogeneous continuum nor, for that matter, simply aleatory, that is to say, without proper consistency or without historical, societal, cultural, and existential weight of its own. On the contrary, that testing existence exacts our thought in ways for which we are still ill prepared is one of the central insights of Ronell's work.

To hammer home the point, *The Test Drive* assesses the psychological as well as political toll that testing takes, but also elicits what potentialities it keeps in store, what future realizations it may yet keep at bay. Ronell leaves no doubt that no simple answers will do, not least because the phenome-non—indeed, the ontological structure—of the test and its ongoing drive is paradoxical, indeed, aporetic at its core. Testing is a self-contradictory push and pull whose punctuated rhythms, slowdowns, and accelerations we have barely begun to understand and whose effects are everywhere to be felt. This explains in part the riddle the book seeks to solve or, at least, the modalities of testing it seeks to tease out in all its complexity and disruption, with and against Nietzsche and the experimental turn he inaugurated or, at least, diagnosed: "Though articulated with unique precision by Nietzsche, the experimental turn should not be seen as the oriented homogeneity of becoming. By its very nature, it interrupts itself, discontinues itself. Es-sentially relational and not static, testing admits of no divine principle of intelligibility, no first word of grace or truth, no final meaning, no privileged signified. How can such a phenomenological lineup of serial "no's" concern us today or speak to our needs?"[18]

It can, Ronell suggests compellingly, because the testing and drive behind (and beyond?) it—which is ultimately also "the thrownness of technology," she writes—"traverses many sectors of existence and does not begin as an explicitly technological life-form." Ronell is all too aware that it is extremely difficult to speak about this cogently, let alone philosophically, not least because, for all its omnipresence from the earliest days of Western thought, "the test has not yet become a philosophical question, though it belongs to an ever-mutating form of questioning." Because there is a sense in which the question, whether in the famous dialectic of question and answer or in the pursuit of open, unanswerable, or merely rhetorical, that is to say, ordi-nary, "questions" (questions without answers versus questions with pregiven answers), belong to the heart of philosophy and, perhaps, of all theoretical inquiry, there might be no point in formulating (or addressing) the question-ing form of the test in theoretical scientific or philosophical terms at all.

But, then, could one do so by other discursive, rhetorical, figurative, or visual means? Would literature or reading (if not "theory") be of greater help? Wisely, Ronell offers no such false hopes. She intimates, rather, that the most responsible—and most exacting—response to our predicament is to put all these disciplinary registers to a different "test" and to look for answers in the interstices between their all too naïvely posited conceptual and institutional demarcations. Hence the need to find several points of entry into—and exit out of—the discursive regime of "testing" at once, mostly by a changing of tones or by playing a discourse's melody back to it; hence also the necessity to understand its "drive" in its multiple and contra-dictory forms, most of which escape the known vocabularies of theories of evolution, processes of learning, or psychoanalytic models of understanding pleasure, aggression, mimetic rivalry, and the like.

Ronell engages this difficulty from several surprising and well-informed perspectives. She offers a wide-ranging panorama, drawing on telling examples from ancient philosophy and speaking (as did Jean-François Lyotard in *Le différend* [*The Differend*]) of the Platonic *elenchus* as a kind of cross-examination for the purpose of disproof. She also discusses the history of science and natural philosophy, especially the conflict between Robert Boyle and Thomas Hobbes over the threat that experimental physics seemed to pose to philosophy defined in terms of causality, that is to say, to physical propositions cast in necessary form in view of universal assent. And, as so often throughout her writings, she returns to the history of literature from Novalis to Kafka, to the use of psychological genealogies in Freud (suggesting that "[p]sychoanalysis belongs in the lexicon of the test drive"), and to the transcendental phenomenological and neo-Kantian philosophies of Husserl and Hermann Cohen. Along the way, she delves into the views of Max Weber, who, in his famous essay on science as a profession and vocation, is especially intrigued by the American academic "compulsion to test everything" and who refers to "material instances of testing such as the Ph.D., written, oral, comprehensive, general and qualifying examinations, teaching evaluations, and the corresponding physical and mental stress tests." She further explores the intricacies of contemporary legal cases and jurisprudence, where scientific (especially DNA) testing has come to be admissible evidence in modern litigation.

These multifarious pulsations of the test drive finally result in interesting observations concerning epistemological matters, such as the dispute over principles of verification, decidability, and falsification from Rudolf Carnap and Kurt Gödel to Carl Hempel and Karl Popper. Ronell recalls how the positions taken in these passionate debates have been reiterated in more recent discussions surrounding computational modeling in the contemporary philosophy of mind and the continued efforts for Artificial Intelligence (AI), even after many fatal philosophical onslaughts, such as Hubert Dreyfus's *Why Computers (Still) Can't Think,* to spell out the minimal requirements for cognitive acceptability and "testability" of just about everything pertaining to human skills and competence in its most existential (for example, aesthetic, erotic, and religious) depths.

* * *

Ronell's philosophical frame of reference is thus at once broad—and hardly limited to so-called "Continental" thinkers (even though Nietzsche, next to

Derrida, remains clearly the most important interlocutor in the book)—and specific, as she expands her inquiry far afield into debates in twentieth-century philosophy of science and analytic and post-analytic Anglo-American thought. The latter, she implies, have by their very own account brought out the structural limitations of epistemic or otherwise normative criteriological restraints upon the concept and experience of testing, whether in the laboratory or with regard to existence and thought in general.

It should come as no surprise, then, that *The Test Drive* originated in preparation for a study primarily devoted to the work of Alan Turing. His remarkable biography as a pioneer of AI, a decoder in the Second World War "Enigma" project, and a gay man who suffered an untimely, violent death not only reveals, Ronell writes, a "phantom body agitating in the scientific corpus," but also "reminds us of the story of the way the state has experimented on the minoritized body and how prison systems to this day continue to function furtively as so many sites for experimental science." However, because the unfolding of the book's larger project and wider claims included nothing less than a full-fledged scientific and philosophical, literary, and figural probing of the most testing instances of the modern material and immaterial world, of existence and its thought, *The Test Drive* moves beyond this remarkable chapter as well.

A recurrent theme in Ronell's study is philosophy's wrestling with the fact that conceptions of rigor and demonstrability have consistently and increasingly been identified with a certain "core of testability." Again, debates around the programs of AI and cognitive science confirm this association of philosophical logic and reason with "computational realizability." Ronell raises the fatal question that all such ambitions must face, and with which they have been confronted within the tradition of Anglo-American analytic and post-analytic philosophy itself, notably in the work of Hilary Putnam, Stanley Cavell, and others, namely: "But what if testing were from the start itself built upon notions of constitutive incompletion, ambiguity, blind runs, and radically provisional cognitive values?" One much-debated early instance of such recognition, Ronell recalls, is Gödel's epochal insight that "statements of number theory, being also statements about statements of number theory, could each misdirect a proof." Put otherwise, Gödel showed demonstratively that "provability 'is a weaker notion of truth,'" or, again, that truth can be rescued from "limitative results of provability." Yet, other non-logico-mathematical instances of this realization abound, in philosophy and ethics, in literature and psychoanalysis, disciplines on which Ronell focuses more centrally.

* * *

The Test Drive is concerned throughout with the ethical and political implications of its theme, even though it wisely steers clear of the facile moralism
and normativism that have so often accompanied the many theoretical
and practical critiques of technological or instrumental reason. In this,
I would suggest, Ronell's writing once again parallels the tone and argument of Deleuze's major work. Indeed, no sweeping invectives against the
"mechanization of the world view" (to cite a title by the Dutch historian of
science Dijksterhuis), no pessimism about modern reason's "iron cage" (to
cite Weber) are to be found here. Ronell's critique of testing reason is far
more topical and, indeed, local in its orientation as it directs our attention
to a sensitivity of singular cases of testing existence and the thought it exacts
from us. This being said, larger political matters are not avoided.

As she had already done in *Finitude's Score,* Ronell takes the Gulf War as
a polemical test case, a case of testing (arms and men and women for) war:
"Technological warfare belongs to the domain of testing as well and does
much to support the thesis that there is little difference between testing and
the real thing."[19] This circumstance, she goes on to note, has wide-ranging
implications for our attempts at understanding the world and others in it,
both in the not so distant past and the all too imminent future: "The test
already functions as a signal to the enemy other. What this means, among
other things, is that the Cold War *was* a war. It also means that George W.
Bush could at once invoke and scramble these codes by announcing, on
9/11, that the attack on the World Trade Center was, in his words, a test:
'This is a test' were his first words after the attack in 2001: 'The resolve of
our great nation is being tested,' he proclaimed."[20]

Bush decided on seemingly clear terms what an opening question in
The Test Drive wisely leaves undecided: "Can faith be tested or is it not
the essence of faith to refuse the test—to go along, precisely on blind faith,
without ground of grade?"[21] Ronell reads Bush's invocation in an interpretive tour de force, a lucid turning of theologico-political tables, and suggests
that by claiming

> the terror attack was a test, President Bush leaves no room for the undecid-
> ability of Abraham, the contestability of Job or the intricated martyrdom
> of Christ. Disturbing the codified usage of the trial to which "the test"
> alludes, the utterance subverts the condition of *being tested* by offering
> that, at the moment of its mention, the test has been passed. The test will
> already have made sense and turned in the result: one would not have

been chosen to withstand it, the logic goes, if one had not *already passed* the test of history countersigned, in this case, by God.[22]

But before we conclude that Ronell sees war everywhere, as if it were truly the sole—or most exacting—case of testing existence, we should ponder the reverse side of this observation as well. Thus, with reference, again, to the Gulf War, Ronell notes:

> war, as it increasingly becomes the technological and tele-topical test site par excellence, has lost its metaphysical status as meaningful production— at least when compared to Hegel's discussion of war as a sort of pregnancy test for historical becoming. If we no longer know how to wage war, in other words, how to legitimate and justify its necessity in history's un- folding (we desist at times from calling our interventions war—they have become police actions or humanitarian runs), we still hold out the hope that it may yield some test results.[23]

Where the test of war is failed, others may still be passed. Such is the logic—and ontological weight—of the test and its drive: it supersedes any of its historical instantiations and reduces even its most exacting instances, namely war, to testing by other (and not the most sophisticated or endur- ing) means.

* * *

There is more. In addition to these polemical and theologico-political mat- ters, Ronell discretely reconstructs the element of gender in the cognitive space of testing and its analogues, an intellectual, discursive, and experien- tial realm that—like Heidegger's *Dasein,* aptly deconstructed by Derrida in several of his most innovative readings—would like to pride itself above all on its sexual neutrality. There is something about testing, Ronell reminds us, that makes it "appear at nearly every juncture to be linked to the mascu- linist themes of *virtu* and *agon.* Always involving a question of endurance and risk, testing also depends upon a decisive urge to test one's strength, try one's limits, and work to failure. Whether you are typed in as male or female or clocking in as yin or yang, these represent masculinist grunts and dilemmas. They are codified culturally as a specific kind or ordeal."

A little later, in a section that discusses the many forms of romantic and liberal "irony" as merely partial abandonings of "theoretical test treaties," she likewise critically engages the writings of Richard Rorty to expose yet another neutralization (this time philosophically rather than politically) of the position of gender: "Irony, with its implications of self-mastery and de- structive *jouissance,* and testing, which rhetorically and operationally feeds on irony, are rarely anchored in post- or parafeminist concern or rewound through *écriture féminine.*" There is surely some distance, however, between avoiding concerns of gender in theoretical discussions—whether this neutralization occurs in an ontological or an ontico-pragmatic-pragmatist point of view—and the "fabled misogyny of lab culture," with which all these philosophical positions here find themselves aligned. (One wonders, is the theme of neutralization or de-transcendentalization a concern that Deleuze, with his sustained emphasis on nonsubjectivized or nonpersonalized individuality, could easily have made his own? Or is perspective part of the added value of Ronell's project of which I spoke above?)

So much is clear: the reader of *The Test Drive* is led through the labyrinths of scientific, textual, controlled, and moral and religious experiments, while passing through several traditions of Western philosophy, but also nineteenth- and twentieth-century literature; several Western and Eastern forms of nonknowledge, such as Zen Buddhism with its trial of the koan; Valéry's "Monsieur Teste" and its creative reinterpretation by Jean-Luc Marion in his critique of visual and conceptual idolatry. Yet in the final analysis, Ronell offers more than an intellectual history of the motif of testing, something different from an inventory of its rearticulation and complexity. Ultimately, her book revolves around the question, briefly indicated earlier, of what *escapes* the test and the trial, at least in its culturally hegemonic understanding and instituted practices whose inventory we have summarized. Such escape can take many forms and Ronell sketches a few.

What if, for example, no test confirms an illness that is clearly being experienced, leaving diagnoses and social *acceptance* of the disease in limbo, demanding an attestation to its truth and truthfulness that no objective protocols warrant? That this happens in everyday lives, indeed, as the very structure of the ordinary, as well as in history's most dismal hours, scarcely needs proof. As if recalling an impasse from which Lyotard sets out in the opening pages of *The Differend*, Ronell speaks of the "tenacity of revisionist prodding," which is "due in large part to its ability to invoke the rhetoric of testing when it comes to the deconstitution of the Shoah as memory and knowledge." Testimony would be more exacting, more exact, than the general requirement for "empirical proof" and epistemic certainty.

* * *

In sum, though *The Test Drive* makes an important contribution to the literary, philosophical, and, more broadly, theoretical interpretation of technology and experimentation and does so in historical and comparative perspective, its aim and interest is first of all systematic and therapeutic.

In its rethinking of the premises and implications of the Baconian *placet experiri* that sounded at the dawn of modern science and formed the very heart of its epistemological and practical justifications, as Horkheimer and Adorno recall in the opening chapters of their *Dialectic of Enlightenment,* Ronell's work offers a wide-ranging critique of testing, in the Kantian sense of the term *critique* by laying bare the simple and complex conditions of possibility of any experience overall as it manifests itself in testing.

In this sense, the test's "drive," for all its articulation in terms of a psycho-analytic (and this means, no doubt, in a larger phylo- no less than individual, ontogenetic) register, reveals an illusionary or, more precisely, imaginary thrust whose foundation is transcendental even though its phenomenality is shot through—and enabled—by an essential historicity made up of turns and tropes, traces and frames.

In steering clear of romantic and apocalyptic claims (though, as Deleuze says in the preface to *Difference and Repetition,* there is a sense in which a book about the structure and meaning of difference and repetition, the event and the test, should be, precisely, "apocalyptic,"[24] even where it avoids "the many dangers in invoking pure differences . . . lapsing into the representations of a beautiful soul"[25]), Ronell offers us a subtle diagnosis and evaluation of the modern techno-scientific predicament that forms the backdrop for so much contemporary theorizing in philosophy, literary and cultural criticism, psychoanalysis, and even the more promising reassessments of the study of religion.

Indeed, as it drives its point home in a variety of experimental ways—adopting the tested phenomenological method of Husserl's own "zigzag" no less than the innovative ventrilocution of the philosophical "DJ"[26]—*The Test Drive* attests that there are fundamentally *two senses* of testing and being tested, of experimenting and being experimented upon, of proving and of being approved, of trying out and being tried. One relies on "the phantasm of testing's groundedness and unquestioned solidity,"[27] that is to say, on its repeated but ultimately static reference to criteriological knowledge and its supposed measure; the other obeys a dynamic rhythm that is, from the start (and in the end), well, far more testing, that is to say, still more demanding because more groundless, fragile, and hence by definition ab-solute, in the sense of absolved, hypothetical in principle, undecided, however fine or luminous its test results may turn out to be.

Just as there are two modes of repetition according to the psychoanalytic model—one repressive or traumatic, one therapeutic or salutary—we should distinguish, in order to understand the impetus and the impasse evinced by *The Test Drive* no less than the thrust of Deleuze's argument in *Difference and Repetition,* between what Bergson called "static" and "dynamic" repetition. The two modes correspond to two different senses or aspects of testing existence and extend into two completely different, yet coexisting and mutually dependent, if not constitutive, modes of "conduct"—next to "points of view"—expressing "non-exchangeable and non-substitutable singularities" as well.[28] Behavior and agency, individuality and spirituality form part and parcel of the alternative—and non-dogmatic—image of thought that is being drawn here, one that avoids individualism and the personal, for example, but testifies to an alternative, resolutely non-Heideggerian, mode of "authentication," based on the belief in "a world in which individuations are impersonal, and singularities are pre-individual: the splendour of the 'ONE'"[29]

Experimentation and the regime of testing are two salient instantiations of the aforementioned polarity, even though one—by virtue of its very freedom—eludes the grasp of all dogmatic images of thought, leaving nothing more (or less) than an "Idea" in the emphatic sense of the term to be hoped for. In the words of Deleuze: "in the dynamic order there is no representative concept, nor any figure represented in a pre-existing space. There is an Idea, and a pure dynamism which creates a corresponding space."[30]

For Deleuze, there is a distinction between the "cadence-repetition [répétition-mesure]" and the "rhythm-repetition,"[31] the first being only the appearance and the effect of the other. In his words:

> The first repetition is repetition of the Same, explained by the identity of the concept or representation: the second includes difference, and includes itself in the alterity of the Idea, in the heterogeneity of an "appresentation." One is negative, occurring by default in the concept, the other affirmative, occurring by excess in the Idea. One is conjectural, the other categorical. One is static, the other dynamic. One is repetition in the effect, the other in the cause. One is extensive, the other intensive. One is ordinary, the other distinctive and singular. One is horizontal, the other vertical. One is developed and explicated, the other enveloped and in need of interpretation. One is revolving, the other evolving. One involves equality, commensurability and symmetry; the other is grounded in inequality, incommensurability and dissymmetry. One is material, the other spiritual, even in nature and in the earth. One is inanimate, the other [carries] the secret of our deaths and our lives, of our enchainments and our liberations, the demonic and the divine. . . . One concerns accuracy, the other has authenticity as its criterion.[32]

For Deleuze, something radically different from a simple dichotomy of differences and their repetitions is at issue. And for Ronell, the stakes of testing existence and exacting thought are roughly the same. Indeed, as we found, much else besides the existential analytic, with its all too familiar appeal to authenticity (or, in Heideggerian parlance, *Eigentlichkeit*), holds sway over the representationalist logic and the dogmatic image of thought it expresses. What interests Deleuze above all is the more creative and strenuous relationship between the two modalities of the dynamic and static—that is to say, in Ronell's idiom, between the two conceptions of the test: its drive and its sedimented result—both of which affect the substance of life, of events and things, and do so in mutually exclusive no less than mutually constitutive ways. What further intrigues Deleuze more than anything else is the specific responsiveness that repetition, this time taken as a comportment, of sorts, implies.

To clarify the first point, he notes:

> The two repetitions are not independent. One is the singular subject, the interiority and the heart of the other, the depth of the other. The other is only the external envelope, the abstract effect. The repetition of dissymmetry is hidden within symmetrical ensembles or effects; a repetition of distinctive points underneath that of ordinary points; and everywhere the Other in the repetition of the Same. This is the secret, the most profound repetition: it alone provides the principle of the other one, the reason for the blockage of concepts.[33]

Again, this secret difference, the other repetition, the repetition of the Other within the very repetition of the Same should, for all its distinctiveness, not be defined in oppositional—that is, negative or dialectical—terms. Though it does not relate analogically, let alone eminently to the first, that is to say, to the abstract repetition that precedes and represses it, the other repetition is not the latter's abstract negation—and hence *mere* other—either. Deleuze makes the most of this point: "It is true that we have strictly defined repetition as difference without concept. However, we would be wrong to reduce it to a difference which falls back into exteriority, because the concept embodies the form of the Same, without seeing that it can be internal to the Idea and possess in itself all the resources of signs, symbols and alterity which go beyond the concept as such."[34]

Mutatis mutandis, the same could be said of the test, of testing existence and the most exacting thought it inspires, requires, and, in a sense, expresses.

In Deleuze, we saw, all this also recalls the doctrine of so-called onto-logico-epistemological parallelism in Spinoza. In the following passage, for example, which resituates the dual-aspect-theory upon which Spinoza's *Ethics* relies by cutting its umbilical cord, that is to say, the correlation, co-implication, or, as Deleuze says, "proportionality"[35] of its two constitutive realms (which are the only ones known to us, according to Spinoza, under the attributes of Thought and Extension): "It is as though everything has two odd, dissymmetrical and dissimilar 'halves,' the two halves of the Symbol, each dividing itself in two; an ideal half submerged in the virtual and constituted on the one hand by differential relations and on the other by corresponding singularities; an actual half constituted on the one hand by the qualities actualising those relations and on the other by the parts actualising those singularities. Individuation ensures the embedding of the two dissimilar halves."[36]

This individuation and the "ethics" of experimentation, of testing and attesting existence, that it requires has nothing of the individualism, personalism, or subjectivism that represent the dogmatic images of thought. On the contrary, as in St. Paul's admonition, which I cited as my epigraph, it suggests that we respect two different—and, prima facie, contradictory—requirements simultaneously, namely to "test everything" while to "hold fast what is good" (I Thessalonians 5:21–22). To do so would mean to live in and through two parallel "worlds" (one of them not this one), none of which we could easily settle for, as long as history and existence take their toll.

In the meantime, testing existence, together with the exacting thought it implies, would impose that one limit one's moral and other exigencies, if not those expressed with regard to oneself—which may know no end—then at least those vis-à-vis others. St. Paul, it would seem, claims as much: "Let each one test his own work, and then his reason to boast will be in him alone and not in his neighbor." (Galatians 6:4).

In so doing, Stanley Cavell adds, one would "test not merely the limits of our identity but the limits of our humanity."[37] Indeed, we would thus be "testing for humanity," just as we would be "testing for automaticity."[38] Discriminating the one, we would be discriminating the other. The dual aspects of our human reality being essentially two sides of the same coin, tossed up in the air—which is nothing but the test or trial—of existence, whose epistemic and normative criteria inevitable fail or (as Cavell says) "disappoint" us, and, hence, exact thought and judgment more than anything else.

NOTES

1. Gilles Deleuze, *Spinoza: Practical Philosophy* (San Francisco: City Lights, 1988), 40.

2. Gilles Deleuze, *Difference and Repetition,* trans. Paul Patton (New York: Columbia University Press, 1994), 158; *Différence et repetition* (Paris: Presses Universitaires de France, 1968), 205–6, trans. modified. The otherwise excellent

English translation renders *les tests* as "examinations," thereby blocking a view of the parallel and virtual dialogue that interests us here.

3. Ibid., 159–60/207.
4. Avital Ronell, *The Test Drive* (Champaign: University of Illinois Press, 2004), 345–46, n. 14. See also Avital Ronell, *American philo: Entretiens avec Anne Dufourmantelle* (Paris: Éditions Stock, 2006), 149.
5. Ronell, *The Test Drive*, 5.
6. Ibid., 50.
7. Ibid.
8. Gilles Deleuze, "Preface to the English Edition," in Deleuze, *Difference and Repetition*, xv.
9. Stuart Hampshire, *Spinoza and Spinozism* (Oxford: Oxford University Press, 2005).
10. Compare Deleuze, *Difference and Repetition*, 293–94/373–76.
11. Alain Badiou, *Deleuze: Le clameur de l'être* (Paris: Hachette, 1997); trans, Louise Burchill, *Deleuze: The Clamor of Being* (Minneapolis: University of Minnesota Press, 2000). The title refers to Deleuze, *Difference and Repetition*, 35/52.
12. "C'est le possible et le réel qui se ressemblent, mais non pas du tout le virtuel et l'actuel" (Deleuze, *Difference and Repetition*, 357).
13. See my *Minimal Theologies: Critiques of Secular Reason in Theodor W. Adorno and Emmanuel Lévinas*, trans. Geoffrey Hale (Baltimore and London: Johns Hopkins University Press, 2005).
14. Ronell, *The Test Drive*, 9.
15. Ibid., 6.
16. Ibid., 7.
17. Cited in ibid., 327, n. 2.
18. Ibid., 9.
19. Ibid., 167, compare 168 and 347, n. 24.
20. Ibid., 167.
21. Ibid., 6.
22. Ibid., 168.
23. Ibid., 347, n. 24.
24. Deleuze, *Difference and Repetition*, xxi/3.
25. Ibid., xx/2.
26. Ronell, *American philo*, 168, 169.
27. Ronell, *The Test Drive*, 184.
28. Deleuze, *Difference and Repetition*, 1/7.
29. Ibid., xxi/4, trans. modified.
30. Ibid., 20/32.
31. Ibid., 21/33.
32. Ibid., 24/36–37, trans. modified.
33. Ibid., 24/37, trans. modified.
34. Ibid., 24–25/37.

35. Ibid., 280/358.
36. Ibid., 279–80/358.
37. Stanley Cavell, *The Claim of Reason* (Oxford and New York: Oxford University Press, 1979), 397, 398, and 265.
38. Ibid., 412.

Thomas Pepper

The Problems of a Generation
or
Thinking and Thanking *Zwang* AND *Drang*

In memory of the victims
of the Bush Wars

A work, no matter how recondite, specialized, or antiquarian, manifests a historical compulsion. Of course, we no longer exist in a way that renders manifestation possible: we have lost access to what is manifested and to manifestation itself. Nothing, today, can be manifested. Except, possibly, the fact that humanity is not yet just. The indecency of a humanism that goes on as if nothing had happened. The task of extremist writing is to put through the call for a justice of the future. Henceforth, justice can no longer permit itself to be merely backward looking or bound in servility to sclerotic models and their modifications (their "future"). A justice of the future would have to show the will to rupture.

"A thinker," Flaubert said, "should have neither religion nor fatherland nor even any social conviction. Absolute scepticism." Radically rupturing, the statement is not merely subversive. It does not depend upon the program that it criticizes. How might one free oneself from the cowardliness pressing upon social convictions of the present, subjugated as they are to reactive, mimetic, and regressive posturings?[1] (*CW*, 21)

Ungrounded Prolegomena of the Abgrund, or Where We Stand

What is a prophet?

And what do *compulsion, Zwang, Drang,* mean?

In writing on and in and with the topos Avital Ronell, these are the most urgent questions that come to the fore. Let me be perfectly clear: in asking "what is a prophet?" I have nothing of the religious in mind—at least not in any sense related to the parodic transcendental cover-up of the wars— "history," as it is called, sadly enough—of the positive-negative monotheisms of Abraham, themselves born of two acts: one of blind obedience to a command to murder the son, the second the erection of the Father's No-No in some communal act of killing and eating him, committed out on some camping trip—the West—destined to go bad.

No, no, go not immediately to the beatifying transcendentalism of those acts of forgetting—nor remember them out of compulsion to repeat (them and the memory of) the Same. My first question, "what is a prophet?," is an entirely earthly one.[2] Some time ago, speaking with a Deleuzean day-tripper friend, I thought I was catching him in the act of smuggling this unconcealed transcendental bomb of prophecy into his immanentist armoire. Annoyed by what I saw as a subreption unworthy of the intelligence of this friend and interlocutor from whom I have learned and continue to learn, I called him on it, point-blank: "What is this 'prophet' and 'prophecy' shit?," I asked, "and how dare you think you can get away with it!?"

To my overheated question my friend replied calmly: "A prophet is one who sees the present more clearly in the present, and enunciates what it sees."—And this regardless of whether the munchkins (see the preface to *DIC*) around at the time of this statement are capable of understanding—or, I add, even of recognizing the event-character of—the statement as such, of recognizing its *assertion as a statement, as an act in its own right.*[3]

Moments like this stick with you. Especially against the everyday gray of the administrative-nihilistic dominant of our time in which, proximally and for the most part, colleagues, students, so-called journalists and politicians, publishers, editors, writers, and keynote speakers have forgotten (enter multiple choice): a. what language is, and the ethics its sharing dictates; b. that it exists; c. how to use it; d. how to read it; e. how to know if and when you are dealing with it.

* * *

187

Avital Ronell has *been with* for many years. Here it is deliberate that the ablated object position of the preposition accompanying this intransitive verb is left empty. We shall have to take recourse to the logics of Heidegger's *Sein und Zeit* in order to understand the primordiality of "*being with*" and "*being in*" in respect of being-there's (*Dasein*'s) being in the world as such.

What is at issue is the very matter of *being with* as a condition of possibility for *Dasein* with or without any specific this or that, this figure or that figure, in any concrete situation: not only witness, but *withness*. This discussion of the primordial structures of existence might seem terribly abstract, which is why there always seems to be such a gaping, yawning abyss—in its own way a kind of *béance causale* between claims toward being about the structure of concrete existence and the analysis of any concretely given situation itself.—About the infinite distance between *being with*, on the one hand, and *being with*—not an x, but *some thing*, something with a name.

After the Second World War, the fructification of this empty place will resurface in France, like a spring in ancient epic, in the concrete analyses of a Lacan, a Blanchot, a Duras, a Deleuze, a Barthes, a Foucault, a Derrida, a Godard. And indeed: it will do so in a certain taking notice or account of act, event, praxis (yes, I dare use this word), writing (as a middle verb), all of which, whether attributed to Jakobson or Austin or both, are names for attempts at a jailbreak from the first lie of a modernity that would have it that the only valid language game is description in sentences of subject-predicate form—of *propositions, sinnvolle Sätze.*

Wittgenstein made us aware of this problem in his *Logico-Philosophical Treatise* (*Logisch-philosophische Abhandlung*). There he compels us to realize that, according to the doctrine expounded in his own very few pages, the very sentences of this book itself—along with all propositions of logic, mathematics, and all tautologies—are themselves, necessarily, without sense, *sinnlos* (which is not at all the same as *nonsensical, unsinnig*, something the stupids—not sublime enough to be idiots—of logical positivism, the Anglo-Twits, systematically erred about in forgetting).

And thus it is no accident at all, but rather what Althusser calls "the becoming necessary of the contingent," that it is Wittgenstein himself who situates the realizing of his own (but not merely) historical compulsion to write the *Philosophische Untersuchungen*, his posthumous *Philosophical Investigations* of 1951, in his working through of Piero Sraffa's response to the Austrian philosopher's own animated setting forth of the aforestated doctrine of what constitutes a meaningful sentence in his own *Treatise*. Sraffa's response, as Wittgenstein himself tells us, was: "What is the meaning of *that?*" where the deictic ictus on the otherwise weak demonstrative pronoun points to Sraffa's giving himself a chin-chuck.[4] In Italian culture, this gesture says something like the following paraphrase of a performative: "I hereby judge what you are telling me to be bullshit, or of no consequence [redundantly: to me]."

Gesture, act, thus trumps "the cat is on the mat" or "the present King of France is bald," in the same way that "let there be light" trumps those silly descriptions of what some Yahweh-Fido created—thises and thatses—on any of the days remaining before Sunday. As Ronell reminds us in *The Test Drive,* Mr. Y. gets bored pretty quickly, which is why he can only take six days of creating before taking a day of rest, and then proceeding to test out his creatura for the time remaining—the *Frist des Daseins,* as Paul, Kierkegaard, Rilke, Heidegger, and Taubes all know (Agamben falls out of this crucial list for his crucial error of forgetting Kierkegaard and being merely a redactor of Taubes). And—as Longinus knows—the First Book of Moses itself only pulls off the trick of following God's performance, in a hortatory subjunctive the subject of which is "light," by anticipating it with "And God said" and following it immediately with "and there was light," thus sandwiching the performative between a proposition of neutral narration on the one hand and the assertion of the postperformance state-of-affairs, a kind of postcoital ah-ah-*Erlebnis,* which seals the matter with a "That was goooooood" on the other.

Philosophical Investigations, written in "the darkness of this time" (a time running thus up through our present), thanking Sraffa, criticizing Frege by name (very rare)—thus, in these thinkings and thankings, comes to remind us that description is but one language game among others. As no one has yet noticed (philosophers are not very good on the mimetic anomalies that key us off to intertextual phantoms), this is why Mr. L.W. (we must use his given initial in order to separate him from other Ws) entitles his book *Philosophische Untersuchungen,* after almost a century (from 1840 to 1923, when Frege wrote the last essay in his posthumous book) during which Trendelenburg, Husserl, and Frege (posthumously) published major works under the title *Logische Untersuchungen.* Unlike L.W.'s wannabe epigones down to this day, it remains for this reader, who is, like Ronell, not merely Anglophone nor Francophone nor Germanophone, but who is differently a stateless stranger, one not entirely at home in any language or other zone (Avital's answering machine for long times of sometimes, some time ago, and perhaps still: "I'm out, you're in"), to remind people in any of those otherwise not completely disabled enough nationalist camps—like most bigots, usually ignorant, proud, and defensive concerning their own ignorance[5]—of their own history, even when they—nationalistic bigidiots—have loved to say, for a long time now, that it is Ronell and those who have stuck it out being in and out with her, and so forth, who do not know or care about history.

Writing in and on With

Better than a reader *of,* or a volume of essays *on,* here the title of the assignment at hand asks, demands a *with.* And thus, in the case of this preposition reassignment, the extreme difficulty of which this wannabe, this *manque-à-être* (isn't everybody?) has joyfully accepted, already Avital Ronell has anticipated the differences between and among such pre-positional particles—with, within, without.

An example or two: In *Crack Wars,* and there rendered most a-cute(ly) in its opening *attacca,* "Hits," and, more precisely or concretely with the gesture toward Heidegger with which these aphoristic meditations end (see *CW,* 33–46), already we are invited, compelled to consider "Being *on* drugs" [my emphasis]. Indeed, for the Munchkin–Old Farts (and in this time of what Ronell calls "reactive posturings," how many of the young, in their overwhelming desire to get through the corporate-academic portal so as to receive a sentence to lifelong mediocrity with ever-decreasing benefits [or worse] are already older than the chronologically old—who at least used to know something?)—this is, no doubt, one of the things that irritates them about Ronell's work, namely that, despite the utterly classical thematic titles of her major works (*Dictations: On Haunted Writing, The Telephone Book: Technology, Schizophrenia, Electric Speech, Crack Wars: Literature, Addiction, Mania, Finitude's Score: Essays for the New Millennium,* or, more recently and iconically—without the colon's immediate promise of supplementary auto-interpretation—*Stupidity, The Test Drive*), these texts, nonetheless, under these controlled signs of unicity, are driven by a compulsion, an urge to expose the foundations of the treatise form itself, to lay them bare, to break them down, to make them strangers like us, thieves in the night.[6]

Here, despite the titular adherence to the rules of thematic appurtenance dictated by the varieties of literary thematics instilled in the author, already before the "merciful end of graduate school" (*DIC,* ix), Ronell's work digs in to the literary-thematic data mine with her dexterous pointer, colon or none, in order to open up a space of potential there, one not capable of being exhausted in or reduced to the reactive "mimetic posturings" of the all-too-common form of infantile leftist—or currently dominant dominance-and-submission oriented, opportunistic, cowardly, and ubiquitous rightist—actings out.

The new and old MOFs might see reading (with) Ronell to be part of a kind of purportedly dangerous—according to their out-petered script—maieutics dangerous to the young and impressionable, lest these be thus seduced to go on and themselves break form, in short, to write—even if (in the work of this thinker and writer Miss Ronell and myself in being with her) composition, proximally and for the most part, is done so well as to serve, for almost three decades now, to bear (in its exquisite sphincter control, never in its letting go) an inimitable signature.—Better, thus, in any case, than the run-of-the-cuisinart academic ephebe might manage.[7] And—oh yeah, I almost forgot: if this interrogation of the *Grund*s of scholarship were not enough, in addition to this, there is, in Ronell, her jewissance, her martyrous passion, her Kierkegaardian refusal of the lie of disinterestedness toward that by which she is compelled. None of today's ubiquitous cynicism here.

Next example: If this were a book in the register *of* or *on* Avital Ronell (what today is all too easily called a *reader:* in choosing what to read it has already read it for you), then this would be a betrayal of the ethics-toward-justice of Ronell's writing practice. This kind of unreflective trotting out of the (forgive me)[8] subjective genitive—Avital's Reader—a lovingly selected congeries of morsels, would indeed be yet another symptom of today's overwhelming compulsion to keep it str8 and simpleton-compatible.

To be just, to be ethical—to the in-mixed, in-folded (not cuisinart) subject-object of our inquiry, the task at hand, the community of thinking, (to) oneself even, to be *with* Avital—we are not allowed to linger with the false intimacy of a set of edited-down (as in dumbed-down, stupided-down) bite-size chunks. Tensely, if not therefore paradoxically, we must take Ronell more in the (or our) objective, a word I use in its perspectival sense of being-a-lens, even if, like the voice (off) of the Godard of *Two or Three Things I Know about Her,* thus we must just as soon interrogate everything and everyone as to the matter of "what is an Object?" so as to go on to interrogate some *Dasein*s as to the nature of this kind of what-is questioning—which last, recently, risks proliferating in and as obscene acts of torture. We must take Avital in, take her, let her be taken in.

Here I counter such proposals for the ubiquitous and further reduction of everything to the propositional with reading *in,* not in the sense of paging or leafing through for the purposes of the cocktail-party *Kultur* of a shallow (cynical, purportedly disinterested) postmodernism, "etc.," or of any other post-it-ism, but rather in the truth of extimacy. I parry such superficial proposals with the compulsion to *over*-read with Ronell, and to read her over and again. To read Ronell *on*—and on. (I am in Ronell. Ronell is in me. We are, and have been, ever since we encountered each other, in this ravishingly powerful knot—*Gefecht*—of an embrace.) This is not to speak of "Avital and me"—as they say these days. This is not, and is not to be (even "merely") "personal." Not one byte. The euphemism of such personalizing-eulogizing tendencies is one of the hallmarks, the greeting cards of false closeness, which should be avoided in the extimacy of the true proximity of those exposed to each other, *auseinandergesetzt*, of proximity in the real of desire, of the desire to think, the desire of thinking—which (surprise! bang!) is *not* personal.

But am I in Ronell? Is Ronell in me? Are we "with" each other? Certainly, in order to be with her at all, it is necessary to ask these most necessary and necessarily extreme and painful questions, which are the kinds of things so deep and so "primitive" in the realm of thinking, hidden—as Klein and Winnicott, let alone DerriDasein and Heidegger-san, know—*at* and *as* and *with* its origins, if there were any. Here we are dealing with what Blanchot calls the "terrifyingly past." If one asks these kinds of questions—and one must, by virtue of the demand of thinking—deal with major anxiety, anxiety so strong it threatens the very bounds of the subject, of the good tit and the bad, as well as with the good in the bad, the bad in the good.

If "one" cannot deal with such anxiety—as to whether one is interrupted, in or out, as to whether one knows or is known, and so on, one projects identifyingly, or projectively identifies, hurling the sticks and stones and bombs from one's ever-tense darkness slingshot with the strength of "one's" "own" rageful destructive drives at any other of convenience.

For these destructive fools—in academe or out: these days, they are every-where, especially among the members of the violence class, namely admin-istrators (Benjamin on *Verwaltung* in Kafka)—there is never *enough*, "they" never "have" enough (precisely because "they" are not *in*, in the sense of "*in* Avital," and thus Avital is not "*in*" them). For these it is imperative—the imperative—not only to consume ever-larger hecatombs, but to swipe the portions—of every course—off the plate of all others onto "their" "own."[9]

It is Ronell who teaches about "their own." In 1992, at the highest pitch of the riots following upon the acquittal of the be(at)ing-on-camera of Rodney King—Ronell wrote an essay, "Trauma TV" (now in *FIN*), for delivery at a conference on "philosophy and literature." As the rhetoric of the Medium[10] was blaring at that time on all frequencies, the people in the ghettos of East L.A. were destroying *their own* property. Clearly this was a card in the race deck (Lacan: "If there's only one card, I can only draw one.") For centuries now, capitalism has defined a person by its "properties."

As Ronell pointed out—in front of live audiences, because the frequencies of the medium were all jammed—of people in ghettos, how can one speak of *their own* property, when it is owned by people somewhere else, in the Green Zone or Beltway? (This was before Giorgio Agamben published *Homo Sacer: Sovereign Power and Bare Life.*[11])

Meanwhile, from the Air above the Abgrund . . .

"Trauma TV" was gathered into *Finitude's Score: Essays for the End of the Millennium* in 1994. The supersonic scream of this book's own occasion is transmitted in its preface, the second paragraph of which reads as follows:

> In case you're thinking, Well, Avital, fuck her, she just lives inside her own head, this work reveals a growing concern over the finite figures that comprise our shared experience. As long as there is something like experience, it is not entirely mine. Nonetheless, if there is a growing sense that the writer is inhabiting an inside that is out of it, this condition cannot simply be debited to the account of the solitary worker but is rather a symptom pointing to *the vanishing of the experienceability of the world*—assuming that, after all is said and done, one can still say "world." In my previous work, I have tried to show in a Heideggerian way the shattering of world and, correspondingly, the extent to which "worldview" (*Weltanschauung*) has been obsolesced. In this work, taking into account the fact of an irredeemably fissured world, I try to consider remappings urged by literature and psychoanalysis but also by the logic of teletopical incursions that has supplanted ground and grounding. On another level, in a requiem for George [H. W.] Bush, I trace the phantasmic history that has led to the relegitimization of war. In order to explore the recodifications of war for which "GeoBush" is responsible, it was necessary to take recourse to psychoanalytic writings on paranoiac aggression and to understand how the Persian Gulf War metonymized the compulsion of the Western logos to "finish with." In this case, GeoBush's personal trauma in World War II was found to coincide with a national crypt which we understand as unmournable Vietnam. More technologically defined, the Gulf War disclosed the essence of the test site and the crucial relatedness of technology to testing. Still, the drama of an unfinished world war, which left wide open the question of airspace, was refitted to Iraq according to the strategic command system of a very personal obsession. GeoBush's obsession with airspace, which led me to inquire why there are so many cowboys in Cyburbia, continued into his last days in office: eerily marking to the day and to the minute the anniversary of his initial bombing of Iraq, Bush

announces that "the skies are safer now." His final utterance on reviewing the military in 1993 was to assure himself and us that closure had been finally, in the final moments, achieved. But what are the terms of such a closure? And has the double history of traumatic repetition been brought to term? Whether or not war can be read any longer as a pregnancy test for historical becoming, we have to come to terms with the possibility that we no longer know how to wage war—which is why one has the uncanny sense of riding the wave of a personal pathology when finding oneself engaged in "war." (*FIN*, ix–x)

Scripsit Ronell 1994. The urgency—*Drang*—of the situation set forth here has only been made more acute by GeoShrub's adjuvant excuse for the invasion of Iraq and the overthrow of Saddam Hussein: "He tried to kill my daddy." While the most clamorous objections to the confabulated and ever-mobile reasons for the continuing crimes against humanity reintensified in Palestine (1948–), Afghanistan (2001–), Iraq II (2003–), Lebanon (2006–), and in many elsewheres have to do with the lies in which such excuses have been (and still are) propagated, it remains nonetheless to take seriously this typically sandbox excrescence of the current placeholder of the hereditary for-profit presidency. For if Shrub's reasons for his own going to war are *personal,* then our W.ARbusto is, in fact, admitting that he is not acting as the representative–democratically elected (which he is not) sovereign of a republic, but as a kinglet of days of yore, whether ancient or feudal or modern or postmodern—it matters not. Thus Bush's burning word (as dictated to him, perhaps in better syntax—which last, as has been noted, only comes on the scene when at least the preconscious becomes involved), in his signing statements, and like that of his precursor *Führer,* is law.[12] The relation between the personal and the political has now indeed been complicated in its being made easy, in its being pancaked.[13]

I put the Ronell passage above, so as to bring it under the interrogation lamp with the following:

> Today it is no longer possible to keep to the traditional representations of space, to think air space, be it that of land or sea, either as a mere contingency or as something superadded. To do so would be to think, in an all too naïve way, from bottom to top [*von unten nach oben gedacht*]. It would be the perspective of an observer, who, from the standpoint of the surface of land or sea, looks into the air and, straining his neck, stares from below to above while the bomber rushing through air space accomplishes its monstrous effect from above to below. Despite whatever differences [existed] between land war and sea war, in both of these previous cases there existed a common plane, and, even spatially, the battle played itself

out in the same dimension, in which the fighting parties stood opposed on the same surface. In contradistinction to this there emerges, in [the case of] air space, its own dimension, its own space, which is not annexed to that to the planes of land and sea, from which it is separated, but leaves the differentiation between itself and these others out of consideration, and already for this reason [*aus diesem Grunde*] is essentially [*wesentlich*] to be differentiated in its structure from the surface spaces of the other two kinds of war. The horizon of air war is another than that of land and sea war; and it is even a question if, in the case of air war, one can still speak of *horizon*. The structural change is all the greater in that both surfaces— of land and of sea—lie undifferentiated beneath the one the successful effects of which [proceed] from air space, from above to below [*von oben nach unten*]. The person to be found upon secure dry land, however, is related to the airplanes having their effect upon him from the air above [*von oben*] more in the way in which a living thing to be found upon the sea bottom is related to the craft upon the sea's surface than it does to one of its own kind.

[Considered] on its own, air war suspends the relation between power's use of violence and the population affected by [such] violence to an extremely greater degree than is the case with blockade in sea war. In bombardment from the air the relationshipless-ness [*Beziehungslosigkeit*], of the agent prosecuting war, to the ground and to the enemy population upon it, becomes absolute; here not even a shadow of the relation between protection and obedience remains any longer. In air war [considered] on its own there is no longer any possibility, for the one side or the other, to establish [such] a relation. Having flown in, the airplane comes and throws its bombs to the ground; the low-flying [aircraft] is allowed to come down to the ground and then once again climbs away; both exercise their function of annihilation [*Vernichtungsfunktion*] and then immediately abandon [*überlassen*] this ground—with people and matters as they are [*Sachen*] to be found upon it—to their fate, that is to say to the powers of the state on the ground. Like an observation of the relation [*Verhältnis*] between the type of war and [its] booty, so [too] an observation of the relation between protection and obedience reveals the absolute disorientation [*Entortung*], and with it the purely annihilating nature, of modern air war.

I cite this passage from the final pages of Carl Schmitt's *The Nomos of the Earth in International Law of the Jus Publicum Europaeum* of 1950.[14] Ronell writes of the "*vanishing of the experienceability of the world*—assuming that, after all is said and done, one can still say 'world.'" Schmitt: "The horizon of air war is a different one from that of land war and sea war; it is even a question whether one can still speak of *horizon* at all." This is no coincidence, nor is it in any way a matter of Ronell's secret sharing with Schmitt. While

195

by 1994 Ronell has perhaps not yet metabolized Schmitt's earlier *Erörterung* of this *Entortung* of *Nomos* (Schmitt is not referred to by name in *Finitude's Score*), indeed his discourse is "eerily mark[ed]" here in a "double history of traumatic repetition."

In the second paragraph from Schmitt the structural transformation brought about by air war is enunciated as the extreme attenuation, break, or absence of (at least) three different kinds of relation: 1. There is the suspension, *Aufhebung*, (to a degree greater than what obtains in sea blockade) of the *Zusammenhang* between the power using violence and the population affected by the violence; 2. in the following sentence this escalates into the *Beziehungslosigkeit*, or relationshiplessness, which becomes absolute in the case of those prosecuting air war vis-à-vis the ground and those upon it; and 3. the observation of the difference, in the case of air war, regarding the relation, *Verhältnis*, between a given kind of war and the booty corresponding to it, just as the comparing observation regarding the relation [*Zusammenhang*] of protection and obedience—both of these reveal the "absolute de-placement and with it the purely annihilating character of modern air war [*absolute Entortung und damit den reinen Vernichtungscharakter des modernen Luftkrieges*]." Absolute de-placing is revealed through the relationshiplessness of the bomber swooping down and then back up again. The lack of hanging together of attacker and attacked, of the ones holding power and those obedient to them, is revealed in comparison of the modes of war and their resultant spoils (in air war there is spoiling but there are no spoils as such). Observations that take all of this into account reveal the *purely annihilatory character* of modern air war. The introduction of the dimension of the vertical, of war in 3–D, is correlated here with three strong attributes of nihilism: the "modern," "absolute de-placement," and "the purely exterminational mode."

Ronell's repetitions of Schmitt—unaware as they are here of being repetitions—are different. If what is being discussed is "*the vanishing of the experienceability of the world*," nonetheless it remains the case that "this work reveals a growing concern over the finite figures that comprise our shared experience." What is shocking here is Ronell's ability not to be "inside her own head" but rather of her being strong enough to tackle the unenviable task of dealing with what is in George H. W. Bush's head—not for the purpose of some pathetic and pointless attempt at the false charity of empathy, but in an attempt to bring him to term, to understand the logic of his own bad(-)object relations, so as to try to prevent them from going on and on. Obviously this has nothing to do with the individual-therapeutic, which, in any case, and as Freud himself realized with Schreber, is impossible in the case of the paranoid. No, not that: Rather Ronell here goes on to see Bush itself as an effect of the larger phantasy of the cowboy flying over the frontiers of subcyburbia so as to secure the oil necessary to the daily commute and its American way of death in life (are there things known, in the civilized world, as sidewalks in Houston?). It is Ronell's enormous strength to be capable of an analysis that takes crucial account not only of the transmogrifications of the technological enhancements in killing potential actualized in air war, but also of the ways in which these themselves are tied in with ideology and with world-destructive paranoid delusion. For Schmitt, as a historian of law and of the law of war, as well as of their transformations, such things are beginning to be thought already just after the First World War. In his definition of the state of exception in *Political Theology*, he enters a Kierkegaardian rhetoric he will never leave behind regarding the impotence of the law as abstract universal which, in every act of judicial decision, must come up against a "concrete" situation.

For Schmitt's work, the extremity of the impasse here is grave indeed. While, on the one hand, he is the preeminent exponent of the legal theory of decisionism, he is at the same time at a loss to account for any kind of ideological capture, for the way in which extreme decisions—and the extremity of decisionism itself, its belonging to what he calls, in the opening pages of *Political Theology* (1921), "the outermost sphere"—capture subjects, whether singularly or in groups. Without Freud, Althusser, and Ronell, Schmitt is shipwrecked. Only psychoanalysis, what Derrida calls the "science of the proper name,"[15] can help us deal with the qualitative abyss, opened up in Kierkegaard's reading of Hegel, between the universal and the particular-become-singular. Althusser himself is dwelling with these problems when, in a discussion of Lucretian atomism, he speaks of "the becoming necessary of the contingent."[16]

The Caves of Being

It turns out that both Schmitt and Ronell are in a chat room with at least one third party, whom Ronell names, with her "in a Heideggerian way," and whom Schmitt, also "in a Heideggerian way," does not. It is Heidegger with whom both Ronell and Schmitt are having intercourse, being *with*. Here is the "transition" [*Übergang*] from the tenth to the eleventh hour of *Was heisst Denken?* It is—quite literally, thus—the annunciation of the last lecture of Heidegger's last university course, the beginning of the eleventh (or twelfth, noonday) hour of his professional career. It is spring-summer [*Sommersemester*] 1952:

Parmenides's saying goes right to what the word *eon* names. This becomes fully clear if we substitute, under the auspices of Parmenides's own usage, the word *eon* for the last word *emmenai*. Grammatically presented, the word is a participle. Consideration showed: *eon* is the participle of participles, the *eon* is the singular and thus most preeminent *metoche* [sharing, participation]. It speaks the twofold: beings being: being of beings [*Seiendes seiend: seiend Seiendes*]. Instead of verbal interpretation [*verbalen Beudeutung*] the language uses the infinitive *emmenai, einai, esse, sein* as well.

The worn-down form of *eon,* which is common in Plato and Aristotle, is: *on, to on,* beings being [*das Seiende seiend*]. Without any trace of a violent act the entirety of Western metaphysics thus may be translated under the title: *to on.* Of course here we must fulfill one condition. From the outset, thus, we must consistently and exclusively hear and read the word *to on* as the preeminent participle, and this even when we do not each time, in philosophical usage, ourselves pronounce it as such.

When we say "Being" [*"Sein"*], then, this means: "the Being of Beings" [*"Sein des Seienden"*]. When we say "Beings," then, this means: Beings in reference to Being [*Seiendes hinsichtlich des Seins*]. We speak always *from* the fold-into-two. This is always already given, for Parmenides as well as for Plato, for Kant as well as for Nietzsche. The fold-into-two has already unfolded the realm within which the relation of Beings to Being becomes representable. This relation can be interpreted and explained in different ways.

Plato gives an interpretation crucial for Western thinking. He says, between Beings and Being there is a *chorismos. He chora* means the place. Plato wishes to say: Beings and Being are in different places. Beings and Being are differently placed. Thus when Plato thinks the *chorismos,* the different placing of Beings and of Being, he is inquiring as to the completely other place of Being in comparison to that of Beings.

In order to be able to put this question about the *chorismos,* about the *differentness* of the placing [*Verschiedenheit der Ortung*] of Beings and Being at all, the *difference,* the fold-into-two [*Zwiefalt*] of both must already have been given, and this in such a way that the fold-into-two itself and as such is not taken account of independently.

The same holds for all transcendence. When we pass over from Beings to Being, we thus measure, in this passage, the twofold of both. The passage nonetheless never allows the fold-into-two to have originated beforehand. The fold-into-two is already in use. It is already in every act of saying and representing, doing and letting what is most used [*das Gebrauchteste*], and thus the applicable [*Gebräuchliche*] itself.

If we hear the word *eon* from behind its folded-into-two meaning, from beyond its grammatical, participial form, then we can translate the saying more clearly:

"It needs the letting-set-forth-before thus (the) taking-into-account also: Beings Being."

In itself even this is still no translation of the concluding words of the saying. We have merely replaced the Greek words with others—by *ens* and *esse* or by "Beings" and "being." In this substitution business we come everywhere to nothing. If we are to hear the saying, if, through it, we shall be brought into questioning, it is not enough to exchange the Greek words for any better-known words of other languages. Rather we must let ourselves be said by the Greek words, [let them] say what it is *they* name. We must displace our hearing into the realm of saying of the Greek language.[17]

We should not shy away from leaving the most difficult for the end, instead of making some kind of false attempt at clearing everything up and bringing it to a false, and falsely final, apocalyptic blowout. There is much to be written (and I am writing it elsewhere, from another place, that is to say, here and now) on the *lassens,* the differentiations in the capitalizations, the need to pluralize Beings in English for *Seiendes* in the German, the difficulties of *Hören,* the entirety of "Western metaphysics," the taking-part of *metoche,* which Heidegger has spent so much time discussing in the previous lecture.[18] Nonetheless, there are important things to be said about this constellation I have assembled *with* Ronell, Schmitt, and Heidegger.

What Ronell names here as her Heidegger channel is also a Freud-Benjamin channel. For in order to read what she asserts above, precisely in its difference from Schmitt and Heidegger, we must take account of the way she (and not they) deploys "psychoanalysis" to transform a consideration of the Heideggerian *Gestell* by linking it to obsession, *Zwang,* and to obsession as *not merely personal.* Ronell's instress on inscape is there so as to draw attention away from itself. And H.W.'s Thing is also, indeed, a structural matter, despite its reeking of a "very personal obsession," and not a matter of some individual trauma victim handing over its shell-schlock. Rather, the *Wiederholungszwang,* which Freud, deliberately slaloming around Nietzsche, not unproblematically discovers in *Beyond the Pleasure Principle,* must be read with the canniness of Benjamin on Baudelaire. For Benjamin, modern lyric, the symptomatic scream of the loss of experience in shock, is that of "a love not so much at first as at last sight."[19]

If the cry—from the speaker of this poem to a woman seen and just as soon lost in the crowd—at the end of Baudelaire's sonnet is "Oh you whom I might have loved, oh you who knew it!," the job of the pilot of the plane is to put the bombardier in position of destroying the target, with the resulting destruction to be filmed by a camera with no one behind the lens. Not even shock belongs to the agent of destruction in air war.[20]

199

The destruction of air war is "absolute" because of the relationshiplessness Schmitt has foregrounded in his consideration of its technics. Let us make some more flybys over Heidegger's text in order to target what is at issue there—not to destroy, but to read *and* to see (they are not at all the same). Heidegger's words come to utterance in the two years following Schmitt's *Nomos*. Despite the apparent difference from the Schmitt in their thematic register, we are, in many important respects, in the same airspace, if not on the same ground or sea. Here too the nihilistic movement at and as the origin of Western metaphysics is prefigured in Heidegger's often-told story about the instrumentalization of the thinking of being in its fall from the infinite and verbal *emmenai* into its on-the-way-toward nounness in the participle *eon,* which itself becomes fully reified in its substantialization in *to on.* This Platonic act of reification—infinitive verb into present participle into gerund with a definite article—is decisive for the fate of metaphysics, "for Parmenides as well as for Plato, for Kant as well as for Nietzsche."

In a passage reminiscent not only of Baudelaire but also of Lucretius, Giorgio de Chirico writes a wonderful transposed epitaph on the last page of his only novel, *Hebdomeros:* ". . . O Hebdomeros, dit-elle, je suis l'Immortalité. Les noms ont leur genre, ou plutôt leur sexe, comme tu as dit une fois avec beaucoup de finesse, et les verbes, hélas, se déclinent."²¹

Verbs, which are conjugated, decline—into nouns, which are, indeed, declined. Usually verbs are conjugated; they hook up. Nouns are fallen, declined. What does it mean when verbs fall? This question has as its stakes nothing less than the matter of the articulation of *Dasein's* irreducible spatiality, the theory of the sign and of reference, the world for Descartes, distance, and discourse, as these begin to be discussed in chapter 3, "The Worldhood of the World," in *Being and Time,* and, in particular, in sections 17–27. It is this very logic of decline, which, in section 27, leads to the discussion of *Dasein's* being-in-the-world in terms of its averageness, leveling down, and the meaningless discourse, *Gerede,* of "The They" ["das Man"]. *Dasein* and *Sein* would seem to be preeminent cruxes of nounverbs and verbnouns.

The fold-into-two [*Zwiefalt*] itself unfolds the space in which "the relation of Beings to Being becomes representable [*vorstellbar*]." Distance belongs to representation—"Where word leaves off, no thing may be" (Heidegger, citing Stefan George)—whereas presentation causes shock because it touches, hits, contaminates, wounds, marks—like love at last sight—and leaves the scar of the poem as trace. The fold-into-two must be conceived as logically prior to the setting up of the *chorismos,* the gap between the completely different realms of Being and Beings.

Despite the ease in doing so, we must not simply be blinded by the uncanny similarity of the air war problematic in Schmitt (1950) and Ronell (1994). This, indeed, would be a very destructive act of pancaking. Yes, there is much to be done in terms of pointing out the horizontal and vertical axes, here dramatized in the vocabulary of "horizon" and "experience" or "the skies" or "the airplane swooping in."

And likewise, the comparison of the uncanny resemblances between Schmitt's discussion of the different situation of airspace in relation to the spaces of the ground, whether land or maritime, and Heidegger's trip about the neglect of the different ways in which Being and Beings are situated, about their different emplacements, is only the clearing of the runway for a reading. This is comparative literature—reading—in its bare bones, but without yet having made a definitive reading or intervention.

The question that *must be asked* is: What does and might it mean for the world, today, to be capable of acknowledging the relations between what happens in all purported transcendences and the purely annihilatory, kakangelic, compulsive, repeated behavior [*andauernd wiederholte Tun*] of air war? Schmitt, Heidegger, Ronell know damn well what they are talking about in these places—just as in many others. Lévinas and William Burroughs and Joseph Beuys did too, when they talked about the allergy of Western metaphysics for the other, or of humanity as a skin disease (with subcutaneous oil reservoirs) of the surface of the earth.

I have not even mentioned yet the militarization of space, which indeed takes all of this into "the outermost sphere," and which has already been in the works for a long time. This, indeed, is the usurpation of the outermost sphere—read: of the quintessence, fifth element—by beings in their forgetting of Being. *This* is nihilism. And nihilism is ubiquitous today. It *is* today. It would seem to be embodied in all acts of purported transcendence: "the skies are safer now," the missile shield will ensure eternal peace. Gore Vidal: *Perpetual War for Perpetual Peace*. If you think of yourself as inhabiting some tower with a great view, I suggest that you and yours think about what, from the Bible until now, tends to happen to high towers, and consider, rather, for example, what is said of people in caves. Because today we are troglodytes, living in caves, and would seem to be doing everything we can to make sure we have to dig them deeper. I, for one, would rather be—privileged to be—surviving with Ronell, without wars, war criminals, or signing statements. May the world live on, and, when justice is come, have the chance to write a requiem for the last victims of the Bushes.

It is the task of the prophets of now to realize the lesson taught to us by the progressive unfolding of the deserts of nihilism: Now that all the places that formerly sheltered the transcendental—sky, space—have been mobilized for death dealing, it is the task of thought today to realize that the other space, place, locality is that of the *act* of thought, which does not happen elsewhere, but is situated, differently, *here*—if anywhere, and is not simply a representation of a state of affairs.

Let us begin our libretto with three mottos from the last millennium:

To complicate a fact is: to act.

A possible world is something specified in a sentence,
     not seen through a telescope.

"Things as they are / Are changed upon the blue guitar."[22]

NOTES

1. I refer to Avital Ronell's works by abbreviation and page number: *Dictations: On Haunted Writing* (Lincoln: University of Nebraska Press, 1993 [1986], *DIC; Crack Wars: Literature, Addiction, Mania* (Lincoln: University of Nebraska Press, 1992), *CW; Finitude's Score* (Lincoln: University of Nebraska Press, 1994), *FIN.*

2. My interlocutor here was Hans Skott-Myhre, whom I thank, and whose slow pupil I remain.

3. A prophetic act is thus what Paul de Man calls text or event. See "Kant and Schiller," in his *Aesthetic Ideology* (Minneapolis: University of Minnesota Press, 1995).

4. For the authoritative checkup on the chin chuck and significance of the repression of its meaning, see Leo Steinberg's magnificent *The Sexuality of Christ in the Renaissance and in Modern Oblivion* (Chicago: University of Chicago Press, 2nd ed., 1997 [1983]).

5. If you are having trouble wrapping your head around this list, you will find some help in a book published around the same time as Husserl's own *Logical Investigations,* called *The Interpretation of Dreams.*

6. Speaking of losses: I take this moment to remember Hans-Georg Gadamer, who, in his lectures at the Collegium Phaenomenologicum in Perugia in 1986, speaking of the *Gedankenkreis* to *Being and Time,* said that during the time of its composition, Heidegger in his lectures repeatedly cited the Gospel: "Do not wait for the savior, he will come like a thief in the night."

7. Hence the envy. Once, during the spring of 1992 in City Lights Bookshop in San Francisco, I witnessed the following invidious love scene: A male Berkeley gradual student hands a female Berkeley gradual student a copy of *Crack Wars,* just published. The female fingers the multicolored ribbon-bookmarks sewn into the spine, turns to her suitor, and says, in the nastiest voice imaginable, "How the fuck does SHE rank!?"

8. I typed this "forgive me" reflexively; but, in its unreflected, reactive character, it does provide the chance to ask the question: Who, among the readers of this essay, of this book, of Ronell, of anything, even knows or cares what the difference between an objective or a subjective genitive is anymore? Who even knows what a genitive is? A verb? A noun? A mode? A case? A tense? A mood?—and most of all, a *tone*. If "diplomacy" has failed and thus led to an unending series of wars on the mobile army of the truth of the other, this is only possible on the basis of the fact that the United States of America is an isolated, illiterate, and ignorant nation, without any significant venue for serious intellectuals to communicate—even among themselves. Germany 1933–45 (including its exiled parts) may have produced much more eloquent writing than the U.S.A. from 1980 on through the now, and until the advent of an unforeseen resituation of what counts as a society, or a life worth living. We are waiting for "the will to rupture." Who knows? If even the so-called elite of the United States is satisfied with the newspaper whose motto is "all the News that's fit to print" and its ubiquitous, if ever more murderous, metonymic displacements, there is very little worth saving, apart from life itself considered as mere potential for something else.

9. I advert to Gore Vidal's sublime utterance in *The Nation* on the occasion of the death of a being rigidly designated by "Nixon," "R.I.P., R.M.N.," now in Vidal, *The Last Empire: Essays 1992–2000* (New York: Doubleday, 2001).

10. The term "Medium" is used here in order to indicate that it, too, is now more than ever an Army of One. As Rei Terada suggested to me in conversation around the beginning of "shock and awe" in 2003, there are no longer media, there is only the medium. Indeed, is not this always already one of the big calling cards of fascism?

11. Stanford, Calif.: Stanford University Press, 1998 (1995).

12. For reasons of theoretical interest, someone somewhere will have to take up what this involves, in a Lacanian problematic, for the relation between S1 and S2, between the master signifier and its chain of metonyms. When it is the metonyms dictating (to) the Master, we should, properly and in the tradition of ideology critique, say that we know who *really* is holding the big dildo. No doubt this has something to do with what Lacan himself noted as the waning of the paternal order. Today some call it blowback.

13. I analyzed and predicted this in my "On the Degradation of the Political Life in a Certain Type of Object Choice Made by Men," *Cultural Critique* 44 (1999), an issue edited by Jochen Schulte-Sasse and devoted to the matter of Clinton's impeachment.

14. Berlin: Duncker and Humblot, 1950, cited from the second edition of 1974. I have retranslated with attention to language, rather than use the existing English translation (by G. L. Ulman, *The Nomos of the Earth in the International Law of the Jus Publicum Europaeum* [New York: Telos Press, 2003]). The paragraphs cited here are to be found in the German at pp. 297–98, and in the English of the published translation at pp. 319–20.

15. See Jacques Derrida, *La Carte postale de Socrate à Freud et au-delà* (Paris: Flammarion, 1980).

16. See his *Sur la philosophie* (Paris: Gallimard, 1993).

17. Martin Heidegger, *Was heisst Denken?* (Martin Heidegger Gesamtausgabe 8), hrsg. von Paola-Ludovica Coriando (Frankfurt am Main: Klostermann, 2002), pp. 232–33. My translation.

18. For some groundwork on these questions of reading Heidegger, see "Anamorphoses of Grammar," in Thomas Pepper, *Singularities* (Cambridge, U.K.: Cambridge University Press, 1997).

19. Benjamin, *Gesammelte Schriften*, I-2 (Frankfurt am Main: Suhrkamp, 1974, 1980), p. 623.

20. The cowardliness of the gesture of covering Picasso's depictions of the fascist aerial destruction of Guérnica during discussion of resolutions authorizing the use of force against Iraq by the United Nations indeed placed those in the chamber of the General Assembly in the position of a pilot on a bombing mission, whose job is to deliver death, not to see it. Indeed this act could be likened to the covering of mirrors in a household where mourning is taking place. Those participating in passing such resolutions were thus removed from the position of the traditional beholder in painting, sparing them thus the witness of their own double act—of murder in Iraq and of suicide inasmuch as their work has reduced that organization to aiding and abetting the very acts it was founded in order to prevent from ever happening again. Shame!

21. Giorgio de Chirico, *Hebdomeros* (Paris: Flammarion, 1964), 130. The main text of the novel is followed by the inscription: "Paris, octobre 1929." For the Ashbery and the translation, see Giorgio de Chirico, *Hebdomeros* (Cambridge, Mass.: Exact Change, 1992).

22. From Paul de Man, *Allegories of Reading* (New Haven, Conn.: Yale University Press, 1979), Saul Kripke, *Naming and Necessity,* First Lecture (Cambridge, Mass.: Harvard University Press, 1980), and Wallace Stevens, "The Man with the Blue Guitar," in Holly Stevens, ed., Wallace Stevens, *The Palm at the End of the Mind* (New York: Vintage, 1967).

Tom Cohen
Roaming (Dis)Charges:
"Catastrophe of the Liquid Oozing"

Abstinence—cold turkey—
opens the medusoid rift.

—CRACK WARS

Coming from her, originating in her, it is nonetheless
a foreign body, ever replacing the newly born body.
Catastrophe of the liquid oozing.

—CRACK WARS

One can approach Avital Ronell as a political scientist of memory transmission whose performative forays—at plague-centers within a *grand mal
d'archive*—negotiate a different relation to the catastrophic. There are vapors
one encounters in this prose, drugs without names of the sort that concern
AR, and one enters corridors within her syntax that beckon, or unravel,
into accelerating *passages*. One could assemble a file of these, trip over
their accumulation and vanishings, get off in uncharted spots at which
the body writes under other names, under the radar of swooping policial
cropdusters. Peel back the analytic riffs and one finds oneself, forgetting
these opiates, at the revocation of imagined histories: legatees are threaded
like beads, epistemo-political machines are exposed, and one is delivered,
if one is, to sites one cannot get back from. One finds oneself—no, I do,
who find sanctuary in a certain tonality—before an array of portals that
whisper again and again one word: *war*. Ronell goes out for drives to test
this perimeter. There are crack wars and drug wars, the tropes of Desert
Gulf, war as illness: one hears the "tensions rumbling through the novel
derive from a secret war against artificial, pathogenic and foreign invasions"
(*Crack Wars*, 115)[1]; "the poetic and war efforts appear often to interlap" (*Stupidity*, 5); the "warrior impulse" (*Stupidity*, 110), and illness is itself "war"
(*Stupidity*, 186).[2] It is a word that recurs like a stamp, suggesting a "civil
war" internal to the archive and contemporaneity, of which *Crack Wars*

is an unlikely cipher and *Stupidity* a strategy of transition. *AR* roams the modern legacyscape inspecting catastrophes of cultural transmission and their cognitive politics the way a ghost returns to a remembered site—from after "the transvaluating machine was left running" (*CW,* 69).

I will examine the slow drip of this word, *war,* but do so by way of the least auspicious trace among Ronell's preoccupations—the black ooze, which haunts the center of *Crack Wars,* coming from the mouth of Emma Bovary's corpse. Site of speech and ingestion, the running fluid that dissolves interiors in literature's famous corpse is like the acid-blood of Ridley Scott's alien, manifesting prefigural properties: ink-like, it seems to precede not just tropes but letteration itself—as if inscriptions were being liquefied.

What I would like to explore is a minor figure in her text, a bile she finds coming from the mouth of Emma Bovary and locates at the center of *Crack Wars*—as if, threading the pharmocopoetics of the "literary" and programmed culture, this figure had something to do with war itself. I will interpret this as a sort of prefigural agency Ronell encounters in secret places—a leakage that evacuates the remaining debris of old models of interiority. I will suggest it also condenses the figure of "anteriority" itself to a mercurial and corrosive ink, a site where inscriptions seem to have melted back. And I will suggest that, in its way, this figure into which traditions may be dissolved, as into an allo-human black hole within memory networks, is connected to a site linked to what Derrida calls *khora,* a nonsite in which the preinscriptions from which reading models and meaning systems derive are set or effaced. Because of this link, the prefigural agency Ronell taps into anticipates coming wars of reinscription that seem palpable on numerous epistemological fronts "today." The war, then, will be in and over archival programs and memory regimes that return, like oil, to the site of "catastrophe of the liquid oozing."

I.

Why can, or must one, return to war in Ronell—even if that is called by other names, like "test drive"? Do others not know this war is going down? What has it to do with wars of transmission and legacies, of the archive and anteriority?

AR is the performative (an)archivist of a certain going under (the jacket of *Stupidity* speaks of "the fading of cognitive empires"). Of course, she will be forced to migrate along the filaments of metaphor: from telephonics and switchboards (s)he is forced from the *terra* itself—which has been dissolved into circuits and cognitive mafias—into orbits, of which the iconic text or "name" thought secure operates as near space-junk and satellite ("Kant," "Wordsworth"). A "satellite" is turned toward the earth teleporting memory or cognitive clichés, but its outer side faces constellations without anthropomorphic echo. AR's appeal to *satellites* mimics the war fantasies of a coming American panopticon, sensors of the "compressed kill chain"—a "Minority Report" scenario of preemption, of temporal loops. I will risk a hypothesis: the war at issue is over inscriptions from which perceptual programs and legibility are generated, and not this or that territorial or colonial skit—drug wars or desert storms, wars on terror or involving academic self-mutilations (for the greatest drug is the ordering of certain cognitive rituals here, certain blinds). *I will risk an obscure remark that may betray my stupidity: she wanders into a preparatory space of auto-sacrifice without a cut, and without a call, in which anteriority as "recognized" is also liquefied.* She has wandered beside a nonsite she calls at times ex-scription. The epistemo-political war that is at issue may be more decisive, if invisible, today than any mere world war, because it condenses the historial labyrinth of the archive of the Book to the point of a non-question.

Yet having said this, I am interested in something very small and irreducible that drifts through her tropology—*a black liquid,* a poison of sheer anteriority, a sort of vomit or voiding of interiors, the home, the family even. As the (an)archivist of a certain going under, AR seems unable to track the inner history of ideational forces, mini-genealogies, without exposing it to something like an encapsulating backglance designed to close out a repetition cycle or mark where it is arrested and bypassed.

Ronell references what she calls "crack wars" to this figure at the omphalous of a seeming canon—the "novel," modernity, Flaubert. That is, to the black ooze coming from Emma's mouth in what one calls death, which triggers a reverse temporal flow. The "catastrophe of the liquid oozing" marks time, is para-menstrual, drains: "it all comes from the issue of her body, the sudden spill of liquid, the way she's stained and shredded by anguish. Coming from her, originating in her, it is nonetheless a foreign body, ever replacing the newly born body. Catastrophe of the liquid oozing" (*CW,* 110).

The literary hit, "woman," the pharmacopia itself implodes here to an inky exteriority, a liquid black hole, a trickle of mnemonic transmission fluid. It alters the aesthetic montage we call body: "Now this drainage which in itself produces nothing—there is no transfer of energy or funds—will terminate only when the cash flow gushes out of her mouth at the scene of her suicide. This is when the concept itself of currency becomes assimilated to her circulatory systems" (*CW,* 111). Even "coffee, a dissolute pleasure, brings up the haunted image of black liquid" (*CW,* 142). And: "(s)he does not manage to eliminate any particular force or figure, though it is said that ink flows from her mouth" (*CW,* 95). Ink-like, the ooze here vomited from Emma, which resists figuration, is not unrelated to the fluids of Norman Bates's oil-like bog—allied, not only to what that film calls a sort of placeless *mother,* but to what the preceding film quips about as a sort of "alphabet soup" in doing so.

AR arrests not just Madame Bovary but a macabre instant of transmission that dissolves then discharges the "book's" intestines. What catapults the repetitions of an addiction—that is, chemical, semantic, referential, and temporal addictions, even those supposedly birthing "modernism" (or its feint)—to a sort of hemorrhagic fever where the borders of cells and organs dissolve?

This gearshift metastasizes in Ronell's reading of Dostoyevsky in *Stupidity,* when Flaubert's book turns up in the pocket of the "idiot" Myshkin. In this "coupling" between the two novelists something passes: "The coupling with the other work seals the suicide pact" (*S,* 223). Ronell reads this empocketing: "Depositing the book near or on his body . . , Myshkin proffers his body as an impossible pre-scription, overwritten, as it were, and conscripted by a drive that comes from elsewhere. (There is no prescription for what he has.) Parasided and harassed, he, like anybody, finds himself borrowed and read as the map of expensive hospitality, an inscription pad where everyone crashes. . . . Sealing and concealing the book, Myshkin signs in and under the name of the other, binding himself irrevocably to this power that comes from elsewhere" (241–42).

Ronell here isolates a unique site, little accessed in today's criticism, an Odradekian petratrope amid her exorbitant traffic and eavesdroppings on teletechnic switchboards and the inner histories of dead-enders, suicides, ecstates, addicts, and those beyond mourning. We witness in AR's detective work on cultural mnemonics the encounter with a *khoratic* agent, where inscriptions have dissolved into a prefigural soup in and from which vehicles of transport are dumped or retrieved. The black fluid dissolves script or letteral shapes to some preoriginary *stuff.* AR draws near to this nonsite to wrest from it other times and lines of force, alternative time-spaces or historial back loops to which the ones we call tradition represent facades and relapses (to use de Man's cancer-prone trope, to which Ronell, with clear antagonism, draws close). One could call de Man a transmorphic repressed of AR, but (s)he names it, virtually dedicates *Stupidity* to that, if with a palpable nausea, as if accessing this anti-poison to Derridean weaves.

The black oozing—what has this ink-like stuff, not quite vomit, to do with a blinding "white" of the page, of (a) *crack,* or the war that is at once, today, invisible and so totalized it seems without temporal or geographical horizon, an epistemographic trance or eddy like the facade of a global war on terror, like white noise? This crack war has been there a long time. Already, *it* was that totalized war that Benjamin responds to in the *Theses* when he speaks of the "enemy" as historicism or a certain media programming of perception (and not, that is, the mere "world" wars of late-colonial fascism in its proto-technic genocidal convulsion). That is, what is totalized in the contemporary fever of mimetic and mediacratic programs, commodified reference, memory regimes.

What *war*, if what "was" itself, *sheer anteriority*, leaks or recongeals—if anteriority, like this black discharge, offers itself, as it is shown in *Crack Wars,* as the cipher of the phantasm of a "modernity" that, today, seems so anesthetized, so drugged? AR chooses the back trails of the literary to operate, in mock-guerilla fashion. She takes what Hillis Miller called a black hole and liquefies it—turns it, or its inertia, into a proactive agent. What is liquefied bursts the cell walls, runs under portals, eludes surveillance.

II.

There is a question about the underlying "Americanness" of Ronell's project. AR writes from after the "transvaluating machine" has been left in default. She assumes a teletechnic switch that displaces and consumes the protocols of the Book, disclosing networks that precede it. (It is typical of Ronell's "books" that she marks, pleasures in, and distances the latter's production as commodified object and memory bomb.) Ronell leaves a marker of this *American* or totalizing effect in the veil put over the body of a simulant, Emma, a disinfectant-effect. That veil is designed to lessen the corpse's smell, to render in slow motion the catastrophe of the oozing liquid from migrating virally. When AR loops back to *Crack Wars* through the dossier of Dostoyevsky's *The Idiot*—through Prince Myshkin, who carries in his pocket a copy of *Madame Bovary* at his collapse—she maps a *contamination* around the tele-networks of the literary, a wholly other model of "literary history" to anything available in the hermeneutic pharmacy. Ronell chooses to focus not on the female corpse of Natasya, an Emma avatar, but a special American *clothe* connected to smell, to interiors: "This body, now reduced to the smell of preservatives, is covered by a medicalized trace called America: 'Do you notice the smell?' . . . 'I covered her with American cloth—good American cloth . . . '" (*S,* xx) The corpse can be lightly concealed by the smell of "Zhdanor's disinfectant." The black ooze is *active,* like a viral agent, leaping from textual bodice to bodice,

accelerating its reclamation of whatever pretended to be extending temporalities by this linkage. There is no sanctuary, no body it does not burn
through or reclaim in a back-wheel of temporal extensions and prefigural
premises. There is no sanctuary, then, from whatever pours from Emma's
lips—whatever used her literary corpse as a vehicle of detransmission. In
another satellite, what we will call "Faulkner," operating within a totalizing
Americanist cloth or canon, the figure of Emma and her black fluid is again
pocketed although with accelerated and jamming results—moreover, *it*
will coalesce as a personified character, a figure, a gangster, an emissary of
graphic animation and pop culture.

Once "literature" is relieved of its iconicity and institutional definition, as Ronell's readings fractally assume and perform, it discloses itself
as a teletechnic of mnemonic networks. These networks do not enforce
mimetic and identificatory, archival, and interiorist reading practices or
knowledges—they may seem abject, "literary," stupid, perhaps impotent
and frenzied before a certain screen they cannot traverse. These are, as
Benjamin says of cinema, de-auratic, which is to say prefigural, before
personification kicks in with its trances and transferences. These are no
longer tropological primarily—which does not make them without some
sort of direction, or at least an irreversible status. They scan transactions
before which the humanistic models, neo-Enlightenment and hermeneutic
programs, appear simply in evaporation—dispersed across other signifying
acts and machines ("A mere copier and data bank attached invisibly to a
larger apparatus, I am programmed to situate the problem and respond
to its call. . . . I am going to have it scan the entirety of the argument as it
sifts and sorts, putting the information into a new order" [*S,* 280]). And
"literature" was always doing this, steeped in the drug trade of mnemonic
regimes and counter-circuits—which is one reason it had been patrolled by
hermeneutic gangs and antiviral software, for which a courier like Ronell
would appear a sort of antibody. *It dissolves into a site, a nonsite, where
diverse temporalities and allo-anthropomorphine traces converge and transit
en route to other systems of sense and event.* AR is the flaneur of an archival
shift—among else, the repositioning of the era of "the Book" as but one dossier and memory regime within the prehistories of teletechnics as such. She
recounts this: "there had been a non-caesaric change. Nobody could scan
the cut because we had experienced an interruption in history altogether
different from the ones that had been prescribed" (*CW,* 69).

There is no sanctuary from the *oozing,* which can deluge a delta like New
Orleans' flood—the incursion of the non-anthropomorphic order into the
homeland. No interior for retreat, vaginal or *green,* no *Ursprung* for that

210

matter. Not if this prefigural ooze is virally embedded as a phantom within every logological sanctum from the concept of trope to that of "woman." As the allo-gendered *Emma* displays, "woman" as constructed remains a poisoned effect in the archive, a locus of *crack war*—where "crack" as a prefigural figure opens a "Medusiod rift" across a pan-cultural nexus of caesurae (semiotic, pharmocopoetic, sexed). Ronell: "'A woman' is the mark of a figure in active living, a thing of the sidelines, beside the point and attracted actively to a substitute for active living. (This shows what a symptom woman continues to be, one in touch with vampiric death threats, for what else can a substitute for 'active living' evoke?)" (101). It is delicate for Ronell to ex-pose this technicity of "woman," of literature, to sacrifice it, and one must always perform slightly other than: that "literature" was never other than a pharmacotopic dossier, a power and node, within a teletechnics of which it—or the genocidal memory regimes of "the Book"—has been but a signal dossier. In offering her things as "books," engineered objects, marked, embellished, exceeding themselves in typographic shifts, the technology of the "book" is also suspended, and one is delivered over to the non-metaphorics of switchboards, satellites, the "voice" of *AR* (at this point not-a-woman). Exciting "objects," opiates of cognition as well as grenades, they disguise something other—not the immutable stupidity of inscriptions but the *fragility of these* in a time where old software has run against its limits, drained reserves and degraded biosystems and cognitive regimes. Concealed in the faux folds of this writing, the cracks, are telegraphed critico-blogs speaking *en famille* of the insider's politics of "transmission" at the point where the success of corporate transit-lines fades into runic mockery—a *time,* let us say, of war, if war always implies a recasting of temporalities. This project stands beyond mourning, like one trapped too long in the revolving doors of a "transvaluating machine." And it offers itself, or *opfers* itself, in the manner of a faux or painted Isaac who knows better, at the rim of a revoked sacrifice (on the trials of having a psychotic Abrahamic father see the closing pages of *Stupidity,* referenced below): it is almost willing to be erased in the name of an other, or at least think about a suicide that expels the ooze ("Madame Bovary committed total suicide" [*CW,* 94]).

This is why the trope of the switchboard levitates into satellites—to militarize, looses gravitas and circulates, but also to scan the archive of the emerging *post*-global surface of a teletechnic earth whose definitions, and consumed futures, are bound to this system. What occurs when a satellite is reprogrammed, brought down, or worse, understood to have "turned" to the enemy side, become hosted by the black ooze? One is still, has always been here, at war—but with, and in the name, of what other?

III.

Faulkner passes *the* book, the book of books (*Madame Bovary*), to another *pocket*. The trickle of black ooze turns into a proactive agent, a *character* in the novel *Sanctuary*. Faulkner seems to have sniffed out the implications of Dostoyevsky's or Myshkin's bulging pocket, and *pan*icked, totalized and engorged the encounter. This time, it is passed to a country lawyer with the name of a classical poet, Horace Benbow, a *literateur* seeking escape, seeking sanctuary in nature, *from* his home, from his *women*—they are out of control and use up or disrespect him, parasites become hosts. He is forced from the house to a "spring" in the country, to nature, where a curious scene of de-origination in *American* allegory and telemnonics is staged. Here the pocketed volume will precede any return of a *narcissist* reflection at the spring, elicits in advance from behind the bushes a prefigural and nonhuman gangster: what is called *Popeye*. In a verbal exchange the black oozing from Emma's mouth is proactively identified, and by smell at that, with the nonfigure of Popeye.

As they leave the spring or redneck *Ursprung*, Benbow gives a name to the Poesque bird ("a shadow with speed") that swooped by Popeye, causing the latter to panic and leap, "clawing" at Benbow's *pocket,* which has been spoken of as having a book in it:

> "It's just an owl," Benbow said. "It's nothing but an owl." Then he said: "They call that Carolina wren a fishingbird. That's what it is. What I couldn't think of back there," with Popeye crouching against him, clawing at his pocket and hissing through his teeth like a cat. He smells *black,* Benbow thought; he smells like that black stuff that ran out of Bovary's mouth and down upon her bridal veil when they raised her head.
>
> A moment later, above a black, jagged mass of trees, the house lifted its stark square bulk against the failing sky.
>
> The house was a gutted ruin rising gaunt and stark out of a grove of unpruned cedar trees. It was a landmark, known as the Old Frenchman place, built before the Civil War. . . . (*Sanctuary,* 7–8)[3]

Black *stuff.* Popeye, now as an animeme, feline, clawing, is linked to the black fluid itself. It reflects the stupidity of American bluntness to name, totalize, to say nothing of smell or personify this unnameable mnemonic drip. It is taken out of the pocket, vaginal or book-lined, or identified with where this mock-interior turns inside out, prolapses. The "*black stuff* that ran out of Bovary's mouth" will, discreetly but inevitably, contaminate every use of the term or figure of *blackness* in Faulkner (including, especially, "race"—where blacks take on the power of telepathic readers). Thus the scene shifts to the house full of *feebs* (as it is said), the media house of Flaubert, the "Old Frenchman," the shapes and letters of whose name anagrammatically permeates that of "Faulkner." But *Emma* has, here, in a series of transformations, become the gangster *animeme,* the cartoon hero-sailor who takes hits of spinach like it were some drug or steroid. Popeye on a hit of this technic has super powers. The literary has warped, dissolving its anteriorities in a sheer technicity personified—or almost, because, as we hear, Popeye's *face* is chinless, like wax melted away by a flame, prefacial. The ruined house of media or "landmark" of the French or "modernist" novel comes from before the Civil War, or at least *a civil war* it is cognizant of using as a marker of times past and to come.

Ronell circles back to this zone of the prefigural, not quite entered into any of its subsequent embodiments or histories, and she tracks it to an impossible wandering metonymy or non-source. Here that is: *Emma,* the letter M, the black ooze, oral and menstrual voiding. But something has happened along the way to "literature," which does not survive itself as an "institution." A question of reading is posed between the lawyer Horace, naming a classic Roman poet, and the mass-cultural Popeye at the hyperbolic *spring* ("Do you read *books*?"). What Horace has in his *pocket,* unlike Popeye's gun, turns out to be the "book":

> The drinking man knelt beside the spring. "You've got a pistol in that pocket, I suppose," he said. Across the spring Popeye appeared to contemplate him with two knobs of black rubber. "I'm asking you," Popeye said. "What's that in your pocket?". . . . "Don't show me," Popeye said. "Tell me." The other man stopped his hand. "It's a book." "What book?" Popeye said. "Just a book. The kind that people read. Some people do." "Do you read books?" Popeye said. (*Sanctuary,* xx)

Let us suspend addressing whatever a *pocket* is or may be—or if this hyper-allegory may not be transferred to any reading encounter, any text marking the instant of transmission and splitting. At the opening of *Sanctuary* the literary seems to recur to a faulted spring or *Quelle*—a Delphic and prosthetic crack. Even if that "spring," here, is as if surrounded by bushes, trees, natural props. *Even if literature is being clutched by the lawyer as another refuge or sanctuary, and precisely its female emissary, too, emits a menstrual flow that is eviscerating still—no sanctuary again.* The famous spectrality of literary or even cinematic networks, like *animation,* is neither a revelation nor a conceit. It is at once a banality and a premise of intervention. It loops back, before arriving, to a prefigural site, which contracts temporal chains and anteriorities. Before the *spring* appears the law, a country lawyer, Horace Benbow, who seeks refuge from his family, from the storm of controls and betrayals and abjections its logics implies, from his allegorized wife, Belle, who always wants shrimp for his tarty stepdaughter, who disses him. He flees from "woman" as sanctuary. He is surprised when across a narcissist pond *something steps out* before any reflection is returned—from behind the supposed natural setting, the bushes. Source of otherness, what greets Horace at the *Quelle* cannot quite be another human. The name and figure of Popeye cites graphic animation, cartoons, as well as a *rupture* ("pop") of the ocular itself in some sense—here, of reading or memory or perceptual programs. The *law* that enters here, like the work's own reader, is a refugee from and courier of literary and hermeneutic virals.

Sanctuary, when it was still possible to market itself as "literature," posed as a potboiler or prosthetic rape "novel." It hid there. It would not then be read, as the name *Popeye* announces, as a semiotic rape of auratic or mimetological premises (one should say *temples*). At the same time, it or "he" signals an invasive precontamination of and by so-called media, a criminalized popular or mass culture (*Popeye the Sailor Man*). It or he remarks a turning out of every interiority or pocket that the *piñatas* of humanist or Americanist criticism seeks to restore—the historial subject *as such,* the South and its *regionalist* voice, literary history as a manageable parade of styles. And he does this with a nod to cinematic animation, the *technic* that graphematically supplants at any hyperbolic spring or *Ursprung* a band of inscriptions inverting the order of "life-death" and with it classical aesthetic models. Popeye's caesura is that of a gangster from Memphis, Egyptoid polis of Tennessee. He or it is the last and crudest American phantom that the frustrated Horace Benbow wants to find emerging from behind the natural setting—as if from a dominating wife and her shrimp. And like the black menstrual blood leaking from E.B.'s lips, he discloses a world with ceaselessly emptied sanctuaries, corncobbed by this prosthetic liquid coalesced to the *black knobs* of Popeye's eyes.

IV.

Horace Benbow comes into contact with a certain zeroid figure, a black hole named for a cartoon character who slashes the eye of ocularcentric programs, as does all *animation,* and who comes from behind the *bushes*— that is, from where a certain faux interior, which is to say sanctuary, was to have been. Faulkner races across temporalities, sheds regional locus as "America" unnames a saturated field—he undoes the hermeneutic *race* epitomized as a circular and sterile ritual in the pre–Civil War positioning, say, in the story called "Was" that opens *Go Down, Moses.* That text or title will name anteriority as such (*was*), yet reaches into the dead ritual of the twin and childless *white* male twins, living like husband and wife, old and faux theophantic binaries, *Amodeus* and *Theophilus*, "Buck" (fauna) and "Buddy" (flora). The two, sucking into themselves all binaries predicated on abdicating male-male plantation logics, are paralyzed in ritual hunts and returns, before a dawning cataclysm that will rearrange all (*civil* war). In the short text, the term "race" is also played as a kind of cartoon slapstick hunt, in which the absurd tracking or reading ritual of "*old* Moses," the hunting dog, chases a pet fox in play around the house, again and again, upending everything. But in a work titled *Go Down, Moses,* where the going under of a certain model of the law or Book that precedes its own inscriptions is named, that the stupid hunting dog is named "old Moses" gives pause:

> And when they got home just after daylight, this time Uncle Buddy [that is, *Amodeus*] never even had time to get breakfast started and the fox never even got out of the crate, because the dogs were right there in the room. Old Moses went right into the crate with the fox, so that both of them went right on through the back end of it. That is, the fox went through, because when Uncle Buddy opened the door to come in, old Moses was still wearing most of the crate around his neck until Uncle Buddy kicked it off of him . . . and they could hear the fox's claws when he went scrabbling up the lean-pole, onto the roof—*a fine race* while it lasted, but the tree was too quick. ("Was," 28)[4]

The only occurrence of the name of the ur-patriarch and stuttering law-giver in the volume so named, named for "his" going down or under is give to a comic house dog. The hound here is a clownish figure that ritually chases a pet fox inside the house, a practice "race" repeated as ritual. *Race,* on which the "house divided" is set or faulted, the entire histories of this agon of binarized being (who or what is the man, the human), is referenced to an aesthetic ritual of a loopy hound named *Old Moses* but recalling more Disney's Goofy—all the violence, all the alibis of race are diverted to a hermeneutic chase doubled back on itself, a dead plantation order of reading. The war to come here *the* Civil War, but it is also the Benjaminian crack wars, for which the so-called "war on 'terror'" remains a screen and distraction—the faux totalization of the double-chase model as evasion of something else, stupider, lacking aura, more desperate or "material." "He" or it (Popeye) *was* there or here already, and *it* has something to do with or at least smells like the black ooze from Bovary's mouth. A book in Benbow's pocket, mistaken for a gun, could in turn be mistaken for a corncob. Rather than threading discrete infratextual labyrinths (as in *The Idiot*), Emma appears as gun, then as corncob.

Ronell comments on the implications of Myshkin's carrying *Emma Bovary* in his pocket at the time of his collapse, as of Dostoyevsky's marking a lethal pact between the two performances: "The coupling with the other work seals the suicide pact, ratifies destruction: Emma, Emilia: dial Em for murder" (*Stupidity*, 223).[5] Leaving aside the temptation to a diversion to Hitchcock here, we may add, update, Americanize, totalize this call: dial M for *Moses*, because as indicated in Faulkner the pregression of "origins" reaches back before that of the progenitor of the era of the Book, and the law, *Moses*, signatory of an antebellum or plantation hermeneutic. Popeye's link to *animation* is heightened when he is likened to an *electric* light, his eyes like black knobs of rubber.

The entire pretext of interiors has been corncobbed here, and together with it a network of hermeneutic programs that contrive the return of the escaped slave or animal. We return to the spring. The two wraiths—the lawyer and the outlaw, the reader and the technic other—have a face-off, a reading contest even, after which the first will be apprehended and led off by the second. The itinerary of crack wars leads here, all but unthinkably, as if the war machines at the edge of the "era" from which AR writes, with understandable fatigue, know this: one writes backward of an antebellum era, the plantation hermeneutics of Amodeus and Theophilus, yet in the writing itself that is already *disinscribed*—presented as a sterile plantation ritual, as Faulkner writes it. At this point, "Was" returns as a stamp rather than title-puzzle, the declaration, on arrival, of being over, past, archivally closed.

Popeye will be in control of everything, a Memphis or hieroglyphic gangster allied to teletechnics and animation whose frenzied impotence leaves him whinnying vicariously over Temple and Red's performance in a brothel. Temples, nature, spring, enclosures, and pockets of all kinds, *sanctuaries* constructed over an occlusion—all in advance violated and disinteriorized. The book in the lawyer's pocket guarantees this. Horace does not want to name *Madame Bovary*, the woman he takes with him to escape from his women, not knowing that the inverse model to himself that Emma incarnates lethally voids the literary "hit" he seeks. The personified "ruin" of a mediatric house is permeated by latent horrors and cinematized crime, impending murder, stupid folk ("feebs"), while conjuring Faulknerian or American writing tout court in its faux modernist moment. *Old Frenchman's place* is an eviscerated structure housing impending violations that epitomize what remains for Popeye, amid the crack wars of prosthetic romance, that defers American or faux modernist writing to an anterior colonization—or simply an anterior, allo-linguistic trace.

What Popeye incarnates does not itself *read*. He is illiterate, like the shriveled telepath, *black* Aunt Mollie of the tale "Go Down, Moses," who is content to stare at a newspaper article about her dead nephew. One is in the "American" weave and trance placed over Natasya, a metonymic corpse needing disinfectant to stop the viral takeovers, over the suicidal pact Ronell inspects between Fyodor and Gustave. With Popeye's appearance at the spring, all of "Faulkner" the regionalist, the southern "writer," the historial "American" voice, and so on, finds itself as *translated back* into the black flow of a bile linked with this "first" modern novel to sheer anteriority.[6] All referential rites are as if liquefied here—including, under the shadow of Old Frenchman's place, the "American" as such. The detail of Bovary's corpse suggests a literature that begins "after" its institutional death and faux mourning: and with that, the archive is opened to reinscription. Naturalism, historiality, psychology, character, ocularcentrism, symbolism—whatever you like that is, still, auratic and blind—is sucked into the (blind) reading of *Popeye's* black knobs. The zero covers a fault where the system has as though corncobbed itself in advance, in a perpetual trance or aestheticized narcosis.

V.

What disinfectant of what viral transmission is or is not covered, is covered and uncovered by this "American clothe" or weave?[7]

But here a different turn. AR stages a different sort of outing—the test drive, (s)he calls it. In tracking the prefigural ooze from Emma's mouth, stupid, material, inscriptive, a detour is activated. In the "Rhetoric of Testing," a cipher chapter for *Stupidity*, a family plot of dead-enders is visited—de Man, Benjamin, and Friedrich Schlegel:

> The welcoming of irony and allegory, as Schlegel's text indicates, is the kiss of death. For not only is there an impertinent emphasis placed on the nonconvergence of any stated meaning and its understanding, but this engagement lets loose a cannonade of demystifications that can ruin a career (the poisoned Socrates, abjected Schlegel, flunked out Benjamin, dead de Man, et al.) or, at the very least, exacts revenge in the form of a total religious conversion. (159)

Begun as a precarious genealogy of *stupidity*, of cultural transmission and resistance, these figurines end in a kind of swamp orgy, a frog-froth of sterile power. With Popeye. AR implies this is being played out in the

anteroom of a step beyond, a "test drive" mutation to which all these legacies point or catalyze. Thus, for AR, one would be perhaps already outside
of this—those who touched the livewires of "allegory" and "irony." She asks
after prophetic mutations in or from this legacy, unmapped speech acts: "To
what extent is the prophetic word indebted to irony? Can there be prophecy without irony, I mean in a nonpsychotic sense?" (157) There is a short
transit between the vacating of "irony" as a specular infinity to something
else, called "prophetic," piercing future timeloops and collapsing temporal
columns. AR knows that knowing knows something against *itself*, at war
with *itself*, that the political, today, involves only epistemological horizons
where alternative programs of memory, sensation, reference, consumption
may be set—that these are anesthetized, perhaps paralyzed by everything
the drug hit (of all sorts) would oppose or counter-rupture.[8] *AR implies
this is being played out before a step beyond to which all these legacies testify:
coming wars of reinscription.* Crack wars.

How does AR, less and more than a telet-archival flaneur, more or less
fatigued, prepare for such wars? How are they, still, anarchival, preferred
as if at the nonsite Derrida calls *khora,* betokened by a efflux of black bile,
where script has been returned to ink? How does (s)he repeal or evade the
anesthetizing traps? By stepping into them and pretending to be vanquished,
then finding the pool of stupidity where the police do not bother to hang out
or patrol, the *spring*—then setting up para-networks of communication for
the readers-to-come who may need such in place? Primitive trope in its way,
the satellite nonetheless revokes metaphor. Kant is such a "satellite." So too
could be "Plato," "Faulkner," and so on. Satellites protect the stratosphere of
informatrices and faux perceptibility and mnemonics. They manage signals,
or histories. And they can crash (*Houston, we have a problem* . . .).

AR has wandered into a charmed spot or nonsite of exscriptions, re-
hearsing rituals of criticism for lack of a genre. All of her weapons are
fronts—literary history, the frog pond of the politics of transmission, self-
dramatizations, the stupid insight that cannot be given shape or name but is
everywhere enshadowing. (S)he has stepped out of the room, the house, and
is left acting like she wants in or back (a motif of expulsion runs through her
text). (S)he paints the edges of her pages with sparklers and rockets, tropes
philosophical names as "satellites," embraces stupid voices she rescinds
("De Man"), clowns too much, probes victimages, inside stories—as if the
figure of the clown the *Genealogy of Morals* recommends as strategy were
a tarrying site. (S)he sustains and rescinds these histories that she experiences as accelerating circuitry, buzzings that return to and evade this ooze.
One expects, among her catalogue of pharmacopes and illnesses, her cor-

nucopia of anarchival fevers (a grand mal d'archive) to encounter a certain palsy—as where an arm or shoulder, part of the mnemonic body, enters a dead zone neither subject to shaking, nor trance, nor mock-jouissance, nor life-death. The unleashed dogs of coming wars of reinscription like "Old Moses"—everything in AR that testifies to and reverse-accelerates against to maintain a position of articulation, not to be targeted, to maintain the freedom to hang up the phone, to ironize the non-call that is implied— these ooze between the lines, and direct AR's syntax. AR has the privilege to clown here, offering cognitive blogs even while "literature" is revoked. And one wonders, in this machinery of indigestibles, what Obradekian monarch in the faux sovereignty of a voice would emerge, like Myshkin, in sacrificial ardor or self-extinction, if these strategies run out: what would speak, be instantly abjected, unrecognized, then return otherwise when the tropology subsides of the necessary chatter of short-lived aesthetic histories like classicism, modernism, humanism—when they suspend their pretense even to be ghosts?

This question underlies the meditation on Isaac that closes *Stupidity*, faux son to faux father—at the limits of familial travesty. It exemplifies the "Medusoid rift" AR sometimes situates herself-himself in, probing perimeters of totalized political spells in the archival orders. Apotropaic, this *rift* refuses orientation, turns toward the dumb, the mute, toward the mutation of inscriptions that set the levers of perceptual and temporal regimes. If Derrida seemed to morph from the analytic of hospitality to an ill or fevered archive and then to a "suicidal auto-immunitary process" that makes the house itself a self-cancelling structure, Ronell drifts outside of the metaphorics of the house, or the family—and looks back, puts on the costumes to see. *Stupidity* speculates on "this that expelled you from your house"—or its pocket—in its final line, after dramatizing the dilemmas of an Isaac "cheated by the call": "Assuming that Abraham was cured and did not sacrifice Isaac (though according to one midrash the son was executed), the question remains of how and whether Isaac survived the near-death experience—how he survived a psychotic father, that is, everybody's primal father, Kafka's, yours, and mine, even, or especially, when they are in sync with the Law" (309).

The "psychotic" father is the one without real paternal identity (which is never biological), who disowns his own premise and may be, in effect, a woman: (s)he undoes the pretext of the familial—that is his open secret (like Derrida's "I am not of the family"). But the reference to the one ex- ception among what may be called the *Isaac Variations* is telling. It is to a midrash that says, Yeah, of course he was sacrificed and all the speculation covers that up for a reason: if Isaac were cut off, as he of course was, the future would have never taken place, and the "present" occupied by the commentators revoked as spectral. The entire memory system by which a certain model of the house or "present" is maintained would turn out, in essence, to have been an implant more or less self-cancelling, accelerated by having been programmed on "real."

The black stuff or ooze, material, stupid, inkish, khoratic, a prefigural agent with prehistorial properties—it exceeds, it preceeds, it contaminates. It leaks through cracks. Perhaps this trickle, which enters Ronell's calculus and possesses it, is about a catastrophe one has to develop a new vocabulary to engage—one that is not monumentalized as past trauma but oozes, proactively mutates and consumes histories, *beyond mourning*. AR's writing can simulate a shoah's ark redux, the viral gossip of a theoretical afterlife pretending it does not know, at every turn, the extinction of the genres it mimes itself out of. No wonder she is fatigued—even where she uses that as a front or day job, like Popeye before eating his anything but organic spinach. But then, once the referential spell is suspended, reading comes to this site, which, as de Man might say, is irreversible.

NOTES

1. Avital Ronell, *Cracks Wars: Literature Addiction Mania* (Lincoln: University of Nebraska Press, 1992).
2. Indeed, *Stupidity* (Urbana and Chicago: University of Illinois Press, 2002) opens with it five times in its first three sentences, two in its first: "The temptation is to wage war on stupidity as if it were a vanquishable object—as if we still knew how to wage war or circumscribe an object in a manner that would be productive of meaning or give rise to futurity." (*Stupidity*, 3)
3. William Faulkner, *Sanctuary* (New York: Vintage, 1978).
4. William Faulkner, *Go Down, Moses* (New York: Vintage, 1970).
5. We will ignore the slippage into Hitchcock, on whose *Rope* Ronell will produce three of the most trenchant pages extant, as if in passing, in *The Test Drive* (Urbana and Chicago: University of Illinois Press, 2005). We will ignore this slippage, into the oeuvre in which telephonics and cinematic teletechnics converge about a certain wheel, circuit, or dial-tone; in which scissors lodge in the back of the intruder; in which ocularcentrism is, from the start, suspended as the graphematic scandal of what is too obvious—that the effect of living is animation, that the black ooze of Emma is instantaneous, exceeds its Flaubertian discharge, lies in the "visible" order of the prefigural mark.
6. In "Go Down, Moses," the final but titular tale in *Go Down, Moses*, we hear of the lawyer Gavin Stevens that the law was his "hobby" and his "serious vocation was a twenty-two year old unfinished translation of the Old Testament *back* into

classic Greek"—that is, a *translation* of the biblical text's (English) translation as though "back" not into an originary language but into the aesthetic language that, nonetheless, precedes Mosaic authority.

7. It will take a century (we are not there yet by this count) for "Faulkner's" gesture to be apprehended: that everything here pretended to in the ritual of the "literary" is closed, never was as pretended to by the parlor-room class of Horace's, by the "law," henpecked.

8. One marvels, still, at one secret in *Stupidity*. That is, AR's use of and alliance with a for some reason loathed "de Man." *Stupidity* is the most accomplished "de Manian" work of its kind in a sense, as well as containing the most distinct dossier on this figure in the recent archive, uniquely reading his work as a reflection on the question of the *techne,* of technicity as such. But what is interesting may be that, while identifying with "Derrida" and as if against "De Man," she inhabits the latter's stupid position to divert the stylistic engulfments of the former—positioning herself, inadvertently, as *the scholar of the active black fluid, of disinscriptions.* Through the catalogues of stupidity Ronell raids a "quarantined" corner of the family crypt, looking for tools. As she notes, what are stupidly taken for the name of tropes in de Man are in fact nothing of the sort, that what was at stake was the "material," the mute, the allo-human: "So what are these debilitators of meaning and being? One can argue that, strictly speaking, 'allegory,' 'anacoluthon,' 'parabasis,' and 'metonymy' should not be misapprehended as the names of tropes. To the extent that they involve no substitutions, they are parafigural. Whereas tropes involve the transport of sense from one signifier to another, the grammatical non-tropes, such as allegory, do not participate in this language of transport of a sense or a meaning." (159)

Elisabeth Weber

"Vectorizing Our Thoughts Toward 'Current Events'": For Avital Ronell

I.

In Ingo Schulze's 1999 text "Handy," published in English as "Cell Phone," the narrator, who will remain nameless throughout the story, and his wife Constanze have rented a bungalow near Berlin, in the village of Prieros, for their summer vacation. The same day that Constanze has been unexpectedly called back to her work in Berlin, five or six strangers arrive in the middle of the night and demolish the front portion of the wooden fence that surrounds the property. The narrator reports: "the fact was that not even a symbolic barrier protected the bungalow now. Given the situation, it was some comfort to have a cell phone. I'd got more familiar with it over the last few days, because I'd brought the envelope that included all the instructions—which Constanze had guarded so jealously—along with me to Prieros and had finally learned how to store numbers and activate my answering machine."[1] The next morning, while surveying the damage, the narrator is approached by a neighbor, Neumann, who, after helping him clean up the destroyed fence, asks for his cell phone number. The narrator never wanted a cell phone, "until Constanze came up with the idea of a one-way phone. To make calls, yes—to be called no, with the exception of her of course." As a consequence, he does not know the number, but sits down to find it in the envelope. A day later, he too returns to Berlin. After several weeks, in late September, again in the middle of the night, the cell phone rings. Neumann is calling to report on the return of the vandals.

This is the occasion on which Constanze learns that her husband has given the cell phone number to someone else. In her profound disappointment, she offers a glimpse into the telephonic structure of contemporary life: "'Think of all those people who could call now. . . . All those neighbors.'" Her husband replies: "'Our number's in the book, a perfectly normal number. Anybody can call us.' 'That's not what I mean. A building is on fire or gets bombed and somebody runs out with nothing but his cell phone, because it happens to be in his jacket or his pants pocket. You can talk with somebody like that now.' I plugged the recharger into the wall socket beside the bed. 'It can very well happen,' Constanze said. Her voice now had that 'teacher' tone of hers. 'Somebody calls you up from Kosovo or Afghanistan or from wherever that tsunami was. Or one of those guys that froze up on Mount Everest. You can talk with him to the bitter end. No one can help him, but you hear his last words.' . . . 'Just imagine who all you'll be dealing with now. Nobody has to be alone anymore.'"[2]

Of course, Constanze is mistaken that all this can happen only because her husband has given his cell phone number away. Her husband is right to say that anyone could call them anytime at home. The destruction of the fence that symbolizes the breaking-into the sphere of intimacy via telephone is in itself nothing new, but defines the telephone. But Constanze points out something else that marks the difference between the telephone and the cell phone. The latter no longer needs an identifiable, permanent location: a building or phone booth. It can be carried anywhere, and is therefore the channel of transmission of disaster par excellence. "No one can help him, but you hear his last words"—this was, as is well known, lived hundreds of times during the attacks on the World Trade Center, the Pentagon, and United Airlines flight 93. The cell phone accomplishes what is often claimed of television but rarely truly the case: a transmission in real time.

What Avital Ronell calls "the dark side of the telephonic structure," "the call as decisive, as verdict, the call as death sentence,"[3] is here strangely reversed: It is the condemned who places the call. According to Ronell, "one need only consult the literatures trying to contain the telephone in order to recognize the persistent trigger of the apocalyptic call. It turns on you: it's the gun pointed at your head."[4] The "more luminous sides—for there are many—of grace and reprieve"[5] are found by Ronell, for example in Benjamin's Berliner Kindheit, where the telephone is associated with "calling back from exile, suspending solitude, and postponing the suicide mission with the 'light of the last hope.'"[6] Luminous sides find no mention in Schulze's text after the cell phone number has been given to the vacation neighbor. From that moment on, those who are on the brink of dying violent deaths invade the most intimate sphere. They are, as far away as they might be, "all those neighbors." The cell phone is defined here as the channel of communication that indissociably connects witnessing with utter paralysis.

The cell phone, one of the media or technical devices that produce "discrete images of space and time,"[7] turns out to be the producer of a medium. Schulze's text shows how the device that gives its name to the short story produces a medium in the material sense, namely, as Wolf Kittler put it in an illuminating commentary on Walter Benjamin's "The Task of the Translator," "a space of translucence and permeability." A medium, then, is "a space in the strict sense of the term, namely not just a limited extension within an unlimited extensity, but a space, to which there is no outside."[8]

This space without outside produced by the cell phone determines our being, through and through, our being within this space and, decisively, our "being-with-others," our "Mitsein."[9] As Constanze says: "Somebody calls you up from Kosovo or Afghanistan or from wherever that tsunami was." "Just imagine who all you'll be dealing with now." What Samuel Weber writes of the effects of GPS, the Global Positioning System, is valid for the cell phone too: "We are in a world overseen, in its planetary totality, by GPS. . . . As mobile as we may be, or become, we are even more localizable. We are, as it were, on call—and from this call it is difficult to imagine any escape."[10] In Schulze's text, the medium from which it is impossible to escape is one that exposes the subject to paralyzed witnessing, or a mutism of a particular kind: the impossibility to respond. Far from being just the accidental result of a mistakenly placed phone call, such paralysis and mutism reveal themselves as determining the cell-phonic structure of today's Mitsein.

This is where Avital Ronell's work sees one of its unrelenting responsibilities. Ronell has pointed out that in spite of the multiplication of communication systems via television, phone, cell phone, and the Internet, "there are no clear transmission systems that would allow us to be heard here"—"here," in the United States. She continues: "The disappearance of the public sphere is a catastrophe of historical dimension. The public sphere—the polis—is where we once located politics. What we have to come to terms with is the vanishing of politics. One of the things that the Gulf War has shown us is our own mutism. It is from this place of silence that I am trying to speak today."[11] This diagnosis, made in a paper delivered on May 17, 1991, is not out of date. The cell phone in Schulze's text exemplifies the paralyzed witnessing and mutism that Ronell identifies as perhaps the biggest challenge for today's scholar. Ronell's work responds to this challenge with a relentless urgency to analyze the conditions of the "transmission systems" that threaten to reduce the scholar's work to mutism (and often succeed). In doing this, Ronell, moreover, detects the subversive potential of certain "transmission systems." When she analyzes, in a close reading of the effects George Holliday's videotape of the beating of Rodney King by LAPD officers had on commercial television during the officers' 1991 trial, and on several Californian cities, where it produced "insurrection on the streets" after the not-guilty verdict, Ronell uncovers "nomadic or testimonial video" as installed in television "as bug or parasite" and producing the "Ethical Scream which television has massively interrupted. This ethical scream that interrupts a discourse of effacement (even if that effacement should indeed thematize crime and its legal, moral, or police resolutions), this ethical scream—and video means for us 'I saw it'—perforates television from an inner periphery, instituting a break in the compulsive effacement to which television is in fact seriously committed. . . . When testimonial video breaks out of concealment and into the television programming that it occasionally supersedes, it is acting as the call of conscience of television."[12]

The cell phone, perhaps especially the newest versions that include still- and video-cameras, may have the potential of transmitting the "Ethical Scream" as well. However, in an age in which, as Samuel Weber has formulated it, "the technology and media that were supposed to bring about the 'global village' have contributed to the revival of 'ethnic cleansing' and religious fundamentalism,"[13] the paralyzed witnessing and resistance manifested in Constanze's reaction call for further reflection, because they are closely related to the "mutism" that Ronell has the courage to acknowledge, to analyze, and to challenge.

Ronell has shown in *The Telephone Book* that the "call" and the "caller" in Heidegger's *Being and Time* have a fundamentally telephonic structure. Schulze's text amplifies this structure for the cell phone caller: "Prior to borrowing a status of metaphysical subject or subject of a police interrogation (name, purpose, etc.), the caller, uncontained and un–at home, is Dasein in its uncanniness: 'Er ist das Dasein in seiner Unheimlichkeit, das ursprüngliche geworfene In-der-Welt-sein als Un-zuhause, das nackte 'Dass' im Nichts der Welt' (compare BT 276–77), ringing primordially as Being-in-the-world that is 'not at home.' . . . The caller is Dasein in its not-at-homeness."[14]

The cell phone call, with its penetration of the intimate sphere (up to the couple's lovemaking toward the end of the story), reveals a condition that might not be new, but that has been considerably aggravated with the advent of new media. In the words of Jacques Derrida:

the global and dominant effect of television, the telephone, the fax machine, satellites, the accelerated circulation of images, discourse, etc., is that the here-and-now becomes uncertain, without guarantee: anchoredness, root-edness, the at-home [le chez-soi] are radically contested. Dislodged. This is nothing new. It has always been this way. The at-home has always been marked [travaillé] by the other, by the guest, by the threat of expropriation. It is constituted only in this threat. But today, we are witnessing such a radical expropriation, deterritorialization, delocalization, dissociation of the political and the local, of the national, of the nation-state and the local, that the response, or rather the reaction, becomes: "I want to be at home, I want finally to be at home, with my own, close to my friends and family." . . . The more powerful and violent the technological expropriation, the delocalization, the more powerful, naturally, the recourse to the at-home, the return toward home. . . . Hence the "regression" which accompanies the acceleration of the technological process, which is always also a process of delocalization—and which in truth follows it like its shadow, practically getting confused with it.[15]

Constanze's final statement, "Nobody has to be alone anymore," is hardly an affirmation of community; it voices regret, if not a threat. Those who do not have "to be alone anymore" constitute a strange community of anonymous, satellite-connected neighbor-strangers, facing on one side cata-strophic deaths and on the other utter powerlessness. "All those neighbors" are dispersed all over the face of the globe, but at the same time irrupt into the most intimate spheres, interrupting the most intimate moments with their despair.

Nietzsche's antidote to Christian "Nächstenliebe" (neighborly love or, literally, love of the closest), the "Nächsten-Flucht" (the flight from the clos-est) and "Fernsten-Liebe" (love of the most distant),[16] is here challenged in serious ways, if not made impossible. The neighborly love imposed by the so-called "global village" has become inescapable, a medium in the sense described above. Precisely because of the impossibility to escape it, the om-nipresence of distance- and difference-abolishing media triggers, according to Derrida, an autoimmune response, that is bound to unleash death and self-destruction. Lacan's reading of the commandment of neighborly love and his endorsement of Freud's rejection of this commandment point in the same direction: ". . . the retreat from 'Thou shalt love thy neighbor as thyself' is the same thing as the barrier to jouissance, and not its opposite. . . . I retreat from loving my neighbor as myself because there is something on the horizon there that is engaged in some form of intolerable cruelty. In that sense, to love one's neighbor may be the cruelest of choices," literally: the "most cruel path."[17]

226

It is important to realize that this "most cruel path" is intrinsically connected to the conditions of transmission systems that define the "global village." The latter would not be possible outside the conditions created by what Derrida has compellingly termed "mondialatinisation," the essentially Christian "globalatinization," that is the "latinization" not just of the "globe" but of the "world," and, to speak with Heidegger, of our "being-in-the-world."

In his analysis of the "two 'ages' of violence," which he sees to be at work in "our 'wars of religion,'" Derrida shows how the acts of violence that appear most "archaic" and those that are technologically most refined can both be described as "autoimmune" reactions and as such obey the same "terrifying but fatal logic" of what he calls "the auto-immunity of the unscathed that will always associate Science and Religion."[18] The analysis of this "logic" yields ways to decipher the brutal acts committed in our days in the name of religion, but also the differently but not less brutal acts of defense against these brutalities.

Derrida starts this analysis by recalling the indispensable question of language: namely the fact that "we are already speaking Latin," whenever we speak about "religion,"[19] and by recalling how "the word 'religion' is calmly (and violently) applied" to experiences and phenomena that have "always been and remain foreign to" "religion" in its necessarily Latin sense.[20] This calm and violent application corresponds to a worldwide propagation of Latinity, "globalatinization"—and we are at the heart of it, whether we are aware of this or not:

> For everything that touches religion in particular, for everything that speaks "religion," for whoever speaks religiously or about religion, Anglo-American remains Latin. Religion circulates in the world, one might say, like an English word that has been to Rome and taken a detour to the United States. Well beyond its strictly capitalist or politico-military figures, a hyper-imperialist appropriation has been underway now for centuries. It imposes itself in a particularly palpable manner within the conceptual apparatus of international law and of global political rhetoric. Wherever this apparatus dominates, it articulates itself through a discourse on religion. . . . Globalatinization (essentially Christian, to be sure), this word names a unique event to which a meta-language seems incapable of acceding, although such a language remains, all the same, of the greatest necessity here.[21]

What Derrida calls globalatinization can, of course, not be thought outside of the "cyberspace," in other words, without a complex and irreversible delocalization. It is therefore through and through dependent on a technological apparatus that works at its propagation and, at the same time, its dissolution. Derrida's thesis is that globalatinization produces in its heart that which threatens it from outside, for example or par excellence terrorism that is carried out in the name of a specific "religion." More precisely, globalatinization produces that what threatens it as autoimmune reaction, as a war against its own mechanisms of defense. As a consequence, the categories of inside and outside, of the center and the periphery, of friend and enemy, lose their perspicuity.

This collapse of space is made particularly palpable in Constanze's description of the consequences that she foresees after her husband has given out his cell phone number. That this collapse facilitates the outburst of archaic forms of violence is explained by the link that Lacan, following Melanie Klein in his text "Aggressiveness in Psychoanalysis," has established between space and aggressiveness. Ronell, in her reading of Lacan's text, relates this link to her analysis of the first war in the Persian Gulf. According to Lacan, in Ronell's formulation, "the domination of space is related to the narcissistic fear of damage to one's own body." Moreover, "the fear of death—the 'absolute Master' according to Hegel—is subordinate to the narcissistic fear of damage to one's own body."[22] The drive to dominate space as a defense against the fear of damage to one's own body and the subordination of the fear of death to this drive exemplifies the dynamics of "autoimmunity" (in Derrida's sense) in a chilling way. Ronell adds an element of criticism aimed directly at the most powerful nation of the world. Commenting on Lacan's remark that the "preeminence of aggressivity in our civilization . . . would be already demonstrated sufficiently by the fact that it is usually confused in 'normal' morality with the virtue of strength," Ronell writes: "The glorification of strength as a social value is a sign of social devastation initiated on a planetary scale and justified by the image of a laissez faire accorded to the strongest predators."[23]

II.

Avital Ronell's work, beyond acknowledging the difficulty of practicing the meta-language that Derrida describes as so urgently needed, and its quasi-impossibility especially in the American context and its transmission systems, sets out to invent such a language. "Running through psychoanalysis, we learn that vectorizing our thoughts toward 'current events' means that we are in fact looking at recurrent events whose eventuation cannot as such be easily located."[24] In other words, we are looking at events that enact repetitions intended, as Freud put it in *Beyond the Pleasure Principle*, to establish, after the fact and therefore in an irrecuperably belated way, a preparedness of the psychic apparatus for a trauma whose force disrupted the latter's protective shields to such an extent that no registration of the trauma could take place.[25] The "eventuation" of the trauma can therefore not be located.

One of the events analyzed by Ronell in 1991 was "Operation Desert Storm." Ronell's analyses set out to show that this war "incorporated many wars and was played out in a spectral battlefield: WWI (the gas masks), WWII (the calculated resurrection of Hitler), the Vietnam syndrome,"[26] but also the war on drugs, and the war on AIDS.[27] According to this reading, a massive repetition compulsion was enacted in the decision to go to war against Iraq, on the individual level, as Ronell shows in her detailed analysis of some of the first President Bush's statements,[28] as well as on the collective level of the "American unconscious."[29]

Ronell argues that "the war in the Persian Gulf has destabilized our understanding of location, and has instituted a teletopical logic: a logic of spaces aligned according to technological mappings, where the near is far and vice versa. Among other things, this means that what seems to be outside our borders is, in fact, occurring on the inside, which is to say that crucial projections are taking place and that what we understand by boundaries will have to be entirely rethought."[30] Ronell reads the Rodney King beating and the innumerable television broadcasts of George Holliday's video as the most glaring example of such a "teletopical logic," and, accordingly, as the most prominent "metonymy" figuring the "survival of the effaced Persian Gulf War."[31]

Ronell's argument is two-fold: "the Rodney King beating is a metonymy of a hidden atrocity, be this the unshown war or the atrocities to which African-Americans are routinely subjected"[32], and "the excess of the Rodney King intrusion upon broadcast television dramatized the rupturing of the protective film with which television habitually covers itself by showing and producing the traumatic scene of 'excessive force.'"[33] This two-fold diagnosis reveals its impact especially when read against the backdrop of an analysis of what was shown on television of the theater of operations during the first war in Iraq.

According to Frank Rich, "'War in the Gulf' was the ratings triumph that put the previously struggling CNN on the map."[34] Lee Edwards pinpoints a complex state of affairs when he asserts that "CNN became a world-class media power with the Persian Gulf War."[35] To the debate around the question, what it was that made CNN's coverage of the Persian Gulf War so hugely popular, to the point that the "Gulf War was the first war to have its own logos, theme music and telegenic overnight stars,"[36] Ronell contributes an analysis that takes as its point of departure the thesis of the effacement of the Gulf War on television, in other words, the thesis that the nonstop coverage was a cover-up that allowed this war to remain "unshown." This effacement had—and continues to have—several layers.

First, what Ronell refers to is the complete absence, on television and in other mainstream U.S. media, of a testimony of the devastating effects of war on the lives of the Iraqi people. Ten years later, during the beginning of the American military campaign in Afghanistan, and fifteen years later, during the second war in Iraq, the "effacement" of the "atrocity" is still the iron rule. Ted Rall is one of the few journalists to denounce this cover-up: "The nanny media, even more prudish since 9/11, covers our millions of eyes to protect us from our own icky deeds. In Afghanistan in 2001, while covering a war that had officially killed 12 civilians, I watched a colleague from a major television network collate footage of a B-52 bombing indiscriminately obliterating a civilian neighborhood. 'If people saw what bombing looks like here on the ground,' he observed, as body parts and burning houses and screaming children filled the screen, 'they would demand an end to it. Which is why this will never air on American television.' But other countries don't have our nanny media. Europeans and Arabs see the horror wreaked in our name on their airwaves, assume that we see the same imagery and hate us for not giving a damn. America's self-censors make anti-Americanism worse."[37]

This is one of the massive facts and effects of the disruption, if not elimination, in Ronell's words, of "clear transmission systems that would allow us to be heard here," and that also would allow us to hear and see. As Freud puts it in his "Zeitgemässes über Krieg und Tod,"[38] "one-sided information" (Freud's euphemism for censorship) is the first result of the "confusion of wartime."[39] The burning question raised by Ronell's thesis is that of a voluntary self-censorship of American media that is massive on the conscious level, but even more massive unconsciously. It is on the unconscious level that Ronell deciphers another, far more powerful layer of the televisual "effacement" of the Gulf War: The "effacement" in question has everything to do with the specificity of the medium "television." According to a compelling analysis by Samuel Weber, the Gulf War made it clear that "the television camera is not a mere observer of something going on independently of it. Rather, it is an integral and essential part of the military action itself."[40] Weber analyzes a particular sequence of images that was shown on television countless times during the war. In this sequence a missile homes in on its target, an Iraqi building. Because the sequence is recorded with a television camera situated in the nose of the missile, "the viewer has a bird

230

or bomb's eye view of the action"[41]: Weber writes: "The television camera is part of the system of guidance and evaluation through which missiles are directed at targets, hits or misses confirmed, and finally, future strikes determined. . . . The television camera and its technology is anything but a mere voyeur in the enormous destructive activity taking place."[42]

The camera-equipped missiles homing in on a target allow the spectator to simulate for the time of their flight the thrust of a kamikaze fighter and his ultimate control over his death, with the fundamental difference, of course, that the television spectator does not die during the destruction of the target, but rather revels in telecommand immortality. What went on behind the target, "that we never saw. When you are invited to play God, you don't want to be worried about such banal terrestrial things as mutilated bodies. . . . The televisual reporting of the Gulf War thus offered its viewers an exhilarating spectacle of 'Command and Control,' one that magnified but also repeated the more ordinary gesture of 'zapping' through which the TV viewer demonstrates his or her freedom of choice (and of elimination, as the word also indicates)."[43]

Weber underlines that in this spectacle, "there is no one behind the camera, not directly at least. So that in television, even more than in film, it is technologically possible to separate vision from the individual body."[44] Television then "intensifies" the "decorporalization of vision." The characteristics of the Gulf War were paradigmatic for this "decorporalization," insofar as it was "a tele-war, fought quite literally at a distance, with the help of television cameras. . . . This kind of war is much more like 'zapping' than hand-to-hand combat. Its conduct, and not just the content of its images, is intrinsically tele-visual. Like video games. Tank commanders shoot at each other by means of television, which transmits numbers as much as images."[45]

Weber's analysis proves to be helpful for a reflection on the American military campaign in Afghanistan (and, in fact, unbeknownst to most Americans, in several other countries[46]). The "tele-war" and its "decorporalization" of vision has reached a new level with the deployment of an unmanned aerial vehicle, the by now infamous "Predator." Under the Clinton administration, the spy plane had flown test flights over Afghanistan, providing "what several administration officials called incomparably detailed real-time video and photographs of the movements of what appeared to be Mr. bin Laden and his aides. The White House pressed ahead with a program to arm the Predator with a missile, but the effort was slowed by bureaucratic infighting between the Pentagon and the C.I.A. over who would pay for the craft and who would have ultimate authority over its use. The dispute, officials said, was not resolved until after Sept. 11."[47] Since then, the Predator has "revolutionize[d] warfare by providing instantaneous intelligence and battlefield control to commanders who are hundreds and even thousands of miles away."[48] In late 2001, the Predator carried out a task that "seemed unthinkable" just a year prior. "In the first search-and-destroy mission of its kind, a Predator attacked and destroyed a target with Hellfire missiles launched from an external weapons rack."[49] As Peter Pae states at the beginning of an article published in the Los Angeles Times, "President Bush has been able to tune in video images of Taliban targets in Afghanistan from the safety and comfort of the White House, giving the commander in chief a powerful capability."[50] Although these "video images" are a "top-secret television feed from the war zone,"[51] they spell out the essence of the hearth of the American home, the television, whose essence is remote control or telecommand: acting over a distance, decorporealized, potentially deadly. This new form of telecommand indeed turns "zapping" into an exercise of elimination and invites the president, to use Samuel Weber's words, to "play God," in perfect accordance with the name originally chosen for the military campaign in Afghanistan: "Infinite Justice," as well as the name given to the missiles, "Hellfire." For in such a war, there is no room for doubting that "we" are on the "good" side and the "others" deserve "hell."[52]

Since then, the Predator's use has been vastly expanded in a highly classi-fied "targeted killing" program whose legality under U.S. and international law is strongly disputed.[53] According to the official line, the "top-secret effort to kill suspected terrorists with drone-fired missiles" is intended as a response to "an increasingly decentralized Al Qaeda." In the words of Lee Strickland, a former CIA counsel who retired in 2004 from the agency's Senior Intel-ligence Service, it is intended to keep pace "with the spread of Al Qaeda commanders." Strickland has, however, to admit that "paradoxically, as a result of our success the target has become even more decentralized, even more diffused and presents a more difficult target—no question about that."[54] Of course, there is nothing "paradoxical" about this state of affairs.[55]

The effacement of the war could hardly be greater today. This is why it is crucial to follow what Ronell calls the "signifying chains"[56] that allow for a reading of the war, and for an interrogation of "our destructive desire, that is, the desire for war, for having a blast, for the apocalypse which is promised to us as the revelation of truth. We should be courageous enough to interrogate the excitement of armageddon, the fluttering hearts of those who ascribe meaning to war."[57] What is at stake is to uncover the signifying chains that conduct the "desire for war" ("desire" to be understood here in the psychoanalytic sense). This is why Ronell describes this particular work as that of a historian of phantasms: "I am tracing a phantasmic history. This is not the result of a whim or an effect of subjective contingency. The phantasmic control systems are out of my hands just as this war left a number of us disarmed." In her deciphering of this "phantasmic history," Ronell recalls that "on the eve of German reunification, Goebbels's phrase 'new world order' lept out of his diaries to be recircuited through the ventrilocating syntax of George Bush."[58] The name of the military operation in Iraq in 1991 can be deciphered along the links of that same signifying chain: "Desert Storm masks itself as a natural catastrophe, it appears to have concealed itself in the language of natural eruption. . . . The move to a natural idiom of calamity tries to efface the symbolic order in which modern warfare is waged."[59] Ronell detects in the name "Desert Storm" and in the comparison of the fighter pilots' missions with "lightning strikes" the "rehabilitation of Nazi signifiers": "the storm and the lightning are not natural borrowings, but an account that America has opened with the past, referring us in this age to the storm troopers and Blitz—lightning—krieg."

This "rehabilitation of Nazi signifiers" has seen a new development in the pursuit of a "new world order" with the younger Bush administration's relentless invocation of the "homeland" after September 11, its dehumanization of the enemy,[60] its arbitrary and indefinite detention of "enemy combatants" to whom any legal recourse is denied, and its claim "that the president had the power to order torture."[61] According to the World Report 2006 of Human Rights Watch, the United States government is today the "only government in the world to seek legislative sanction to treat detainees inhumanely," in other words, to use torture.[62] As Alfred McCoy writes in his scathing account of the CIA's secret fifty-year effort to develop more efficient methods of torture, that was finally crowned with success in Guantánamo Bay, "there is no longer any need, well into the war on terror, to ask whether the United States has engaged in the systematic torture of suspected terrorists."[63] A third level of what Ronell calls the war's "effacement" on television can be found here, that is more glaring today, after (and, significantly, in spite of) the revelations of prisoner abuse at Guantánamo Bay and Abu Ghraib, than at the time of the redaction of Ronell's text in 1991. It is the effacement of the extent and brutality of torture performed by U.S. officials, and, correspondingly, the television-led erosion, if not effacement, of the American public's unconditional rejection of torture. Television's leading role in this effacement following the September 11 attacks is eloquently described in an essay by Alfred McCoy that deserves to be quoted extensively:

> With the horrific reality of the Twin Towers attack still resonating and endless nuclear-bomb-in-Times-Square/ticking-bomb interrogation sce-

narios ricocheting around the media and pop culture, torture seems to have gained an eerie emotional traction. Polls taken over the last three years have confirmed this. With a complex reality reduced to a few terrifyingly simple, fantasy-ridden scenarios, torture in defense of the "homeland" has gained surprisingly wide acceptance, while the torture debate has been reframed—to the administration's great advantage—as a choice between public safety and the lives of millions or private morality and bleeding-heart qualms over a few slaps up the side of the head. In this way, old-fashioned morality has been made to seem little short of immoral. Through the invisible tendrils that tie a state to its society, the media has often reflected aspects of administration policy on such subjects. Television, in particular, has had a powerful effect in its repeated portrayals of harsh, even abusive interrogations as effective and morally justified acts—when, in fact, they are neither. After years of watching television shows such as NYPD Blue and 24 with plots that mimic the ticking-bomb scenario, millions of ordinary Americans seem to believe that we have entered an era when abuse, or even torture, is necessary to save lives. Each week, for instance, up to 20 million Americans have watched the fictional detectives of NYPD Blue use harsh methods to "tune up" suspects in the "pokey," or interrogation room, risking their careers to extract information that regularly saved lives and made the city safer. Accepting the need to torture just one criminal in this week's episode, or just one terrorist with a ticking bomb in Fox Television's popular CIA drama 24, opens ordinary Americans to consider whether the torture of real terrorists is not only justifiable but imperative. It seems likely that these televised scenarios have lent a hand in creating a public climate tolerant of governmental torture.[64]

What Ronell wrote of "Operation Desert Storm" has lost nothing of its perspicuity when read in the context of the current wars in Iraq and Afghanistan, and the so-called "war on terror": "The only way that this return of the regressive, truth-promising values of war could make claims for a future order would be by disavowing our history: this entails the repression of those disasters which have rendered possible the Occident. In short, we do not know how to think war as something we should wage, which is why we think we can conduct warfare as if it were extraneous, momentary, simulated, and not engaging the very core of our being. This, incidentally, is no longer Hegelian, this thought of remaining outside of our own war and external to it as though one were not fundamentally marked by it. War in the Hegelian context produced History and implicated our very being; if this war, by contrast, has something to teach us, it is that we no longer have access to it."[65]

One of Ronell's most persistent endeavors is to think the wars we are engaged in, and to reclaim "access" to wars that, as it becomes more evident every day, cannot not, irrevocably, "engage the very core of our being."

NOTES

1. Ingo Schulze, "Cell Phone," in: *Chicago Review, New Writing in German*, 48:2/3 (Summer 2002), p. 266.
2. Ibid, 271f.
3. Avital Ronell, *The Telephone Book: Technology, Schizophrenia, Electric Speech* (Lincoln: University of Nebraska Press, 1989), p. 6.
4. Ibid., p. 6.
5. Ibid., p. 6.
6. Ibid., p. 7.
7. Wolf Kittler, "The Middle Voice: Steady and Discrete Manifolds in Walter Benjamin." Working Paper 3.25, Center for German and European Studies, University of California, Berkeley, 1996, p. 22.
8. Kittler, "The Middle Voice," p. 4.
9. Heidegger analyzes "Mitsein" as constitutive of "Dasein" in *Being and Time*, trans. J. Stambaugh (Albany: State University of New York Press, 1996), for example, p. 110.
10. Samuel Weber, *Mass Mediauras* (Stanford, Calif.: Stanford University Press, 1996), p. 5.
11. Avital Ronell, "Activist Supplement: Papers on the Gulf War," in *Finitude's Score: Essays for the End of the Millennium* (Lincoln: University of Nebraska Press, 1994), p. 293f.
12. "TraumaTV: Twelve Steps Beyond the Pleasure Principle," in *Finitude's Score*, pp. 311–12.
13. Weber, *Mass Mediauras*, p. 7.
14. *The Telephone Book*, pp. 67–68. The quote continues: "Heidegger adds 'the naked that-it-is,' translated as the 'bare' that-is. The nuance may be significant, the decision notably to read nackt not as naked but as bloss, bare. The stark nakedness of the unsolicited call doubles for a mystified version of what das Man might recognize as the obscene phone call." This passage resonates well with the following assessment of television: "If TV has taught us anything . . . the teaching principally concerns, I think, the impossibility of staying at home. In fact, the more local it gets, the more uncanny, not at home, it appears. Television, which Heidegger, when he was on, once associated with the essence of his thinking, chaining you and fascinating you by its neutral gleam, is about being-not-at-home, telling you that you are chained to the deracinating grid of being-in-the-world. Perhaps this explains why, during his broadcast season, Lacan spoke of homme-sickness. We miss being-at-home in the world, which

never happened anyway, and missing home, Lacan suggests, has everything to do in the age of technological dominion with being sick of homme." Avital Ronell, "Trauma TV," p. 310.

15. Jacques Derrida and Bernard Stiegler, *Echographies of Television,* trans. Jennifer Bajorek. (Cambridge, Mass.: Polity Press, 2002), pp. 79–80, translation slightly modified.

16. Friedrich Nietzsche, *Also Sprach Zarathustra,* quoted in "Von der Nächstenliebe," Kritische Studienausgabe, vol. 4, ed. G. Colli and M. Montinari (Berlin and New York: Deutscher Taschenbuch Verlag, 1988), pp. 77–79.

17. Jacques Lacan, *The Seminar of Jacques Lacan, Book VII: The Ethics of Psychoanalysis,* trans. Dennis Porter (New York: Norton, 1992), p. 194.

18. Jacques Derrida, "Faith and Knowledge," in *Acts of Religion,* ed. Gil Anidjar (New York and London: Routledge, 2002), p. 80.

19. Derrida, "Faith and Knowledge," 66.

20. Ibid., 67.

21. Ibid., 66f.

22. "Activist Supplement: Papers on the Gulf War," p. 303. Compare Jacques Lacan, *Ecrits: A Selection,* trans. Bruce Fink (New York: Norton, 2002), p. 29.

23. "Activist Supplement: Papers on the Gulf War," p. 303.

24. "TraumaTV," pp. 322–23.

25. Sigmund Freud, "Beyond the Pleasure Principle," in *The Standard Edition of the Complete Psychological Works of Sigmund Freud,* ed. J. Strachey, vol. 18 (London: Hogarth Press, 1955), pp. 31–32.

26. "Activist Supplement: Papers on the Gulf War," p. 303.

27. Compare *Finitude's Score,* pp. 301 and 307, and 303.

28. Throughout her text "Support our Tropes," Ronell gives many examples for this repetition compulsion.

29. "Support our Tropes," p. 272.

30. "Activist Supplement: Papers on the Gulf War," p. 293.

31. "TraumaTV," pp. 318 and 324.

32. "TraumaTV," p. 324.

33. "TraumaTV," p. 323.

34. Frank Rich, "The Real Reality TV," *New York Times Magazine,* October 29, 2000, p. 60.

35. Lee Edwards, *Mediapolitik: How the Mass Media have Transformed World Politics* (Washington, D.C.: CUA Press, 2001), p. 76.

36. Frank Rich, *New York Times Magazine,* October 29, 2000, p. 60. The quote continues: ". . . (whether leading men like Colin Powell or Robert Duvall-esque character types like Peter Arnett). Most important, it played out in real time before a mass audience—the first instance history had been shaped (and spun, often by the military brass) on the spot into a dramatic 24/7 TV mini-series."

37. Ted Rall, "The Bland Leading the Blind: The Nanny Press and the Cartoon

Controversy," Wednesday, February 8 2006, http://www.commondreams.org/views06/0208-20.htm, accessed February 8, 2006.

38. Translated, rather imprecisely, as "Thoughts on War and Death," in *The Standard Edition of the Complete Psychological Works of Sigmund Freud,* ed. J. Strachey, vol. 14 (London: Hogarth, 1957), p. 275.

39. Freud's explicit denunciation of censorship deserves to be quoted extensively, given that it has, ninety years later after its redaction in 1915, lost nothing of its perspicacity: "Peoples are more or less represented by the states which they form, and these states by the governments which rule them. The individual citizen can with horror convince himself in this war of what would occasionally cross his mind in peace-time—that the state has forbidden to the individual the practice of wrong-doing, not because it desires to abolish it, but because it desires to monopolize it, like salt and tobacco. A belligerent state permits itself every such misdeed, every such act of violence, as would disgrace the individual. It makes use against the enemy not only of the accepted ruses de guerre, but of deliberate lying and deception as well—and to a degree which seems to exceed the usage of former wars. The state exacts the utmost degree of obedience and sacrifice from its citizens, but at the same time it treats them like children by an excess of secrecy and a censorship upon news and expressions of opinion which leaves the spirits of those whose intellects it thus suppresses defenceless against every unfavourable turn of events and every sinister rumour. It absolves itself from the guarantees and treaties by which it was bound to other states, and confesses shamelessly to its own rapacity and lust for power, which the private individual has then to sanction in the name of patriotism." Ibid., p. 279. For a compelling reading of this text, see Samuel Weber, "Wartime," in *Violence, Identity, and Self-Determination,* ed. Hent de Vries and Samuel Weber (Stanford, Calif.: Stanford University Press, 1997), pp.80–105.

40. Samuel Weber, "The Media and the War," in *Surfaces: Electronic Journal,* published by Les Presses de l'Université de Montréal, director: Jean-Claude Guédon, vol. 1, 1991, p. 8.

41. Weber, "The Media and the War," p. 9.

42. Weber, "The Media and the War," p. 8. Avital Ronell and Samuel Weber add crucial perspectives that are completely absent in the otherwise often interesting reflections of media and television critics on the Persian Gulf War. See, for example, A. Trevor Thrall, *War in the Media Age* (Cresskill, N.J.: Hampton Press, 2000); Edwards, *Mediapolitik;* the collection edited by Abbas Malek, News media and foreign relations: a multifaceted perspective (Norwood, N.J.: Ablex, 1997), and the volume edited by Robert L. Bateman III, Digital War. A view from the front lines (Novato, Calif.: Presidio, 1999).

43. Weber, *Mass Mediauras,* p. 165.

44. Ibid., p. 166.

45. Ibid.

46. Josh Meyer, "CIA Expands Use of Drones in Terror War," *Los Angeles Times*, January 29, 2006 (http://www.latimes.com/news/nationworld/world/la-fg -predator29jan29,0,5819230.story?coll=la-home-headlines), accessed February 8, 2006: Commenting on the highly classified "targeted killing program" that relies on unmanned Predator drones armed with Hellfire missiles to eliminate "suspected terrorists," a former counter-terrorism official who worked at the CIA and State Department (which coordinates such efforts with other governments), and who was speaking "on condition of anonymity," said that "We have the plans in place to do them globally. . . . In most cases, we need the approval of the host country to do them. However, there are a few countries where the president has decided that we can whack someone without the approval or knowledge of the host government. The CIA and the Pentagon have deployed at least several dozen of the Predator drones throughout Iraq, Afghanistan and along the borders of Pakistan, U.S. officials confirmed. The CIA also has sent the remote-controlled aircraft into the skies over Yemen and some other countries believed to be Al Qaeda havens, particularly those without a strong government or military with which the United States can work in tandem, a current U.S. counter-terrorism official told *The Times*. Such incursions are highly sensitive because they could violate the sovereignty of those nations and anger U.S. allies, the official said, speaking on condition of anonymity." See below for longer quotes from the same article.

47. Judith Miller, "Many Say U.S. Planned for Terror but Failed to take Action," *New York Times*, December 30, 2001, p. B4.

48. Peter Pae, "Future is Now for Creator of Predator," *Los Angeles Times*, January 3, 2002. See http://www.latimes.com/news/printedition/front/la-010302atomic .story, accessed February 8, 2006. In line with his usual anti-intellectual demagogy, President Bush "lauded the Predator's abilities, singling it out as an example of how the conflict in Afghanistan 'has taught us more about the future of our military than a decade of blue-ribbon panels and think-tank symposiums.'" (ibid.)

49. Peter Pae, "Future is Now for Creator of Predator," *Los Angeles Times*, January 3, 2002.

50. Ibid.

51. Ibid.

52. For Samuel Weber's reading of these names, see "War, Terrorism, and Spectacle," *South Atlantic Quarterly* 101:3 (Summer 2002), p. 455.

53. Josh Meyer, "CIA Expands Use of Drones in Terror War," *Los Angeles Times*, January 29, 2006.

54. Ibid.

55. Confirming Samuel Weber's analysis on another point, it is worth mentioning that the drones "are often operated by CIA or Pentagon officials at computer consoles in the United States." Meyer, "CIA Expands Use of Drones in Terror War." The following is a longer excerpt from Josh Meyer's article: "Despite pro-

tests from other countries, the United States is expanding a top-secret effort to kill suspected terrorists with drone-fired missiles as it pursues an increasingly decentralized Al Qaeda, U.S. officials say. The CIA's failed Jan. 13 attempt to assassinate Al Qaeda second-in-command Ayman Zawahiri in Pakistan was the latest strike in the 'targeted killing' program, a highly classified initiative that officials say has broadened as the network splintered and fled Afghanistan. The strike against Zawahiri reportedly killed as many as 18 civilians, many of them women and children, and triggered protests in Pakistan. Similar U.S. attacks using unmanned Predator aircraft equipped with Hellfire missiles have angered citizens and political leaders in Afghanistan, Iraq and Yemen. Little is known about the targeted-killing program. The Bush administration has refused to discuss how many strikes it has made, how many people have died, or how it chooses targets. No U.S. officials were willing to speak about it on the record because the program is classified. Several U.S. officials confirmed at least 19 occasions since Sept. 11 on which Predators successfully fired Hellfire missiles on terrorist suspects overseas, including 10 in Iraq in one month last year. The Predator strikes have killed at least four senior Al Qaeda leaders, but also many civilians, and it is not known how many times they missed their targets. Critics of the program dispute its legality under U.S. and international law, and say it is administered by the CIA with little oversight. U.S. intelligence officials insist it is one of their most tightly regulated, carefully vetted programs. . . . The CIA does not even acknowledge that such a targeted-killing program exists, and some attacks have been explained away as car bombings or other incidents. It is not known how many militants or bystanders have been killed by Predator strikes, but anecdotal evidence suggests the number is significant. In some cases, the destruction was so complete that it was impossible to establish who was killed, or even how many people. . . ."

56. "Support our Tropes," p. 271.

57. "Activist Supplement: Papers on the Gulf War," p. 296.

58. "Support our Tropes," p. 272.

59. "Activist Supplement: Papers on the Gulf War," p. 294.

60. See, among many incidents that could be quoted here, the description of suspected terrorists as rodents, by members of the Bush administration: "They will try to hide, they will try to avoid the United States and our allies—but we're not going to let them. They run to the hills; they find holes to get in. And we will do whatever it takes to smoke them out and get them running, and we'll get them." "President Urges Readiness and Patience." Camp David, September 15th 2001. 11.30.05 www.whitehouse.gov/news/releases/2001/09/20010915–4.html, accessed February 8, 2006.

61. Kenneth Roth, "Justifying Torture," in Kenneth Roth and Minky Worden, eds., Torture (New York: The New Press, 2005), p. 185.

62. *Human Rights Watch, World Report 2006.* Events of 2005 (New York: Human Rights Watch and Seven Stories Press, 2006), p. 502.

63. Alfred McCoy, "A question of torture: CIA Interrogation," from the *Cold War to the War on Terror* (New York: Metropolitan Books, 2006), p. 188.
64. Tomdispatch: Alfred McCoy on How Not to Ban Torture in Congress, http://www.tomdispatch.com/index.mhtml?pid=57336, accessed February 8, 2006.
65. "Activist Supplement: Papers on the Gulf War," p. 297f.

Contributors

PIERRE ALFERI lives and writes in Paris. He has written five books of poetry, two novels, and a collection of essays. He is the founder, with Suzanne Doppelt, of the literary review *Détail*, and of *la Revue de littérature générale* with Olivier Cadiot. He has collaborated with the artist Jacques Julien, and has recorded and performed with musician Rodolphe Burger. He has also translated works by John Donne, Giorgio Agamben, and Meyer Schapiro into the French.

GIL ANIDJAR is associate professor in the Department of Middle East and Asian Languages and Cultures at Columbia University. He is the author of *The Jew, the Arab: A History of the Enemy* (Stanford University Press, 2003) and *Semites: Race, Religion, Literature* (Stanford University Press, 2008) and the editor of Jacques Derrida's *Acts of Religion* (Routledge, 2002). He has been studying with Avital Ronell since 1992.

SAUL ANTON is completing a doctoral dissertation on the relation between aesthetics and history in French Enlightenment philosophy and literature at Princeton University. He has written for *Artforum, Frieze, Parkett,* and many other journals, and he has taught critical studies at the City University of New York and the Tyler School of Art, Temple University. He is the translator of Jean-Luc Nancy's *The Discourse of the Syncope: 1. Logodaedalus* (2008).

SUSAN BERNSTEIN is professor of comparative literature and German studies at Brown University. She is author of *Virtuosity of the Nineteenth Century: Performing Music and Language in Heine, Liszt and Baudelaire, Housing Problems: Writing and Architecture in Goethe, Walpole, Freud, and Heidegger,* as well as essays on Nietzsche, Kant, Heine, Shelley, and others.

JUDITH BUTLER is Maxine Elliot Professor in the Departments of Rhetoric and Comparative Literature at the University of California, Berkeley. She is the author of many books, including *Gender Trouble: Feminism and the*

Subversion of Identity (Routledge, 1990), *The Psychic Life of Power: Theories of Subjection* (Stanford University Press, 1997), *Excitable Speech* (Routledge, 1997), *Undoing Gender* (Routledge, 2004), *Precarious Life: Powers of Violence and Mourning* (Verso, 2004), *Giving an Account of Oneself* (Fordham University Press, 2005), and recently, *Who Sings The Nation State?* (Seagull Books, 2007), with Gayatri Chakravorty Spivak.

TOM COHEN is professor of English at State University of New York at Albany and cofounder of the Institute on Critical Climate Change (IC3), which advances hybrid and transnational experimentation with the import of "climate change" on coming critical discourse. He is author of *Anti-Mimesis from Plato to Hitchcock* (Cambridge University Press, 1994), *Ideology and Inscription: "Cultural Studies" after Benjamin, de Man, and Bakhtin* (Cambridge University Press, 1998), *Hitchcock's Cryptonymies 1: Secret Agents* and *Hitchcock's Cryptonymies 2: War Machines* (University of Minnesota Press, 2005); he is also a contributing editor of *Material Events: Paul de Man and the Afterlife of Theory* (University of Minnesota Press, 2000) and *Jacques Derrida and the Humanities: a Transdisciplinary Reader* (Cambridge University Press, 2002).

DIANE DAVIS is an associate professor of rhetoric & writing, English, and communication studies at the University of Texas at Austin, and she holds the Kenneth Burke Chair at the European Graduate School in Saas-Fee, Switzerland. She is the author of *Breaking Up Totality: A Rhetoric of Laughter,* co-author of *Women's Ways of Making it In Rhetoric and Composition* (with Michelle Ballif and Roxanne Mountford), and editor of *The UberReader: Selected Works of Avital Ronell.*

CATHARINE DIEHL is a Ph.D. candidate in the Department of Comparative Literature at Princeton University. She is completing a dissertation on theories of intensity in aesthetics, epistemology, and metaphysics from Leibniz to Hermann Cohen. She has translated articles on Agamben and Hermann Cohen, and has just completed an essay on the zero in structuralist linguistics.

PETER FENVES is Joan and Sarepta Harrison Professor of Literature and professor of German and Jewish studies at Northwestern University. He is the author of *A Peculiar Fate: Metaphysics and World-History in Kant* (Cornell University Press, 1991), *"Chatter": Language and History in Kierkegaard* (Stanford University Press, 1993), *Arresting Language: From Leibniz to Benjamin* (Stanford University Press, 2001), and *Late Kant: Towards Another Law of the Earth* (Routledge, 2003). He is also the editor of *Raising the Tone of Philosophy: Late Essays by Kant, Transformative Critique by Derrida* (Johns Hopkins University Press, 1993), coeditor of *"The Spirit of Poesy": Essays on Jewish and German Literature and Philosophy in Honor of Géza von Molnár* (Northwestern University Press, 2000), and translator of Werner Hamacher's *Premises: Literature and Philosophy from Kant to Celan* (Harvard University Press, 1996).

WERNER HAMACHER is director of the Institute for General and Comparative Literature at the Goethe-University in Frankfurt, Germany, and holds the Emmanuel Lévinas Chair at the European Graduate School. He has taught at the Free University Berlin, the Johns Hopkins University, Yale University, and as Global Distinguished Professor at New York University. He is author of *Pleroma—Reading in Hegel* (Athlone/Stanford University Press, 1998) and *Premises: Essays on Philosophy and Literature from Kant to Celan* (Harvard University Press, 1996/Stanford University Press, 1999), and editor of *Paul Celan* (Suhrkamp, 1987), *Nietzsche aus Frankreich* (DVA, 2007), and *Jean Daive: W* (Urs Engeler, 2006). He is the editor of the Stanford University Press series *Meridian—Crossing Aesthetics*.

ELISSA MARDER is associate professor of French and comparative literature at Emory University. Her book *Dead Time: Temporal Disorders in the Wake of Modernity (Baudelaire and Flaubert)* was published by Stanford University Press in 2001. She has published essays on diverse topics in literature, literary theory, feminism, film, photography, and psychoanalysis, and is currently completing a book tentatively entitled *The Mother in the Age of Mechanical Reproduction: Essays on Technology, Psychoanalysis, and Literature.* She is also working on a project devoted to early nineteenth-century French literature entitled *Revolutionary Perversions: Literary Sex Acts 1789–1848* and a study of Walter Benjamin's "French" writings.

JEAN-LUC NANCY is professor of philosophy at the University of Strasbourg and visiting professor at the University of California, Berkeley. He is author of numerous books, many of which have been translated into English, including *The Literary Absolute* (with Philippe Lacoue-Labarthe, State University of New York Press, 1988), *The Inoperative Community* (University of Minnesota Press, 1991), *The Title of the Letter* (with Lacoue-Labarthe, State University of New York Press, 1992), *Birth To Presence* (Stanford University Press, 1993), *The Gravity of Thought* (Humanities, 1997), *The Experience of*

Freedom (Stanford University Press, 1993), *The Sense of the World* (University of Minnesota Press, 1997), *Being Singular Plural* (Stanford University Press, 2000), *The Speculative Remark: One of Hegel's Bon Mots* (Stanford University Press, 2001), *Hegel: The Restlessness of the Negative* (University of Minnesota Press, 2002), *The Ground of the Image* (Fordham University Press, 2005), and *Listening* (Fordham University Press, 2007).

SHIREEN R. K. PATELL is clinical assistant professor and associate director of the Trauma and Violence Transdisciplinary Studies Department at New York University. She earned her Ph.D. under Ronell's direction at University of California, Berkeley in 2001 and is the author of several essays, which have appeared in *Poiesis, The New Centennial Review,* and the *Cardozo Law Review.*

THOMAS PEPPER is a professor in the Department of Cultural Studies and Comparative Literature at the University of Minnesota. He is author of *Singularities: Extremes of Theory in the Twentieth Century (Essays on Heidegger and Derrida, Adorno, Blanchot, Celan, de Man)* (Cambridge University Press, 1997) and *Male Midwifery: Maieutics in Kierkegaard's "The Concept of Irony" and "Repetition"* (Kierkegaard Studies Monograph Series, 2, de Gruyter, 1993). He is a contributing editor of *The Place of Maurice Blanchot* (Yale French Studies, no. 93, 1998).

LAURENCE A. RICKELS is professor of German and comparative literature at the University of California at Santa Barbara and a practicing psychotherapist. He is the author of many books, including *Aberrations of Mourning: Writing on German Crypts* (Wayne State University Press, 1988), *The Case of California* (Johns Hopkins University Press, 1991), *The Vampire Lectures* (University of Minnesota Press, 1999), *Nazi Psychoanalysis,* 3 volumes: *Only Psychoanalysis Won the War, Crypto-Fetishism,* and *Psy Fi* (University of Minnesota Press, 2002), *Ulrike Ottinger: The Autobiography of Art Cinema* (University of Minnesota Press, 2008), and *The Devil Notebooks* (University of Minnesota Press, 2008).

HENT DE VRIES holds the Russ Family Chair in the Humanities and is professor of philosophy at the Johns Hopkins University. He is also professor ordinarius of systematic philosophy and the philosophy of religion at the University of Amsterdam and program director at the Collège International de Philosophie, Paris. He is the author of *Minimal Theologies: Critiques of Secular Reason in Adorno and Lévinas* (Johns Hopkins University Press,

2005), *Religion and Violence: Philosophical Perspectives from Kant to Derrida* (Johns Hopkins University Press, 2002), and *Philosophy and the Turn to Religion* (Johns Hopkins University Press, 1999). He is the editor of *Religion: Beyond a Concept* (Fordham University Press, 2008). Among the volumes he has coedited are, with Lawrence E. Sullivan, *Political Theologies: Public Religions in a Post-Secular World* (Fordham University Press, 2006) and, with Samuel Weber, *Religion and Media* (Stanford University Press, 2001) and *Violence, Identity, and Self-Determination* (Stanford University Press, 1998).

ELISABETH WEBER is professor of German and comparative literature at the University of California at Santa Barbara. She is author of *Verfolgung und Trauma. Zu Emmanuel Lévinas' Autrement qu'être ou au-delà de l'essence* (1990) and editor of *Jüdisches Denken in Frankreich* (1994, published in French as *Questions au Judaïsme*, 1996, and in English as *Questioning Judaism*, Stanford University Press, 2004), a collection of interviews with Jacques Derrida, Jean-François Lyotard, Emmanuel Lévinas, Pierre Vidal-Naquet, and others. She is the coeditor of *Das Vergessen(e) Anamnesen des Undarstellbaren* (1997), the editor of several works by Jacques Derrida, and German translator of texts by Jacques Derrida, Emmanuel Lévinas, and Félix Guattari. She was the co-organizer of a six-month-long series of public events on "Torture and the Future" at UCSB.

SAMUEL WEBER is Avalon Foundation Professor of Humanities at Northwestern University and codirector of its Paris program in critical theory. He is the author of many books, including *The Legend of Freud* (University of Minnesota Press, 1982), *Institution and Interpretation* (Stanford University Press, 1987), *Return to Freud: Jacques Lacan's Dislocation of Psychoanalysis* (Cambridge University Press, 1991), *Mass Mediauras: Form, Technics, Media* (Stanford University Press, 1996), *Theatricality as Medium* (Fordham University Press, 2004), *Targets of Opportunity* (Fordham University Press, 2005), and *Benjamin's -abilities* (Harvard University Press, 2008).

Index

The University of Illinois Press
is a founding member of the
Association of American University Presses.

———————————————————————

Composed in 10/13 Adobe Minion Pro
with Myriad Pro display
by Jim Proefrock
at the University of Illinois Press
Designed by Copenhaver Cumpston

Manufactured by Cushing-Malloy, Inc.
University of Illinois Press
1325 South Oak Street
Champaign, IL 61820-6903
www.press.uillinois.edu